THE TOP
10
OF EVERYTHING
2006

THE TOP
10
OF EVERYTHING
2006

The Ultimate Book of Lists

RUSSELL ASH

LONDON, NEW YORK, MUNICH, MELBOURNE, DELHI

Senior Editor Dawn Henderson
DTP Designer Adam Walker
Production Controller Shane Higgins

Managing Editor Julie Oughton
Managing Art Editor Heather McCarry
Category Publisher Stephanie Jackson

Produced for Dorling Kindersley by
The Bridgewater Book Company,
The Old Candlemakers, West Street,
Lewes, East Sussex BN7 2NZ

Project Editor Emily Casey Bailey
Project Designer Lisa McCormick
Designer Bernard Higton
Picture Research Vanessa Fletcher

Author's Project Manager Aylla Macphail

First American Edition, 2005
05 06 07 08 09 10 9 8 7 6 5 4 3 2 1

Published in the United States by DK Publishing, Inc.,
375 Hudson Street, New York, New York 10014

DK books are available at special discounts for bulk
purchases for sales promotions, premiums, fund-
raising, or educational use. For details, contact:
DK Publishing Special Markets, 375 Hudson Street,
New York, NY 10014. SpecialSales@dk.com

A catalog record for this book is available from the
Library of Congress

ISBN 0-7566-1321-3 (hardcover edition)
ISBN 0-7566-1322-1 (paperback edition)

Reproduction by ImageScanhouse Global
Services, Malaysia

Printed and bound by Toppan, China

Discover more at
www.dk.com

Contents

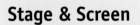

3

The Human World

4

Town & Country

5

Culture & Learning

8

Commercial World

9

Transportation & Tourism

10

Sports

BANQUE
DE LUXEMBOURG

Introduction

The Top 10 of Everything has been published annually since 1989, so this is the 17th edition. When I began compiling it, I set myself the task of ensuring that every featured Top 10 list was definitive. In most instances, that means quantifiable; hence the Top 10 movies, for example, are generally ranked according to how much each has earned internationally. No lists are subjective, so it is not a book of "bests" except those that are measurably bestsellers, while "worsts" in such categories as murders and disasters are similarly quantified, usually by numbers of victims. Alongside these lists are a variety of "firsts" or "latests" that recognize the pioneers and the most recent achievers in various fields of endeavor.

THE PACE OF CHANGE

This new collection of Top 10 lists features the latest updates of established favorites alongside hundreds of entirely new lists. They range from the most expensive pop lyrics, the countries with most executions, the fastest-growing cities, and the biggest beer drinkers to the world's longest-running shows, the richest Russians, the top video games, and the most successful skateboarders. Since the last edition, many momentous events have occurred, including the tragedy of the worst-ever tsunami. After a post-Cold War lull, military spending is escalating again, while in the realm of entertainment we have had the first-ever animated film (*Shrek 2*) to earn more than $900 million and the first documentary (*Fahrenheit 9/11*) to make over $200 million worldwide. The inexorable rise of DVD—sales of which can now outstrip box office earnings—continues, and record charts now take account of the new phenomenon of legal downloading.

FACTS AND FIGURES

In every instance, the figures are the latest available, although we are occasionally thwarted when new figures have not been released in time, or where a sporting season is still in progress as we go to press. Where

SPECIAL FEATURES

■ Completely redesigned in an exciting and user-friendly style

■ Top 10 Close-ups feature major single lists, ranging from the most valuable comics to medal-winning countries at the summer Olympics

■ FirstFacts and FastFacts throughout—from the first billionaire to the largest whale ever measured

■ Further Information—invaluable website links on Top 10 topics

certain figures differ from those published elsewhere, the discrepancy may derive from varying methods of measurement and definitions (in measuring a skyscraper, for example, do you include or exclude a building's spires, and what are the precise boundaries of a city?). Some disagreements may arise from the immense difficulty of accurately calculating certain statistics (how many Muslims are there in the world, and how many people in the US are named "Smith"?). Figures for country and city populations are based on the latest available census, with estimates for increases where officially available, while in most instances "countries" should be taken as meaning "countries, colonies, and dependent territories."

THANKS FOR EVERYTHING

The question most commonly asked of authors of fiction is "Where do you get your ideas?" The question I hear most frequently is "Where do you get your information?" It comes from a huge variety of sources, from organizations, commercial companies and research bodies, specialized and often obscure publications, and, especially, a network of individuals around the world who have shared their knowledge of subjects from birds to bridges. As always, I acknowledge their invaluable contribution (see page 255 for full list of credits), as well as the many people who have been involved with the book at all stages of its development over its 17-year history.

CONTACT ME

Your comments, corrections, and suggestions for new lists are always welcome. Contact me via the publishers or visit my website:
http://www.top10ofeverything.com

Russell Ash

Chapter

01234

top 10 largest bodies in the solar system: page 16

56789 1

The Universe & The Earth

top 10 longest spacewalks: page 19

Elements

top 10 LIGHTEST SOLID ELEMENTS

ELEMENT	DISCOVERER / COUNTRY	YEAR DISCOVERED	DENSITY*
1 Lithium	Johan August Arfvedson, Sweden	1817	0.533
2 Potassium	Sir Humphry Davy, UK	1807	0.859
3 Sodium	Sir Humphry Davy	1807	0.969
4 Calcium	Sir Humphry Davy	1808	1.526
5 Rubidium	Robert Wilhelm Bunsen/ Gustav Kirchoff, Germany	1861	1.534
6 Magnesium	Sir Humphry Davy	1808[#]	1.737
7 Phosphorus	Hennig Brandt, Germany	1669	1.825
8 Beryllium	Friedrich Wöhler, Germany/ Antoine-Alexandré Brutus Bussy, France	1828[†]	1.846
9 Cesium	Robert Wilhelm Bunsen/ Gustav Kirchoff	1860	1.896
10 Sulfur	—	Prehistoric	2.070

* g per cm³ at 20°C

[#] Recognized by Joseph Black, 1755, but not isolated

[†] Recognized by Nicholas Vauquelin, 1797, but not isolated

Osmium, the heaviest element, is over 42 times heavier than lithium, the lightest solid. Lithium, a metal, is not only extremely light, but also so soft that it can be easily cut with a knife. It is half as heavy as water, and lighter even than certain types of wood. Lithium is used in the aerospace industry to make alloys and in the air filtration systems in spacecraft, while the hydrogen in hydrogen bombs is a compound of lithium—lithium hydride. The "dilithium crystals" employed in the warp drives of starships in *Star Trek* are, however, pure fiction.

➔ Lighter than air
Although the most common and lightest of all elements, hydrogen is too explosive to use in balloons. In consequence, hot-air balloons dominate the sport, with helium reserved for wealthy purists.

top 10 MOST COMMON ELEMENTS IN THE UNIVERSE

ELEMENT / PARTS PER MILLION*

1 Hydrogen 750,000 2 Helium 230,000

3 Oxygen 10,000 4 Carbon 5,000 5 Neon 1,300

6 Iron 1,100 7 Nitrogen 1,000 8 Silicon 700

9 Magnesium 600 10 Sulfur 500

* mg per kg

top 10 ELEMENTS WITH THE **HIGHEST** BOILING POINT

ELEMENT	BOILING POINT (°F)	(°C)
1 Rhenium	10,105	5,596
2 Tungsten	10,031	5,555
3 Tantalum	9,856	5,458
4 Osmium	9,054	5,012
5 Thorium	8,708	4,820
6 Niobium	8,571	4,744
7 Molybdenum	8,382	4,639
8 Hafnium	8,317	4,603
9 Iridium	8,002	4,428
10 Zirconium	7,968	4,409

Source: WebElements

top 10 ELEMENTS WITH THE **LOWEST** BOILING POINT

ELEMENT	BOILING POINT (°F)	(°C)
1 Helium	−452.07	−268.93
2 Hydrogen	−423.17	−252.87
3 Neon	−410.94	−246.08
4 Nitrogen	−320.42	−195.79
5 Fluorine	−306.62	−188.12
6 Argon	−302.40	−185.80
7 Oxygen	−297.20	−182.90
8 Krypton	−243.80	−153.22
9 Xenon	−162.00	−108.00
10 Radon	−79.10	−61.70

Source: WebElements

← High light
Familiar as the filament in incandescent light bulbs, tungsten has a high melting point and hardness that also make it valuable for drills and cutting tools.

→ Low-melting mercury
Although mercury is the only metal that is liquid at room temperature, below its melting point it becomes solid and can be bent like steel.

top 10 ELEMENTS WITH THE **HIGHEST** MELTING POINTS

ELEMENT	MELTING POINT (°F)	(°C)
1 Carbon	6,381	3,527
2 Tungsten	6,192	3,422
3 Rhenium	5,767	3,186
4 Osmium	5,491	3,033
5 Tantalum	5,463	3,017
6 Molybdenum	4,753	2,623
7 Niobium	4,491	2,477
8 Iridium	4,471	2,466
9 Ruthenium	4,233	2,334
10 Hafnium	4,051	2,233

Other elements that melt at high temperatures include chromium (3,465°F/1,907°C), iron (2,800°F/1,538°C), and gold (1,947°F/1,064°C). For comparison, the surface of the Sun attains 9,626°F (5,330°C).

top 10 ELEMENTS WITH THE **LOWEST** MELTING POINTS*

ELEMENT	MELTING POINT (°F)	(°C)
1 Mercury	−37.8	−38.8
2 Bromine	19.0	−7.3
3 Francium	80.6	27.0
4 Cesium	83.1	28.4
5 Gallium	85.5	29.7
6 Rubidium	103.7	39.3
7 Phosphorus	111.6	44.2
8 Potassium	146.1	63.4
9 Sodium	207.9	97.7
10 Iodine	236.7	113.7

* Nongaseous only

Among other familiar elements that melt at relatively low temperatures are tin (449.4°F/231.9°C) and lead (621.5°F/327.5°C).

Stars & Comets

the 10 MOST RECENT OBSERVATIONS OF HALLEY'S COMET

1 1986 The Japanese *Suisei* probe passed within 93,827 miles (151,000 km) of its 9-mile (15-km) nucleus on March 8, 1986, revealing a whirling nucleus within a hydrogen cloud emitting 20–50 tons of water per second. The Soviet probes *Vega 1* and *Vega 2* passed within 5,524 miles (8,890 km) and 4,990 miles (8,030 km), respectively. The European Space Agency's *Giotto* passed as close as 370 miles (596 km) on March 14. All were heavily battered by dust particles, and it was concluded that Halley's comet is composed of dust bonded by water and carbon dioxide ice.

2 1910 Predictions of disaster were widely published, with many people convinced that the world would come to an end. Mark Twain, who was born at the time of the 1835 appearance and believed that his fate was linked to that of the comet, died when it reappeared this year.

3 1835 Widely observed, but noticeably dimmer than in 1759.

4 1759 The comet's first return as predicted by Halley, thus proving his calculations correct.

5 1682 Observed in Africa and China, and extensively in Europe, where it was observed from September 5 to 19 by Edmond Halley, who predicted its return.

6 1607 Seen extensively in China, Japan, Korea, and Europe, described by German astronomer Johannes Kepler, and its position accurately measured by amateur Welsh astronomer Thomas Harriot.

7 1531 Observed in China, Japan, and Korea, and in Europe from August 13 to 23 by Peter Appian, German geographer and astronomer, who noted that comets' tails point away from the Sun.

8 1456 Observed in China, Japan, and Korea, and by the Turkish army that was threatening to invade Europe. When the Turks were defeated by Papal forces, the comet was seen as a portent of victory.

9 1378 Observed in China, Japan, Korea, and Europe.

10 1301 Seen in Iceland, parts of Europe, China, Japan, and Korea.

⬆ **Early warning**
The appearance of Halley's comet in 1066, shown here in the Bayeux Tapestry, was seen as a portent of King Harold's defeat by William the Conqueror.

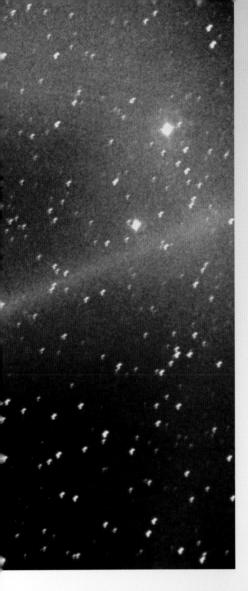

top 10 COMETS COMING **CLOSEST** TO EARTH

COMET	DATE*	(AU#)	DISTANCE (MILES)	(KM)
1 Comet of 1491	Feb. 20, 1491	0.0094	873,784	1,406,220
2 Lexell	July 1, 1770	0.0151	1,403,633	2,258,928
3 Tempel-Tuttle	Oct. 26, 1366	0.0229	2,128,688	3,425,791
4 IRAS-Araki-Alcock	May 11, 1983	0.0313	2,909,516	4,682,413
5 Halley	Apr. 10, 837	0.0334	3,104,724	4,996,569
6 Biela	Dec. 9, 1805	0.0366	3,402,182	5,475,282
7 Grischow	Feb. 8, 1743	0.0390	3,625,276	5,834,317
8 Pons-Winnecke	June 26, 1927	0.0394	3,662,458	5,894,156
9 Comet of 1014	Feb. 24, 1014	0.0407	3,783,301	6,088,633
10 La Hire	Apr. 20, 1702	0.0437	4,062,168	6,537,427

* Of closest approach to Earth

\# Astronomical Units: 1 AU = mean distance from Earth to the Sun (92,955,793 miles/149,597,870 km)

← Last sighting
Halley's comet's 76-year orbit means it was last seen in 1986 and is scheduled to reappear in 2061.

top 10 **BRIGHTEST** STARS*

STAR	CONSTELLATION	DISTANCE#	APPARENT MAGNITUDE
1 Sirius	Canis Major	8.65	−1.46
2 Canopus	Carina	313	−0.62
3 Alpha Centauri	Centaurus	4.35	−0.27
4 Arcturus	Boötes	36	−0.04
5 Vega	Lyra	25	+0.03
6 Capella	Auriga	42	+0.08
7 Rigel	Orion	773	+0.18
8 Procyon	Canis Minor	11.4	+0.38
9 Achernar	Eridanus	144	+0.46
10 Beta Centauri	Centaurus	525	+0.61

* Excluding the Sun

\# From Earth in light years

Source: Peter Bond, Royal Astronomical Society

This Top 10 is based on apparent visual magnitude as viewed from Earth—the lower the number, the brighter the star. At its brightest, the star Betelgeuse is brighter than some of these, but its variability means that its average brightness disqualifies it from the Top 10. The absolute magnitude of Cygnus OB2 No. 12, discovered in 1992, may make it the brightest star in the galaxy, but it is 5,900 light-years away.

top 10 GALAXIES **CLOSEST** TO EARTH

	GALAXY	DISCOVERED	APPROXIMATE DIAMETER*	DISTANCE#
1	Sagittarius Dwarf	1994	10,000	82,000
2	Large Magellanic Cloud	Prehist.	30,000	160,000
3	Small Magellanic Cloud	Prehist.	16,000	190,000
4	= Draco Dwarf	1954	3,000	205,000
	= Ursa Minor Dwarf	1954	2,000	205,000
6	Sculptor Dwarf	1937	3,000	254,000
7	Sextans Dwarf	1990	4,000	258,000
8	Carina Dwarf	1977	2,000	330,000
9	Fornax Dwarf	1938	6,000	450,000
10	Leo II	1950	3,000	660,000

* In light years

\# From Earth in light years

Source: Peter Bond, Royal Astronomical Society

These galaxies are members of the so-called "Local Group," although with such vast distances, "local" is clearly a relative term. Since our solar system and Earth are at the outer edge of the Milky Way, this galaxy is excluded. Over the next hundred million years, the Sagittarius Dwarf—our nearest neighboring galaxy—will be progressively absorbed into the Milky Way.

Planets, Moons & Asteroids

top 10 BODIES* FARTHEST FROM THE SUN

BODY	AVERAGE DISTANCE FROM THE SUN (MILES)	(KM)
1 Pluto	3,675,000,000	5,914,000,000
2 Neptune	2,794,000,000	4,497,000,000
3 Uranus	1,784,000,000	2,871,000,000
4 Chiron	1,740,000,000	2,800,000,000
5 Saturn	887,000,000	1,427,000,000
6 Jupiter	483,600,000	778,300,000
7 Mars	141,600,000	227,900,000
8 Earth	92,955,793	149,597,870
9 Venus	67,200,000	108,200,000
10 Mercury	36,000,000	57,900,000

* In the Solar System, excluding satellites and asteroids

↺ Over the moon
Named after the discoverer of Saturn's moon Titan, the Huygens probe reached Titan (top) on January 14, 2005. With a diameter of 3,200 miles (5,150 km), Titan is larger than both our own Moon (2,159 miles/3,475 km) and the planet Pluto (1,485 miles/2,390 km).

the 10 FIRST PLANETARY MOONS TO BE DISCOVERED

MOON	PLANET	DISCOVERER / COUNTRY	YEAR
1 Moon	Earth	—	Ancient
2 Io	Jupiter	Galileo Galilei, Italy	1610
3 Europa	Jupiter	Galileo Galilei	1610
4 Ganymede	Jupiter	Galileo Galilei	1610
5 Callisto	Jupiter	Galileo Galilei	1610
6 Titan	Saturn	Christian Huygens, Netherlands	1655
7 Iapetus	Saturn	Giovanni Cassini, Italy/France	1671
8 Rhea	Saturn	Giovanni Cassini	1672
9 Tethys	Saturn	Giovanni Cassini	1684
10 Dione	Saturn	Giovanni Cassini	1684

While Earth's moon has been observed since ancient times, it was not until the development of the telescope that Galileo was able to discover (on January 7, 1610) the first moons of another planet. These, which are Jupiter's four largest, were named by German astronomer Simon Marius and are known as the Galileans.

top 10 LARGEST ASTEROIDS

NAME	YEAR DISCOVERED	DIAMETER (MILES)	(KM)
1 Ceres	1801	568	914
2 Pallas	1802	325	524
3 Vesta	1807	312	502
4 Hygeia	1849	267	430
5 Davida	1903	210	338
6 Interamnia	1910	207	334
7 Europa	1858	194	312
8 Eunomia	1851	169	272
9 Sylvia	1866	168	270
10 Psyche	1852	164	264

Asteroids, sometimes known as "minor planets," are fragments of rock orbiting between Mars and Jupiter. The orbits of over 96,000 have been calculated and some 12,000 officially named. Each of the four Beatles has an asteroid named after him, as do Bruce Springsteen, James Bond, and the members of the Monty Python team. The first and largest to be discovered was Ceres, which was found by Giuseppe Piazzi (1746–1826), director of the observatory in Palermo, Sicily, on New Year's Day, 1801.

top 10 OBJECTS COMING CLOSEST TO THE EARTH

	NAME / DESIGNATION	DUE DATE	DISTANCE* (MILES)	(KM)
1	2004 MX2	July 17, 2050	3,700	6,000
2	2003 MH4	June 12, 2132	9,300	15,000
3	2004 KH17	June 11, 2099	46,600	75,000
4	2004 KH17	June 10, 2187	74,600	120,000
5	2000 WO107	Dec. 2, 2169	83,900	135,000
6	=2004 KH17	June 11, 2090	93,200	150,000
	=2000 EH26	Apr. 21, 2106	93,200	150,000
8	=2004 KH17	June 10, 2096	102,500	165,000
	=2000 TU28	Apr. 16, 2051	102,500	165,000
10	2000 QK130	Mar. 15, 2089	111,800	180,000

* Minimum possible distance from Earth

Source: NASA

It is widely accepted that an asteroid impact with Earth some 65 million years ago was responsible for the extinction of the dinosaurs. It is believed that there are up to 2,000 "Near-Earth Objects" (mostly asteroids and comets) over one kilometer (about ⅔ mile) in diameter, and many thousands of smaller ones that approach Earth's orbit and could potentially impact with our planet, with those listed here predicted to make the closest approaches. Asteroids approaching Earth are divided into three groups: Apollos (orbit-crossers), Amors (those that approach but do not cross) and Atens (within our orbit). The "Doomsday Scenario" of an asteroid's colliding with Earth, as presented by such movies as *Armageddon* (1998), would probably involve an Apollo.

⊕ **Collision course?**
Small meteoroids usually break up on contact with the atmosphere, but a body over 50 yards (46 m) in diameter could cause a catastrophe on Earth.

top 10 **LARGEST BODIES**
IN THE SOLAR SYSTEM

BODY / MAXIMUM DIAMETER (MILES / KM)

1 Sun 865,036 miles / 1,392,140 km

2 Jupiter 88,846 miles / 142,984 km

3 Saturn 74,898 miles / 120,536 km

10 Titan 3,200 miles / 5,150 km

9 Ganymede 3,274 miles / 5,269 km

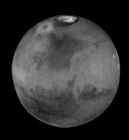

Most of the planets are visible with the naked eye and have been observed since ancient times. The exceptions are Uranus, discovered on March 13, 1781 by British astronomer Sir William Herschel; Neptune, found by German astronomer Johann Galle on September 23, 1846 (Galle was led to his discovery by the independent calculations of French astronomer Urbain Leverrier and British mathematician John Adams); and—outside the Top 10—Pluto, located using photographic techniques by American astronomer Clyde Tombaugh. Pluto's discovery was announced on March 13, 1930; its diameter is uncertain, but is thought to be approximately 1,430 miles (2,300 km). Mercury, also outside the Top 10, has a diameter of 3,032 miles (4,880 km). Ganymede is the largest of Jupiter's 63 satellites, and Titan the largest of Saturn's 34.

8 Mars 4,222 miles / 6,794 km

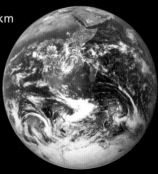

7 Venus 7,520 miles / 12,103 km

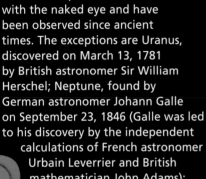

6 Earth 7,926 miles / 12,756 km

5 Neptune 30,778 miles / 49,532 km

4 Uranus 31,763 miles / 51,118 km

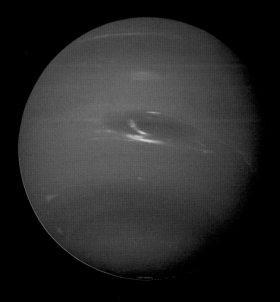

Astronauts & Cosmonauts

top 10 YOUNGEST ASTRONAUTS AND COSMONAUTS*

	ASTRONAUT OR COSMONAUT / COUNTRY#	FIRST FLIGHT	AGE (YRS	MTHS	DAYS)
1	**Gherman S. Titov**	Aug. 6, 1961	25	10	25
2	**Valentina V. Tereshkova**	June 16, 1963	26	3	10
3	**Boris B. Yegorov**	Oct. 15, 1964	26	10	19
4	**Yuri A. Gagarin**	Apr. 12, 1961	27	1	3
5	**Helen P. Sharman**, UK	May 18, 1991	27	11	19
6	**Mark R. Shuttleworth**, South Africa	Apr. 25, 2002	28	7	7
7	**Dumitru D. Prunariu**, Romania	May 14, 1981	28	7	24
8	**Valery F. Bykovsky**	June 14, 1963	28	10	19
9	**Salman Abdel Aziz Al-Saud**, Saudi Arabia	June 17, 1985	28	11	20
10	**Vladimir Remek**, Czechoslovakia	Mar. 2, 1978	29	5	6

* To Jan. 1, 2005

All Soviet, unless otherwise stated

⊕ Blast off

In the space shuttle's 24-year history, 113 launches have achieved a cumulative total of 1,031 days in space.

top 10 COUNTRIES WITH THE MOST EXPERIENCE OF SPACEFLIGHT

	COUNTRY	ASTRONAUTS	TOTAL DURATION OF MISSIONS* (DAYS	HRS	MINS	SECS)
1	**USSR/Russia**	97	16,858	17	8	24
2	**US**	275	9,380	10	4	48
3	**France**	9	384	23	38	0
4	**Kazakhstan**	2	349	14	59	3
5	**Germany**	10	309	17	8	56
6	**Canada**	8	122	13	30	58
7	**Japan**	5	88	6	0	40
8	**Italy**	4	76	6	34	9
9	**Switzerland**	1	42	12	5	32
10	**South Africa**	1	24	22	28	22

* To Oct. 24, 2004 landing of Soyuz TMA-4

The USSR, and now Russia, has clocked up its considerable lead on the rest of the world (with 60.2 percent of the total time spent by humans in space) largely through the long-duration stays of its cosmonauts on board the Mir space station.

top 10 LONGEST SPACE SHUTTLE FLIGHTS*

	FLIGHT	DATES	(DAYS	DURATION HRS	MINS	SECS)
1	**STS-80 Columbia**	Nov. 19–Dec. 7, 1996	17	8	53	18
2	**STS-78 Columbia**	June 20–July 7, 1996	16	21	48	30
3	**STS-67 Endeavor**	Mar. 2–18, 1995	16	15	9	46
4	**STS-107 Columbia#**	Jan. 16–Feb. 1, 2003	15	22	20	0
5	**STS-73 Columbia**	Oct. 20–Nov. 5, 1995	15	21	53	16
6	**STS-90 Columbia**	Apr. 17–May. 3, 1998	15	21	15	58
7	**STS-75 Columbia**	Feb. 22–Mar. 9, 1996	15	17	41	25
8	**STS-94 Columbia**	July 1–17, 1997	15	16	46	1
9	**STS-87 Atlantis**	Sept. 25–Oct. 6, 1997	15	16	35	1
10	**STS-65 Columbia**	July 8–23, 1994	14	17	55	0

* To Jan. 1, 2005   # Destroyed on re-entry

The abbreviation STS (Space Transportation System) has been used throughout the Shuttle programme. The first nine flights were simply numbered STS-1 (April 12–14, 1981) to STS-9. Thereafter a more complex system was employed: the first of the double-digit numbers shows the fiscal year (October 1–September 30) in which the launch took place; the number 1 indicates that it was made from the Kennedy Space Center, 2 from Vandenberg Air Force Base, and the letter the order in which the flights were scheduled, starting with A (although this does not necessarily show the actual sequence in which the mission occurred, due to occasional delays). The ill-fated STS-51-L *Challenger* was the last to be so numbered; all subsequent launches have reverted to the original system of STS + number alone and assigned sequentially to each mission, but the flights do not follow this order precisely.

⬇ Spacewalk

US astronaut Mark C. Lee uses a jetpack to conduct a free spacewalk from *Discovery* (1994); those who performed the longest-duration EVAs have all been tethered to shuttles.

top 10 LONGEST SPACEWALKS*

	ASTRONAUTS[#]	SPACECRAFT	DATE	DURATION (HRS:MIN)
1	James Voss, Susan Helms	STS-102/ISS[†]	Mar. 10–11, 2001	8:56
2	Thomas D. Akers, Richard J. Hieb, Pierre J. Thuot	STS-49	May 13, 1992	8:29
3	John M. Grunsfeld, Steven L. Smith	STS-103	Dec. 22, 1999	8:15
4	C. Michael Foale, Claude Nicollier	STS-103	Dec. 23, 1999	8:10
5	John M. Grunsfeld, Steven L. Smith	STS-103	Dec. 24, 1999	8:08
6	Daniel T. Barry, Tamara E. Jernigan	STS-96/ISS	May 29, 1999	7:55
7	Jeffrey A. Hoffman, F. Story Musgrave	STS-61	Dec. 4, 1993	7:54
8	Steven S. Smith, Rex J. Walheim	STS-110/ISS	Apr. 11, 2002	7:48
9	Thomas D. Akers, Kathryn C. Thornton	STS-49	May 14, 1992	7:44
10	Takao Doi, Winston E. Scott	STS-87	Nov. 24, 1997	7:43

* To Jan. 1, 2005 [#] All US exc. C. Michael Foale who has dual US/UK citizenship [†] International Space Station

All of these EVAs (Extra-Vehicular Activities) were from NASA space shuttles, most of them concerned with capture or repairs to satellites and other equipment, including the Hubble space telescope, and from the International Space Station. The longest EVA on the Moon lasted 7 hours 37 minutes. It was conducted by Eugene A. Cernan (Commander) and Harrison H. Schmitt (Lunar Module Pilot) on December 12, 1972 during Apollo 17's 75-hour stay on the lunar surface—the last occasion on which humans set foot on the Moon.

Oceans & Seas

top 10 LARGEST OCEANS AND SEAS

OCEAN OR SEA	APPROXIMATE AREA* (SQ MILES)	(SQ KM)
1 Pacific Ocean	64,186,600	166,242,500
2 Atlantic Ocean	33,420,160	86,557,800
3 Indian Ocean	28,350,640	73,427,800
4 Arctic Ocean	5,105,740	13,223,800
5 South China Sea	1,148,499	2,974,600
6 Caribbean Sea	971,400	2,515,900
7 Mediterranean Sea	969,120	2,510,000
8 Bering Sea	873,020	2,261,100
9 Sea of Okhotsk	589,800	1,527,570
10 Gulf of Mexico	582,100	1,507,600

* Excluding tributary seas

Geographers' opinions vary as to whether certain bodies of water are regarded as seas in their own right, or as parts of a larger ocean. For example, the Coral, Weddell, and Tasman seas would be eligible for this list, but most authorities consider them part of the Pacific Ocean, whereas the Bering Sea is more commonly identified as an independent sea.

top 10 SMALLEST SEAS

SEA* / OCEAN	APPROXIMATE AREA (SQ MILES)	(SQ KM)
1 Gulf of California, Pacific Ocean	59,100	153,070
2 Persian Gulf, Indian Ocean	88,800	230,000
3 Yellow Sea, Pacific Ocean	113,500	293,960
4 Baltic Sea, Atlantic Ocean	147,500	382,000
5 North Sea, Atlantic Ocean	164,900	427,090
6 Red Sea, Indian Ocean	174,900	452,990
7 Black Sea, Atlantic Ocean	196,100	507,900
8 Andaman Sea, Indian Ocean	218,100	564,880
9 East China Sea, Pacific Ocean	256,600	664,590
10 Hudson Bay, Atlantic Ocean	281,900	730,120

* Excludes landlocked seas

top 10 COUNTRIES WITH THE LARGEST AREAS OF CORAL REEF

COUNTRY	REEF AREA (SQ MILES)	(SQ KM)	PERCENTAGE OF WORLD TOTAL
1 Indonesia	19,699	51,020	17.95
2 Australia	18,903	48,960	17.22
3 The Philippines	9,675	25,060	8.81
4 French overseas territories*	5,513	14,280	5.02
5 Papua New Guinea	5,343	13,840	4.87
6 Fiji	3,868	10,020	3.52
7 Maldives	3,444	8,920	3.14
8 Saudi Arabia	2,571	6,660	2.34
9 Marshall Islands	2,359	6,110	2.15
10 India	2,235	5,790	2.04
World total (including those not in Top 10)	*109,768*	*284,300*	*100.00*

* Clipperton, French Polynesia, Guadeloupe, Martinique, Mayotte, New Caledonia, Réunion, and Wallis and Futuna Islands

Source: *World Atlas of Coral Reefs*

Coral reefs thrive in shallow and clear waters and the sea temperatures found in the tropics. Among the richest of the world's ecosystems, they are extremely vulnerable to human intervention, with overfishing, pollution, and the consequences of global warming presenting the biggest threats to their existence.

⬆ **Coral reef residents**
The world's coral reefs support a diverse range of life, including many exotic fish, in a delicately balanced ecosystem that is vulnerable to outside influences.

top 10 **SHALLOWEST** OCEANS AND SEAS

OCEAN OR SEA* / LOCATION	AVERAGE DEPTH (FT)	(M)
1 **Yellow Sea**, Pacific Ocean	121	36.8
2 **Baltic Sea**, Atlantic Ocean	180	54.8
3 **Hudson Bay**, Atlantic Ocean	305	92.9
4 **North Sea**, Atlantic Ocean	308	93.8
5 **Persian Gulf**, Indian Ocean	328	99.9
6 **East China Sea**, Indian Ocean	620	188.9
7 **Red Sea**, Indian Ocean	1,764	537.6
8 **Gulf of California**, Pacific Ocean	2,375	723.9
9 **Sea of Okhotsk**, Pacific Ocean	3,192	972.9
10 **Arctic Ocean**	3,407	1,038.4

* Excludes landlocked seas

With a maximum depth of 500 ft (152 m), the Yellow Sea will probably not remain on the Top 10 list of shallowest oceans and seas forever—it is likely that environmental changes in the next few millennia will result in the total disappearance of the sea.

◷ **Shallow yellow** The Yellow Sea between Korea and China gets its distinctive color from the sand particles carried into it from the Yellow River (Huang He), its shallowness causing them to be dispersed slowly.

top 10 **DEEPEST** OCEANS AND SEAS

OCEAN OR SEA	GREATEST DEPTH (FT)	(M)	AVERAGE DEPTH (FT)	(M)
1 **Pacific Ocean**	35,837	10,924	13,215	4,028
2 **Indian Ocean**	24,460	7,455	13,002	3,963
3 **Atlantic Ocean**	30,246	9,219	12,880	3,926
4 **Caribbean Sea**	22,788	6,946	8,685	2,647
5 **South China Sea**	16,456	5,016	5,419	1,652
6 **Bering Sea**	15,659	4,773	5,075	1,547
7 **Gulf of Mexico**	12,425	3,787	4,874	1,486
8 **Mediterranean Sea**	15,197	4,632	4,688	1,429
9 **Japan Sea**	12,276	3,742	4,429	1,350
10 **Arctic Ocean**	18,456	5,625	3,953	1,205

The deepest point in the deepest ocean is the Marianas Trench in the Pacific, at a depth of 35,837 ft (10,924 m), according to a recent survey. However, the slightly lesser depth of 35,814 ft (10,916 m) was recorded on January 23, 1960 by Jacques Piccard (Switzerland) and Donald Walsh (US) in their 58-ft- (17.7-m-) long bathyscaphe *Trieste 2* during the deepest-ever ocean descent. Whichever is correct, it is close to 6.8 miles (11 km) down, or almost 29 times the height of the Empire State Building.

First Fact

The first craft capable of exploring the world's deepest oceans was the bathyscaphe (from the Greek words for "depth" and "ship"), invented by Auguste Piccard (Switzerland, 1884–1962). The holder of the world balloon altitude record, he adapted design elements from his balloon gondola to the bathyscaphe, taking it down to record depths. Its successor, *Trieste 2*, was the craft in which Piccard's son Jacques set the unbeatable depth record in 1960. In 1999, Auguste's grandson Bertrand Piccard took part in the first balloon circumnavigation of the globe.

Rivers & Lakes

top 10 GREATEST RIVER SYSTEMS*

	RIVER SYSTEM	CONTINENT	AVERAGE DISCHARGE AT MOUTH (CU M / SEC)
1	Amazon	South America	180,000
2	Congo (Zaïre)	Africa	42,000
3	Yangtze (Chang Jiang)	Asia	35,000
4	Orinoco	South America	28,000
5	Brahmaputra (Tsangpo)	Asia	20,000
6	Yenisei/Angara	Asia	19,600
7	Río de la Plata/Paraná/Uruguay	South America	19,500
8	Mississippi/Missouri	North America	17,545
9	Lena	Asia	16,400
10	Mekong	Asia	15,900

* Based on rate of discharge at mouth

Source: River Systems of the World

top 10 LONGEST RIVER SYSTEMS

	RIVER SYSTEM	CONTINENT	APPROXIMATE LENGTH (MILES)	(KM)
1	Nile	Africa	4,160	6,695
2	Amazon	South America	4,007	6,448
3	Yangtze (Chang Jiang)	Asia	3,964	6,378
4	Mississippi/Missouri	North America	3,870	6,228
5	Ob'	Asia	3,460	5,570
6	Yenisei/Angara	Asia	3,448	5,550
7	Huang He (Yellow)	Asia	3,395	5,464
8	Río de la Plata/Paraná/Uruguay	South America	2,920	4,700
9	Amur	Asia	2,744	4,415
10	Lena	Asia	2,734	4,400

The source of the Nile was discovered in 1858, when British explorer John Hanning Speke reached Lake Victoria Nyanza, in what is now Burundi. It was not until 1953 that the source of the Amazon was identified as a stream called Huarco, which flows from the Misuie glacier in the Peruvian Andes mountains.

⊃ Great lake
Once called the Hyrcanian Ocean, the Caspian Sea, seen here from space, is a saltwater lake that has been landlocked for over five million years. It is fed by the Volga (top left) and other rivers.

top 10 LAKES WITH THE GREATEST VOLUME OF WATER

	LAKE / LOCATION	VOLUME (CU MILES)	(CU KM)
1	Caspian Sea, Azerbaijan/Iran/Kazakhstan/Russia/Turkmenistan	18,882	78,707
2	Baikal, Russia	5,517	22,995
3	Tanganyika, Burundi/Tanzania/Dem. Rep.of Congo/Zambia	4,391	18,304
4	Superior, Canada/US	2,921	12,174
5	Michigan/Huron, Canada/US	2,642	8,449
6	Nyasa (Malawi), Malawi/Mozambique/Tanzania	1,865	7,775
7	Victoria, Kenya/Tanzania/Uganda	604	2,518
8	Great Bear, Canada	550	2,292
9	Great Slave, Canada	542	2,258
10	Issyk Kul, Kyrgyzstan	420	1,725

The Caspian Sea is the world's largest inland sea or lake, containing some 40 percent of all the planet's surface water and receiving more water than any other landlocked body of water—an average of 82 cu miles (340 cu km) per year, which is causing a steady rise in sea level. This environmental change, along with pollution and the overfishing of the Caspian's famed sturgeon population, is among the many threats to its future.

top 10 **LARGEST** LAKES

LAKE / LOCATION	APPROXIMATE AREA (SQ MILES)	(SQ KM)
1 Caspian Sea Azerbaijan/Iran/Kazakhstan/ Russia/Turkmenistan	143,000	371,000
2 Michigan/Huron* Canada/US	45,342	117,436
3 Superior Canada/US	31,700	82,103
4 Victoria Kenya/Tanzania/Uganda	26,828	69,485
5 Tanganyika Burundi/Tanzania/Dem. Rep. of Congo/Zambia	12,700	32,893
6 Baikal Russia	12,162	31,500
7 Great Bear Canada	12,096	31,328
8 Malawi (Nyasa) Tanzania/Malawi/Mozambique	11,150	28,880
9 Great Slave Canada	11,030	28,568
10 Erie Canada/US	9,910	25,667

* Now considered two lobes of the same lake

Lake Michigan/Huron is the world's largest freshwater lake. Lake Baikal (or Baykal) in Siberia, with a depth of as much as 1.08 miles (1.74 km) in parts, is the world's deepest. As recently as 1960, the Aral Sea (Kazakhstan/ Uzbekistan), with an area, including lake islands, of some 26,371 sq miles (68,300 sq km) was the fourth largest lake in the world, but as a result of the diverting of rivers for irrigation, it has dropped to 6,625 sq miles (17,158 sq km).

FastFact Sealed 13,125 ft (4,000 m) beneath the Antarctic, Lake Vostok may be one of the largest lakes on Earth. Despite its location, it is liquid, rather than frozen. It covers an area of some 5,400 sq miles (14,000 sq km) and has a volume of 1,295 cu miles (5,400 cu km). Discovered in 1996 through radar observations from space, it has not been investigated because drilling through the ice into the lake may force it to gush to the surface, contaminating water that has remained undisturbed for up to a million years.

top 10 **DEEPEST** LAKES

LAKE / LOCATION	GREATEST DEPTH (FT)	(M)
10 Hornindals Norway	1,686	514
9 Toba Sumatra, Indonesia	1,736	529
8 Crater Oregon	1,932	589
7 Matana Sulawesi, Indonesia	1,936	590
6 Great Slave Canada	2,015	614
5 Issyk-kul Kyrgyzstan	2,191	668
4 Malawi Malawi/Mozambique/Tanzania	2,316	706
3 Caspian Sea Azerbaijan/Iran/Kazakhstan/ Russia/Turkmenistan	3,363	1,025
2 Tanganyika Burundi/Tanzania/ Dem. Rep. of Congo/ Zambia	4,825	1,471
1 Baikal Russia	5,712	1,741

Islands

top 10 SMALLEST ISLAND COUNTRIES

COUNTRY / LOCATION	AREA (SQ MILES)	(SQ KM)
1 **Nauru**, Pacific Ocean	8	21
2 **Tuvalu**, Pacific Ocean	10	26
3 **Marshall Islands**, Pacific Ocean	70	181
4 **Maldives**, Indian Ocean	116	300
5 **Malta**, Mediterranean Sea	124	321
6 = **Grenada**, Caribbean Sea	131	339
= **St. Vincent and the Grenadines**, Caribbean Sea	131	339
8 **St. Kitts and Nevis**, Caribbean Sea	139	360
9 **Barbados**, Caribbean Sea	166	430
10 **Antigua and Barbuda**, Caribbean Sea	170	440

Source: US Census Bureau, International Database

◑ Marshall Islands
One of the world's smallest island countries, the Marshall Islands—a group of 34 coral atolls and islands—has been an independent country since 1986.

top 10 LARGEST LAKE ISLANDS

ISLAND / LAKE / LOCATION	AREA (SQ MILES)	(SQ KM)
1 **Manitoulin** Huron, Ontario	1,068	2,766
2 **René-Lavasseur** Manicouagan Reservoir, Quebec	780	2,020
3 **Olkhon** Baikal, Russia	282	730
4 **Samosir** Toba, Sumatra, Indonesia	243	630
5 **Isle Royale** Superior, Michigan	209	541
6 **Ukerewe** Victoria, Tanzania	205	530
7 **St. Joseph** Huron, Ontario	141	365
8 **Drummond** Huron, Michigan	134	347
9 **Idjwi** Kivu, Dem. Rep. of Congo	110	285
10 **Ometepe** Nicaragua, Nicaragua	107	276

Not all islands are surrounded by sea: many sizable islands are situated in lakes. Vozrozhdeniya Island, Uzbekistan, previously second in this list with an area of roughly 900 sq miles (2,300 sq km), has grown as the Aral Sea contracts, and is now linked to the surrounding land to become a peninsula. There are even larger islands in freshwater river outlets, including Marajó in the mouth of the Amazon, Brazil (18,533 sq miles/48,000 sq km), and Bananal in the Araguaia River, Brazil (7,722 sq miles/20,000 sq km).

top 10 LARGEST ISLANDS

ISLAND / LOCATION	AREA* (SQ MILES)	(SQ KM)
1 **Greenland (Kalaatdlit Nunaat)**, North Atlantic	840,004	2,175,600
2 **New Guinea**, Southwest Pacific	303,381	785,753
3 **Borneo**, West mid-Pacific	288,869	748,168
4 **Madagascar**, Indian Ocean	226,917	587,713
5 **Baffin Island**, North Atlantic	194,574	503,944
6 **Sumatra**, Northeast Indian Ocean	171,068	443,065
7 **Great Britain**, off coast of Northwest Europe	88,787	229,957
8 **Honshu**, Sea of Japan	87,182	225,800
9 **Victoria Island**, Arctic Ocean	85,154	220,548
10 **Ellesmere Island**, Arctic Ocean	71,029	183,964

* Mainlands, including areas of inland water, but excluding offshore islands

Australia is regarded as a continental land mass rather than an island; otherwise it would rank first, at 7,618,493 sq km (2,941,517 sq miles), or 35 times the size of Great Britain. The largest US island is Hawaii, which measures 10,456 sq km (4,037 sq miles), and the largest off mainland USA is Kodiak, Alaska, at 9,510 sq km (3,672 sq miles).

top 10 **MOST ISOLATED** ISLANDS

ISLAND / LOCATION / ISOLATION INDEX

The United Nations' isolation index is calculated by adding together the square roots of the distances to the nearest island, group of islands, and continent. The higher the number, the more remote the island.

Source: United Nations

Gough Island,
South Atlantic,
Isolation index: 125

=9

Bouvet Island,
South Atlantic,
Isolation index: 125

Far away
The United Nations' isolation index identifies these islands as the most remote on the planet.

Palmyra Island,
Central Pacific,
Isolation index: 125

=9

Kiritimati,
Line Islands,
Central Pacific,
Isolation index: 129

3

Jarvis Island,
Central Pacific,
Isolation index: 128

4

=5

Kosrae, Micronesia,
Pacific,
Isolation index: 126

Starbuck, Line Islands,
Central Pacific,
Isolation index: 126

=5 **Malden**, Line Islands,
Central Pacific,
Isolation index: 126

Vostok, Line Islands,
Central Pacific,
Isolation index: 126

Easter Island,
South Pacific,
Isolation index: 149

2

1

Rapa Iti, Tubuai Islands,
South Pacific,
Isolation index: 130

 Solitary sentinels
The most isolated place on Earth, Easter Island is "guarded" by more than 600 curious statues or *moai*, some over 32 ft (9.8 m) high and weighing 100 tons.

Mountains & Other Land Features

top 10 **LARGEST** METEORITE CRATERS

	CRATER / LOCATION	DIAMETER (MILES)	DIAMETER (KM)
1	**Vredefort**, South Africa	186	300
2	**Sudbury**, Ontario	155	250
3	**Chicxulub**, Yucatán, Mexico	107	170
4 =	**Manicouagan**, Quebec	62	100
=	**Popigai**, Russia	62	100
6	**Acraman**, Australia	56	90
7	**Chesapeake Bay**, Virginia	53	85
8	**Puchezh-Katunki**, Russia	50	80
9	**Morokweng**, South Africa	43	70
10	**Kara**, Russia	40	65

Source: Canada Geological Survey, Continental Geoscience Division

Unlike on the Solar System's other planets and moons, many astroblemes (collision sites) on Earth have been weathered over time and obscured. Thus, one of the ongoing debates in geology is whether or not certain craterlike structures are of meteoric origin or are the remnants of long-extinct volcanoes. The Vredefort Ring, for example, long thought to be meteoric, was declared in 1963 to be volcanic, but has since been claimed as a definite meteor crater, as are all the giant meteorite craters in the Top 10 (along with 106 others) by the International Union of Geological Sciences Commission on Comparative Planetology.

top 10 **DEEPEST** DEPRESSIONS

	DEPRESSION / LOCATION	MAXIMUM DEPTH BELOW SEA LEVEL (FT)	MAXIMUM DEPTH BELOW SEA LEVEL (M)
1	**Dead Sea**, Israel/Jordan	1,312	400
2	**Lake Assal**, Djibouti	511	156
3	**Turfan Depression**, China	505	154
4	**Qattâra Depression**, Egypt	436	133
5	**Mangyshlak Peninsula**, Kazakhstan	433	132
6	**Danakil Depression**, Ethiopia	383	117
7	**Death Valley**, California	282	86
8	**Salton Sink**, California	235	72
9	**Zapadny Chink Ustyurta**, Kazakhstan	230	70
10	**Prikaspiyskaya Nizmennost'**, Kazakhstan/Russia	220	67

The shore of the Dead Sea is the lowest exposed ground below sea level, but the bed of the sea actually reaches 2,388 ft (728 m) below sea level, and that of Lake Baikal, Russia, extends 4,872 ft (1,485 m) below sea level. Much of Antarctica is below sea level (some as low as 8,326 ft/2,538 m), but the land there is covered by an ice cap that averages 6,890 ft (2,100 m) thick. The lowest points on continents outside those appearing in the Top 10 include South America's Peninsula Valdés, Argentina (131 ft/40 m below sea level), Europe's Caspian Sea shore (92 ft/28 m), and Australia's Lake Eyre (52 ft/12 m).

top 10 **LONGEST** CAVES

CAVE / LOCATION / TOTAL KNOWN LENGTH (MILES / KM)

The world's longest cave systems compared with the as-the-crow-flies 230-mile (370-km) distance between London and Paris.

SCALE   64 MILES / 100 KM   128 MILES / 200 KM   192 MILES / 300 KM

10 Ozernaja, Ukrainskaja, Ukraine, 76 miles / 122 km
9 Sistema Ox Bel Ha, Quintana Roo, Mexico, 83 miles / 133 km
8 Siebenhengste-hohgant, Bern, Switzerland, 92 miles / 149 km
7 Fisher Ridge System, Kentucky, 107 miles / 172 km
6 Wind Cave, South Dakota, 113 miles / 182 km
5 Lechuguilla Cave, New Mexico, 114 miles / 183 km
4 Hölloch, Schwyz, Switzerland, 117 miles / 189 km
3 Jewel Cave, South Dakota, 129 miles / 207 km
2 Optimisticeskaja, Ukrainskaja, Ukraine, 133 n

Source: Bob Gulden

top 10 HIGHEST MOUNTAINS

MOUNTAIN / LOCATION	FIRST ASCENT	TEAM NATIONALITY	HEIGHT* (FT)	HEIGHT* (M)
1 Everest Nepal/China	May 29, 1953	British/ New Zealand	29,035	8,850
2 K2 (Chogori) Pakistan/China	July 31, 1954	Italian	28,238	8,607
3 Kangchenjunga Nepal/India	May 25, 1955	British	28,208	8,598
4 Lhotse Nepal/China	May 18, 1956	Swiss	27,923	8,511
5 Makalu I Nepal/China	May 15, 1955	French	27,824	8,481
6 Lhotse Shar II Nepal/China	May 12, 1970	Austrian	27,504	8,383
7 Dhaulagiri I Nepal	May 13, 1960	Swiss/ Austrian	26,810	8,172
8 Manaslu I (Kutang I) Nepal	May 9, 1956	Japanese	26,760	8,156
9 Cho Oyu Nepal	Oct. 19, 1954	Austrian	26,750	8,153
10 Nanga Parbat (Diamir) Kashmir	July 3, 1953	German/ Austrian	26,660	8,126

* Height of principal peak; lower peaks of the same mountain are excluded

top 10 MOST ACTIVE VOLCANOES*

VOLCANO / LOCATION	CONTINUOUSLY ACTIVE SINCE
1 Mount Etna, Italy	c. 1500 BC
2 Stromboli, Italy	c. 4
3 Yasur, Vanuatu	c. 1204
4 Piton de la Fournaise, Reunion	1920
5 Santa Maria, Guatemala	1922
6 Dukono, Indonesia	1933
7 Sangay, Ecuador	1934
8 Ambrym, Vanuatu	1935
9 Suwanose-jima, Japan	1949
10 Tinakula, Solomon Islands	1951

* Based on years of continuous eruption

Source: John Seach, www.volcanolive.com

Sicily's 10,991-ft (3,350-m) Mount Etna may have been erupting for more than half a million years, with occasional dormant periods. Continuous activity has been recorded for the past 3,500 years, the eruption of 1843 killing 56, with a further nine in 1979 and two in 1987.

256 MILES / 400 KM

4 km

Edouard-Alfred Martel

Edouard-Alfred Martel (1859–1938), a French lawyer, invented the science of speleology (cave exploration). From 1888 onward, he explored numerous caves in Europe—many for the first time—discovering underground lakes and streams and developing some of the first caving equipment, including portable ladders and collapsible canoes. In 1889 he became the first to enter the spectacular Gouffre de Padirac, France, and in 1898 he established it as France's first cave open to the public.

➲ Cave man
In an illustration by Lucien Rudeaux, Martel is shown during the first exploration of Great Britain's largest cavern, Gaping Gill, Yorkshire, 1895.

1 Mammoth Cave System, Kentucky, 360 miles / 579 km

World Weather

top 10 COLDEST PLACES—EXTREMES

	LOCATION*	LOWEST RECORDED TEMPERATURE (°F)	(°C)
1	**Vostok**[#], Antarctica	−128.6	−89.2
2	**Sovietskaya**[#], Antarctica	−124.1	−86.7
3	**Oymyakon**, Russia	−96.2	−71.2
4	**Verkhoyansk**, Russia	−93.6	−69.8
5	**Northice**[#], Greenland	−87.0	−66.0
6	**Eismitte**[#], Greenland	−85.0	−64.9
7 =	**Snag**, Yukon, Canada	−81.4	−63.0
=	**Bulunkul Lake**, Tajikistan	−81.4	−63.0
9	**Mayo**, Yukon, Canada	−80.0	−62.2
10	**Prospect Creek**, Alaska	−79.8	−62.1

* Maximum of two places per country listed

Present or former scientific research base

Source: Philip Eden/Roland Bert

Vostok, a Russian research station, recorded the lowest temperature on Earth on July 21, 1983, and—though unofficial—an even colder one of −132°F (−91°C) in 1997. It is situated at an altitude of 11,220 ft (3,420 m) and is subject to katabatic (downhill) winds that can reach up to 200 mph (322 km/h).

top 10 CLOUDIEST PLACES*

	LOCATION[#]	PERCENTAGE OF MAXIMUM POSSIBLE SUNSHINE	AVERAGE ANNUAL HOURS OF SUNSHINE
1	**Ben Nevis**, Scotland	16	736
2	**Hoyvik**, Faeroes, Denmark	19	902
3	**Maam**, Ireland	19	929
4	**Prince Rupert**, British Columbia, Canada	20	955
5	**Riksgransen**, Sweden	20	965
6	**Akureyri**, Iceland	20	973
7	**Raufarhöfn**, Iceland	21	995
8	**Nanortalik**, Greenland	22	1,000
9	**Dalwhinnie**, Scotland	22	1,032
10	**Karasjok**, Norway	23	1,090

* Lowest yearly sunshine total, averaged over a long period of years

Maximum of two places per country listed

Source: Philip Eden

The least sunny places on Earth tend to be in northern latitudes and at elevations that make them susceptible to cloud cover. As a result, Ben Nevis receives about one-sixth of the total sunshine hours of the world's desert areas.

top 10 PLACES WITH THE HEAVIEST DAILY DOWNPOURS*

LOCATION[#] / HIGHEST RAINFALL IN 24 HOURS (IN / MM)

1 Chilaos, Réunion 73.6 in / 1,870 mm

2 Baguio, Philippines 46.0 in / 1,168 mm

3 Alvin, Texas 43.0 in / 1,092 mm

4 Cherrapunji, India 41.0 in / 1,041 mm

5 Smithport, Pennsylvania 39.9 in / 1,013 mm

6 Crohamhurst, Australia 35.7 in / 907 mm

7 Finch-Hatton, Australia 34.6 in / 879 mm

8 Suva, Fiji 26.5 in / 673 mm

9 Cayenne, French Guyana 23.5 in / 597 mm

10 Aitutaki, Cook Islands 22.5 in / 572 mm

* Based on limited data

Maximum of two places per country listed

Source: Philip Eden

→ Desert blooms
At certain times of the year, the barren desert surrounding Yuma, the world's sunniest inhabited place, supports a profusion of wildflowers.

top 10 **HOTTEST** PLACES—EXTREMES

	LOCATION*	HIGHEST RECORDED TEMPERATURE (°F)	(°C)
1	**Al'Azīzīyah**, Libya	136.4	58.0
2	**Greenland Ranch**, Death Valley, California	134.0	56.7
3	= **Ghudamis**, Libya	131.0	55.0
	= **Kebili**, Tunisia	131.0	55.0
5	**Tombouctou**, Mali	130.1	54.5
6	= **Araouane**, Mali	130.0	54.4
	= **Mammoth Tank**#, California	130.0	54.4
8	**Tirat Tavi**, Israel	129.0	54.0
9	**Ahwāz**, Iran	128.3	53.5
10	**Agha Jārī**, Iran	128.0	53.3

* Maximum of two places per country listed

\# Former weather station

Source: Philip Eden/Roland Bert

top 10 **SUNNIEST** PLACES*

	LOCATION#	PERCENTAGE OF MAXIMUM POSSIBLE SUNSHINE	AVERAGE ANNUAL HOURS OF SUNSHINE
1	**Yuma**, Arizona	91	4,127
2	**Phoenix**, Arizona	90	4,041
3	**Wadi Halfa**, Sudan	89	3,964
4	**Bordj Omar Driss**, Algeria	88	3,899
5	**Keetmanshoop**, Namibia	88	3,876
6	**Aoulef**, Algeria	86	3,784
7	**Upington**, South Africa	86	3,766
8	**Atbara**, Sudan	85	3,739
9	**Mariental**, Namibia	84	3,707
10	**Bilma**, Niger	84	3,699

* Highest yearly sunshine total, averaged over a long period of years

\# Maximum of two places per country listed

Source: Philip Eden

Natural Disasters

the 10 WORST AVALANCHES AND LANDSLIDES*

LOCATION / INCIDENT / DATE / ESTIMATED NO. KILLED

1. **Alps, Italy**
Avalanche, Oct. 218 BC
18,000

2. **Yungay, Peru**
Landslide, May 31, 1970
17,500

3. **Alps, Italy**
Avalanche, Dec. 13, 1916
10,000

4. **Huarás, Peru**
Avalanche, Dec. 13, 1941
5,000

5. **Nevada Huascarán, Peru**
Avalanche, Jan. 10, 1962
3,500

6. **Chiavenna, Italy**
Landslide, Sept. 4, 1618
2,427

7. **Plurs, Switzerland**
Avalanche, Sept. 4, 1618
1,496

8. **Goldau Valley, Switzerland**
Landslide, Sept. 2, 1806
800

9. **Medellín, Colombia**
Landslide, Sept. 27, 1987
683

10. **Chungar, Peru**
Avalanche, Mar. 19, 1971
600

* Excluding those where most deaths resulted from flooding, earthquakes, volcanoes, etc, associated with landslides

the 10 WORST HURRICANES, TYPHOONS, AND CYCLONES

LOCATION / DATE / ESTIMATED NO. KILLED

1. **East Pakistan (Bangladesh)**
Nov. 13, 1970
500,000–1,000,000

2. **Bengal, India**
Oct. 7, 1737
>300,000

3. **Haiphong, Vietnam**
1881
300,000

4. **Bengal, India**
Oct. 31, 1876
200,000

5. **Bombay, India**
June 6, 1882
>100,000

6. **Southern Japan**
Aug. 23, 1281
68,000

7. **Northeast China**
Aug. 2–3, 1922
60,000

8. **Calcutta, India**
Oct. 5, 1864
50,000–70,000

9. **Bengal, India**
Oct. 15–16, 1942
40,000

10. **East Pakistan (Bangladesh))**
May–June 1965
35,000–40,000

the 10 COSTLIEST HURRICANES TO STRIKE THE US

HURRICANE / YEAR / COST OF DAMAGE*

1. **"Great Miami"**
1926
$83,814,000,000

2. **Andrew**
1992
$44,878,000,000

3. **North Texas**
1900
$36,096,000,000

4. **North Texas**
1915
$30,585,000,000

5. **New England**
1938
$22,549,000,000

6. **Southwest Florida**
1944
$22,070,000,000

7. **Southeast Florida/ Lake Okeechobee**
1928
$18,708,000,000

8. **Betsy**
1965
$16,863,000,000

9. **Donna**
1960
$16,339,000,000

10. **Camille**
1969
$14,870,000,000

* Adjusted to 2003 dollars

Source: Atlantic Oceanographic and Meteorological Laboratory/National Oceanic and Atmospheric Administration

⊙ Eye of the storm
A cyclone seen from space: the size and power of these and related meteorological phenomena cause loss of life and property on an often massive scale.

the 10 WORST EARTHQUAKES

LOCATION / DATE / ESTIMATED NO. KILLED

1 **Near East/Mediterranean**
May 20, 1202
1,100,000

2 **Shenshi, China**
Feb. 2, 1556
820,000

3 **Calcutta, India**
Oct. 11, 1737
300,000

4 **Antioch, Syria**
May 20, AD 526
250,000

5 **Tangshan, China**
July 28, 1976
242,419

6 **Nanshan, China**
May 22, 1927
200,000

7 **Yeddo, Japan**
Dec. 30, 1703
190,000

8 **Kansu, China**
Dec. 16, 1920
180,000

9 **Messina, Italy**
Dec. 28, 1908
160,000

10 **Tokyo/Yokohama, Japan**
Sept. 1, 1923
142,807

There are some discrepancies between the "official" death tolls in many of the world's worst earthquakes and the estimates of other authorities. For example, 750,000 is sometimes quoted for the Tang-shan earthquake of 1976, and totals of 58,000–250,000 are given for the quake that devastated Messina in 1908. Several other earthquakes in China and Turkey resulted in deaths of 100,000 or more, and an Armenian quake (December 7, 1988) and an Iranian one (June 21,1990) caused more than 55,000/50,000 deaths, respectively.

 Killer wave
Familiar from the images of Japanese artist Hokusai, tsunamis can reach great heights. One caused by an earthquake in Lituya Bay, Alaska, on July 9, 1958, traveled at 100 mph (160 km/h) and surged to 1,720 ft (524 m), but only two people were killed.

the 10 WORST TSUNAMIS

LOCATIONS AFFECTED / DATE / ESTIMATED NO. KILLED

1 Southeast Asia, Dec. 26, 2004   **287,534**
2 Krakatoa, Sumatra/Java*, Aug. 27, 1883   **36,380**
3 Sanriku, Japan, June 15, 1896   **28,000**
4 Agadir, Morocco#, Feb. 29, 1960   **12,000**
5 Lisbon, Portugal, Nov. 1, 1755   **10,000**
6 Papua New Guinea, July 18, 1998   **8,000**
7 Chile/Pacific islands/Japan, May 22, 1960   **5,700**
8 Philippines, Aug. 17, 1976   **5,000**
9 Hyuga to Izu, Japan, Oct. 28, 1707   **4,900**
10 Sanriku, Japan, Mar. 3, 1933   **3,000**

* Combined effect of volcanic eruption and tsunamis
# Combined effect of earthquake and tsunamis

Tsunamis (from the Japanese *tsu,* meaning "port," and *nami,* meaning "wave"), are powerful waves caused by undersea disturbances such as earthquakes or volcanic eruptions. They are often mistakenly called tidal waves, which are a different phenomenon. Tsunamis can be so intense that they frequently cross entire oceans, devastating islands and coastal regions in their paths. Triggered by a massive undersea earthquake in the Indian Ocean, the 2004 tsunami was exceptionally powerful and destructive. It devastated coastal settlements in low-lying areas of Indonesia, Sri Lanka, Thailand and other countries as far away as Africa, resulting in loss of life on an unprecedented scale.

top 10 heaviest flighted birds: page 38

Chapter

2

top 10 fastest mammals: page 37

top 10 deadliest spiders: page 41

the 10 places where most people
are attacked by sharks: page 35

Life on Earth

top 10 types of pet in the US: page 45

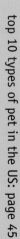

Aquatic Animals

top 10 **HEAVIEST** MARINE MAMMALS

MAMMAL / SCIENTIFIC NAME	LENGTH (FT)	(M)	WEIGHT (TONS)
1 Blue whale, *Balaenoptera musculus*	110.0	33.5	151.0
2 Bowhead whale (Greenland right), *Balaena mysticetus*	65.0	20.0	94.8
3 Northern right whale (black right), *Balaena glacialis*	60.0	18.6	85.6
4 Fin whale (common rorqual), *Balaenoptera physalus*	82.0	25.0	69.9
5 Sperm whale, *Physeter catodon*	59.0	18.0	48.2
6 Gray whale, *Eschrichtius robustus*	46.0	14.0	38.5
7 Humpback whale, *Megaptera novaeangliae*	49.2	15.0	38.1
8 Sei whale, *Balaenoptera borealis*	60.0	18.5	32.4
9 Bryde's whale, *Balaenoptera edeni*	47.9	14.6	22.0
10 Baird's whale, *Berardius bairdii*	18.0	5.5	13.3

Source: Lucy T. Verma

Probably the largest animal that ever lived, the blue whale dwarfs even the other whales listed here—all but one of which far outweigh the biggest land animal, the elephant. The elephant seal, with a weight of 3.9 tons, is the largest marine mammal that is not a whale.

Fast Fact

No blue whale has ever been weighed intact, and size estimates come from measurements of specimens that have been killed and cut up by whalers. Based on this method, the largest was a 90-ft 6-in (27.6-m) female weighing up to 209 tons (190 metric tons) caught by the Russian *Slava* whaling fleet off South Georgia on March 20, 1947. It produced 73 tons of meat and 33 tons of blubber; its skeleton alone weighed 29 tons and its tongue 4.7 tons.

⬆ Big blue
The blue whale is longer than and weighs four times as much as a Boeing 737 aircraft.

top 10 **FASTEST** FISH

⬇ Designed for speed
The skeleton of a sailfish tailfin. Its powerful structure and the streamlined shape of its body are perfectly designed to enable the sailfish to travel in water at speeds faster than a cheetah can attain on land.

FISH / SCIENTIFIC NAME	MAXIMUM RECORDED SPEED (MPH)	(KM/H)
1 Sailfish, *Istiophorus platypterus*	69	112
2 Striped marlin, *Tetrapturus audax*	50	80
3 Wahoo (peto, jack mackerel), *Acanthocybium solandri*	48	77
4 Southern bluefin tuna, *Thunnus maccoyii*	47	76
5 Yellowfin tuna, *Thunnus albacares*	46	74
6 Blue shark, *Prionace glauca*	43	69
7 =Bonefish, *Albula vulpes*	40	64
=Swordfish, *Xiphias gladius*	40	64
9 Tarpon (ox-eye herring), *Megalops cyprinoides*	35	56
10 Tiger shark, *Galeocerdo cuvier*	33	53

Source: Lucy T. Verma

Flying fish are excluded: they have a top speed in the water of only 23 mph (37 km/h), but airborne they can reach 35 mph (56 km/h). Many sharks qualify for the list, but only two are listed here to prevent the list from becoming overly shark-infested.

the 10 PLACES WHERE **MOST PEOPLE** ARE ATTACKED BY SHARKS

	LOCATION	FATAL ATTACKS	LAST FATAL ATTACK	TOTAL ATTACKS*		LOCATION	FATAL ATTACKS	LAST FATAL ATTACK	TOTAL ATTACKS*
1	US (excluding Hawaii)	39	2004	761	6	Papua New Guinea	25	2000	48
2	Australia	134	2004	294	7	New Zealand	9	1968	45
3	South Africa	41	2004	204	8	Mexico	20	1997	35
4	Hawaii	15	2004	100	9	Iran	8	1985	23
5	Brazil	20	2004	85	10	Bahamas	1	1968	22

* Confirmed unprovoked attacks, including nonfatal

Source: International Shark Attack File/American Elasmobranch
Society/Florida Museum of Natural History

The International Shark Attack File monitors worldwide incidents,
a total of 1,969 of which have been recorded since the 16th
century. The 1990s had the highest attack total (514) of any
decade, while 61 unprovoked attacks were recorded
in 2004 alone. This upward trend is believed to reflect
the growth in the numbers of people encountering them
rather than an increase in the aggressive behavior of sharks.

➔ Jaws of death
Led by the great white, shark attacks
worldwide have increased as the amount of
time humans spend in the water has increased.

top 10 **HEAVIEST** SPECIES OF SALTWATER FISH CAUGHT

SPECIES / SCIENTIFIC NAME	ANGLER / LOCATION / DATE	WEIGHT (LB / OZ)		(KG / G)	
1 **Great white shark**, *Carcharodon carcharias*	Alfred Dean, Ceduna, South Australia, Apr. 21, 1959	2,664	0	1,208	380
2 **Tiger shark**, *Galeocerdo cuvier*	Kevin James Clapson, Ulladulla, Australia, Mar. 28, 2004	1,785	11	810	0
3 **Greenland shark**, *Somniosus Microcephalus*	Terje Nordtvedt, Trondheimsfjord, Norway, Oct. 18, 1987	1,708	9	775	0
4 **Black marlin**, *Istiompax marlina*	Alfred C. Glassell, Jr., Cabo Blanco, Peru, Aug. 4, 1953	1,560	0	707	610
5 **Bluefin tuna**, *Thunnus thynnus*	Ken Fraser, Aulds Cove, Nova Scotia, Canada, Oct. 26,1979	1,496	0	678	580
6 **Atlantic blue marlin**, *Makaira nigricans*	Paulo Amorim, Vitoria, Brazil, Feb. 29,1992	1,402	2	636	0
7 **Pacific blue marlin**, *Makaira nigricans*	Jay W. de Beaubien, Kaaiwi Point, Kona, May 31, 1982	1,376	0	624	140
8 **Shortfin mako shark**, *Isurus oxyrinchus*	Luke Sweeney, Chatham, Massachusetts, July 21, 2001	1,221	0	553	840
9 **Sixgilled shark**, *Hexanchus griseus*	Clemens Rump, Ascension Island, Nov. 21, 2002	1,298	0	588	760
10 **Swordfish**, *Xiphias gladius*	Louis Marron, Iquique, Chile, May 7, 1953	1,182	0	536	150

Source: International Game Fish Association, World Record Game Fishes, 2005

Land Animals

top 10 FASTEST-GESTATING MAMMALS

	MAMMAL* / SCIENTIFIC NAME	AVERAGE GESTATION (DAYS)
1	**Short-nosed bandicoot**, *Isoodon obesulus*	12
2	**Black-shouldered opossum**, *Caluromysiops irrupta*	12–14
3 =	**Long-nosed bandicoot**, *Perameles nasuta*	12.5
=	**Narrow-footed marsupial mouse (striped-face dunnart)**, *Sminthopsis macroura*	12.5
5	**Virginia (common) opossum**, *Didelphis virginiana*	12.5–13
6	**Common (northern common) cuscus**, *Phalanger orientalis*	13
7	**Dusky (montane) shrew**, *Sorex monticolus*	13–28
8	**Raffray's bandicoot**, *Peroryctes rafrayana*	15
9	**Mountain (short-eared) brushtail possum (bobuc)**, *Trichosurus caninus*	15–17
10	**Western quoll (chuditch, western native cat)**, *Dasyurus geoffroii*	16–23

* One example per genus listed

top 10 WILD MAMMALS WITH THE LARGEST LITTERS

	MAMMAL / SCIENTIFIC NAME	AVERAGE LITTER
1	**Common tenrec**, *Tenrec ecaudatus*	25
2	**Virginia (common) opossum**, *Didelphis virginiana*	21
3	**Southern (black-eared) opossum**, *Didelphis marsupialis*	10
4 =	**Ermine**, *Mustela erminea*	9
=	**Prairie vole**, *Microtus ochrogaster*	9
=	**Syrian (golden) hamster**, *Mesocricetus auratus*	9
7	**African hunting dog**, *Lycaon pictus*	8.8
8 =	**Dhole (Indian wild dog)**, *Cuon alpinus*	8
=	**Pygmy opossum**, *Marmosa robinsoni*	8
=	**South American mouse opossum**, *Gracilinanus agilis*	8

⬅ Playing possum

The Virginia opossum, North America's
only marsupial, has a short gestation period
and produces large litters. After birth, the
young transfer to a pouch and later cling
to the mother's back for several months.

Fast Fact

Nature appears to confer on most mammals a lifetime's supply of approximately 800 million heartbeats. Small creatures such as shrews have a remarkably fast heart rate of 900–1,400 beats a minute. They thus "use up" their heartbeats and so have an average life span of less than two years. The shrew's metabolism also demands that it feeds constantly to survive: it seldom sleeps and can die of starvation if it does not eat for a few hours.

Shrew chew
A tiny pygmy shrew, the smallest of all land mammals, makes a meal of a worm many times its own length.

top 10 **LIGHTEST** TERRESTRIAL MAMMALS

MAMMAL* / SCIENTIFIC NAME	LENGTH		WEIGHT#	
	(IN)	(MM)	(OZ)	(G)
1 Pygmy shrew, *Sorex hoyi*	1.8–3.9	46–100	0.07–0.63	2.1–18
2 Pygmy shrew, *Suncus etruscus*	1.4–1.9	35–48	0.22	2.5
3 African pygmy mouse, *Mus minutoides*	1.8–3.2	45–82	0.09–0.42	2.5–12.0
4 Desert shrew, *Notiosorex crawfordi*	1.9–2.7	48–69	0.1–0.17	3.0–5.0
5 Forest musk shrew, *Sylvisorex* sp.	1.8–3.9	45–100	0.1–0.42	3.0–12.0
6 White-toothed shrew, *Crocidura suaveolens*	1.6–3.9	40–100	0.1–0.46	3.0–13.0
7 Asiatic shrew, *Soriculus salenskii*	1.7–3.9	44–99	0.17–0.21	5.0–6.0
8 Delany's swamp mouse, *Delanymys brooksi*	1.9–2.5	50–63	0.18–0.23	5.2–6.5
9 Birch mouse, *Sicista* sp.	1.9–3.5	50–90	0.21–0.49	6.0–14
10 Pygmy mouse, *Baiomys* sp.	1.9–3.2	50–81	0.24–0.59	7.0–8.0

* Lightest species per genus

Ranked by lightest in range; some jerboas are smaller, but no precise weights have yet been recorded

top 10 *FASTEST* MAMMALS

Along with its relatively slow rivals, the cheetah can deliver its astonishing maximum speed over only relatively short distances. For comparison, the human male 100-meter record (Tim Montgomery, US, 2002) stands at 9.78 seconds, equivalent to a speed of 23 mph (37 km/h), so all the mammals in the Top 10, and several others, are capable of outrunning a man. If a human ran the 100 meters at the cheetah's speed, the record would fall to 3 seconds.

MAMMAL / SCIENTIFIC NAME /
MAXIMUM RECORDED SPEED (MPH / KM/H)*

1 **Cheetah**, *Acinonyx jubatus*, 71 mph / 114 km/h

2 **Pronghorn antelope**, *Antilocapra americana*, 57 mph / 95 km/h

=3 **Blue wildebeest (brindled gnu)**, *Connochaetes taurinus* /
Lion, *Panthera leo* / **Springbok**, *Antidorcas marsupialis*, 50 mph / 80 km/h

=6 **Brown hare**, *Lepus capensis* / **Red fox**, *Vulpes vulpes*, 48 mph / 77 km/h

=8 **Grant's gazelle**, *Gazella granti* /
Thomson's gazelle, *Gazella thomsonii*, 47 mph / 76 km/h

10 **Horse**, *Equus caballus*, 45 mph / 72 km/h

Flying start
The cheetah's metabolism, extended claws, and body structure are perfectly adapted to enable it to achieve phenomenal acceleration and bursts of speed. As it runs, all four legs leave the ground for as much as half the distance it travels.

* Of those species for which data available at time of collection

Birds

top 10 FASTEST BIRDS

BIRD* / SCIENTIFIC NAME	MAXIMUM RECORDED SPEED (MPH)	(KM/H)
1 **Common eider**, *Somateria mollissima*	47	76
2 **Bewick's swan**, *Cygnus columbianus*	44	72
3 = **Barnacle goose**, *Branta leucopsis*	42	68
= **Common crane**, *Grus grus*	42	68
5 **Mallard**, *Anas platyrhynchos*	40	65
6 = **Red-throated loon**, *Gavia stellata*	38	61
= **Wood pigeon**, *Columba palumbus*	38	61
8 **Oystercatcher**, *Haematopus ostralegus*	36	58
9 = **Ring-necked pheasant**, *Phasianus colchichus*	33	54
= **White-fronted goose**, *Anser albifrons*	33	54

* By species

Source: Chris Mead

Heaviest and fastest
A swan ranks as the heaviest flighted bird and a duck as the fastest in level flight—although some birds may achieve greater speeds in dives.

Recent research reveals that, contrary to popular belief, swifts are not fast fliers, just very efficient, with long thin wings like gliders and low wing-loading. Fast fliers generally have high wing-loading and fast wingbeats. The fastest-swimming birds are penguins, which can achieve speeds of 21 mph (35 km/h). The fasting-running bird is the ostrich, which can reach a speed of 44 mph (72 km/h), and maintain it for 20 minutes—ostrich racing with human jockeys or drawing chariots is pursued in South Africa and other countries.

top 10 HEAVIEST FLIGHTED BIRDS

BIRD* / SCIENTIFIC NAME	WINGSPAN (IN)	(CM)	WEIGHT (LB / OZ)		(KG)
1 **Mute swan**, *Cygnus olor*	93	238	49	6	22.50
2 **Kori bustard**, *Ardeotis kori*	106	270	41	8	19.00
3 = **Andean condor**, *Vultur gryphus*	126	320	33	1	15.00
= **Great white pelican**, *Pelecanus onocrotalus*	141	360	33	1	15.00
5 **European black vulture**, *Aegypius monachus*	116	295	27	5	12.50
6 **Sarus crane**, *Grus antigone*	110	280	26	9	12.24
7 **Himalayan griffon (vulture)**, *Gyps himalayensis*	122	310	26	5	12.00
8 **Wandering albatross**, *Diomedea exulans*	137	350	24	9	11.30
9 **Steller's sea eagle**, *Haliaeetus pelagicus*	104	265	19	8	9.00
10 **Marabou stork**, *Leptoptilos crumeniferus*	113	287	19	6	8.90

* By species

Source: Chris Mead

First Fact The first observation of migrating birds in the New World was made by the sailors of Christopher Columbus's ships, the *Niña*, *Pinta*, and *Santa Maria*. On October 7, 1492 they encountered huge flocks of migrating (and now extinct) Eskimo curlews and American golden plovers, some of which landed on deck. Realizing that these were land birds, *Pinta* captain Martín Alonso Pinzón urged the fleet to turn its course to the southwest, the direction the birds were flying. As a result, Columbus made landfall on San Salvador, rather than mainland America.

top 10 LONGEST BIRD MIGRATIONS

BIRD* / SCIENTIFIC NAME	APPROXIMATE DISTANCE (MILES)	(KM)
1 **Pectoral sandpiper**, *Calidris melanotos*	11,800[#]	19,000
2 **Wheatear**, *Oenanthe oenanthe*	11,200	18,000
3 **Slender-billed shearwater**, *Puffinus tenuirostris*	10,875[#]	17,500
4 **Ruff**, *Philomachus pugnax*	10,300	16,600
5 **Willow warbler**, *Phylloscopus trochilus*	10,125	16,300
6 **Arctic tern**, *Sterna paradisaea*	10,100	16,200
7 **Parasitic jaeger**, *Stercorarius parasiticus*	9,700	15,600
8 **Swainson's hawk**, *Buteo swainsoni*	9,450	15,200
9 **Knot**, *Calidris canutus*	9,320	15,000
10 **Barn swallow**, *Hirundo rustica*	9,260	14,900

* By species

[#] Thought to be only half of the path taken during a whole year

Source: Chris Mead

This list is of the likely extremes for a normal migrant. All migrant birds fly far longer than is indicated by the direct route. Many species fly all year, except when they come to land to breed, or, in the case of seabirds, to rest on the sea. Such species include the albatross, petrel, tern, and some types of swift and house martin. The annual distance covered by these birds may range from 93,200 miles (150,000 km) to almost 186,400 miles (300,000 km).

◐ Long-haul traveler
The entire world population of wheatears migrates to Africa and India in the winter, returning to Greenland and the North American Arctic for the summer.

➲ Big bird
The ostrich, a native of Africa (but with an introduced population in Australia), is the heaviest and tallest of all living birds. It also has the longest legs and is capable of outrunning a racehorse.

TOP 10 HEAVIEST FLIGHTLESS BIRDS

BIRD* / SCIENTIFIC NAME	WEIGHT (LB / OZ)		(KG)
1 **Ostrich (male)**, *Struthio camelus*	343	9	156.0
2 **Northern cassowary**, *Casuarius unappendiculatus*	127	9	58.0
3 **Emu (female)**, *Dromaius novaehollandiae*	121	6	55.0
4 **Emperor penguin (female)**, *Aptenodytes forsteri*	101	4	46.0
5 **Greater rhea**, *Rhea americana*	55	2	25.0
6 **Flightless steamer (duck)**, *Tachyeres brachypterus*	13	7	6.2
7 **Flightless cormorant**, *Nannopterum harrisi*	9	15	4.5
8 **Kiwi (female)**, *Apteryx haastii*	8	4	3.8
9 **Takahe (rail)**, *Porphyrio mantelli*	7	2	3.2
10 **Kakapo (parrot)**, *Strigops habroptilus*	7	1	3.2

* By species

Source: Chris Mead

Insects & Spiders

top 10 SMALLEST BUTTERFLIES

BUTTERFLY / SCIENTIFIC NAME	AVERAGE WINGSPAN (IN)	(MM)
1 **Dwarf blue**, *Brephidium barberae*	0.55	14
2 **Western pygmy blue**, *Brephidium exilis*	0.62	15
3 **Western square-dotted blue**, *Euphilotes battoides*	0.66	17
4 **Pallid dotted-blue**, *Euphilotes pallescens*	0.70	18
5 = **Bernardino dotted-blue**, *Euphilotes bernardino*	0.74	19
= **Cyna blue**, *Zizula cyna*	0.74	19
= **Intermediate dotted-blue**, *Euphilotes intermedia*	0.74	19
= **Little metalmark**, *Calephelis virginiensis*	0.74	19
= **Rita dotted-blue**, *Euphilotes rita*	0.74	19
= **Small dotted-blue**, *Philotiella speciosa*	0.74	19
= **Telea hairstreak**, *Chlorostrymon teleai*	0.74	19

top 10 LARGEST BUTTERFLIES

BUTTERFLY / SCIENTIFIC NAME	AVERAGE WINGSPAN (IN)	(MM)
1 **Queen Alexandra's birdwing**, *Ornithoptera alexandrae*	11.0	280
2 **African giant swallowtail**, *Papilio antimachus*	9.1	230
3 **Goliath birdwing**, *Ornithoptera goliath*	8.3	210
4 = **Buru opalescent birdwing**, *Troides prattorum*	7.9	200
= *Trogonoptera trojana*	7.9	200
= *Troides hypolitus*	7.9	200
7 = **Chimera birdwing**, *Ornithoptera chimaera*	7.5	190
= *Ornithoptera lydius*	7.5	190
= *Troides magellanus*	7.5	190
= *Troides miranda*	7.5	190

⊘ Little and large
The rare Queen Alexandra's birdwing, found in Papua New Guinea, is the largest known butterfly and the heaviest, at up to 0.42 oz (12 g). In contrast, the pygmy blue (shown above to scale), a native of the region from the southern US to Guatemala, is one of the smallest.

top 10 FASTEST INSECT FLYERS

INSECT* / SCIENTIFIC NAME	MAXIMUM RECORDED SPEED (MPH)	(KM/H)
1 Hawkmoth, *Sphingidae*	33.3	53.6
2 = Deer bot fly, *Cephenemyia pratti*	30.0	48.0
= West Indian butterfly, *Nymphalidae prepona*	30.0	48.0
4 Deer bot fly, *Chrysops*	25.0	40.0
5 West Indian butterfly, *Hesperiidae* sp.	18.6	30.0
6 Lesser Emperor dragonfly, *Anax parthenope*	17.8	28.6
7 = Dragonfly, *Aeschna*	15.6	25.2
= Hornet, *Vespa*	15.6	25.2
9 = Honey bee, *Apis millefera*	13.9	22.4
= Horsefly, *Tabanus bovinus*	13.9	22.4

* By species; of those for which data are available

Few accurate assessments of insect flying speed have ever been attempted, and this Top 10 represents only the results of the handful of scientific studies that are widely recognized by entomologists. Some experts have also suggested that the male horsefly (*Hybomitra linei wrighti*) is capable of traveling at 90 mph (145 km/h) when in pursuit of a female, while there are exceptional examples such as that of a dragonfly allegedly recorded by Dr. R.J. Tilyard as flying at a speed of 61 mph (98 km/h). Many so-called records are clearly flawed, however: in 1917, for example, Charles Townsend estimated the flying speed of the deer bot fly at an unbelievable 818 mph (1,317 km/h). If this were true, the fly would have broken the sound barrier!

⊙ Evil bunch
The deadly and aggressive Brazilian wandering spider is also known as the banana spider because it frequently stows away on fruit boats.

top 10 DEADLIEST SPIDERS

SPIDER / SCIENTIFIC NAME / RANGE

1. **Banana spider**, *Phoneutria nigriventer*, Central and South America
2. **Sydney funnel web spider**, *Atrax robustus*, Australia
3. **Wolf spider**, *Lycosa raptoria/erythrognatha*, Central and South America
4. **Black widow spider**, *Latrodectus* sp., Widespread
5. **Violin spider/Recluse spider**, *Loxesceles reclusa*, Widespread
6. **Sac spider**, *Cheiracanthium punctorium*, Central Europe
7. **Tarantula**, *Eurypelma rubropilosum*, Neotropics
8. **Tarantula**, *Acanthoscurria atrox*, Neotropics
9. **Tarantula**, *Lasiodora klugi*, Neotropics
10. **Tarantula**, *Pamphobeteus species*, Neotropics

This list ranks spiders according to their "lethal potential"—their venom yield divided by their venom potency. The banana spider, for example, yields 6 mg of venom, with 1 mg the estimated lethal dose in man. However, few spiders are capable of killing humans—there were just 14 recorded deaths caused by black widows in the United States in the entire 19th century. Their venom yield is relatively low compared with that of the most dangerous snakes—the tarantula, for example, produces 1.5 mg of venom, but its lethal dose for an adult human is 12 mg. Originally applied to the wolf spider, the name "tarantula" is confusingly used for various members of the *Theraphosidae* family and *Lycos tarantula*, the spider once believed to cause the disease tarantism.

top 10 **HEAVIEST** TERRESTRIAL MAMMALS

	MAMMAL* / SCIENTIFIC NAME	LENGTH (FT)	(M)	WEIGHT (LB)	(KG)
1	**African elephant** *Loxodonta africana*	24.6	7.5	16,534	7,500
2	**Hippopotamus** *Hippopotamus amphibius*	16.4	5.0	9,920	4,500
3	**White rhinoceros** *Ceratotherium simum*	13.7	4.2	7,937	3,600
4	**Giraffe** *Giraffa camelopardalis*	15.4	4.7	4,255	1,930
5	**American buffalo** *Bison bison*	11.4	3.5	2,205	1,000
6	**Moose** *Alces alces*	10.1	3.1	1,820	825
7	**Grizzly bear** *Ursus arctos*	9.8	3.0	1,720	780
8	**Arabian camel (dromedary)** *Camelus dromedarius*	11.3	3.4	1,521	690
9	**Siberian tiger** *Panthera tigris altaica*	10.8	3.3	793	360
10	**Gorilla** *Gorilla gorilla gorilla*	6.5	2.0	606	275

* Heaviest species per genus

This Top 10 list excludes domesticated cattle and horses. It also avoids comparing close kin such as the African and Indian elephants, highlighting instead the "sumo stars" within distinctive large mammal groups such as the bears, big cats, primates, and bovines (oxlike mammals).

⬅ The heavy brigade

The elephant, hippopotamus, and rhinoceros head the list of the heaviest land mammals while the gorilla is the heaviest primate, and thus humans' closest super-sized relative. The widespread use of "Jumbo"—originally the name of a huge elephant—to describe oversized objects, and the iconic image of King Kong as a giant gorilla, underline our respect for nature's heavyweights.

Perfect Pets

top 10 **PET BIRD** POPULATIONS

COUNTRY	ESTIMATED PET BIRD POPULATION, 2003*
1 China	72,547,000
2 US	29,000,000
3 Japan	21,250,000
4 Brazil	17,500,000
5 Italy	13,000,000
6 Spain	7,873,000
7 Australia	7,500,000
8 France	6,450,000
9 Germany	4,700,000
10 UK	3,020,000

* In those countries for which data available

Birds of a feather
Caged birds have been kept as pets worldwide since ancient times.

A boy and his dog
The US dog population is equivalent to one animal for every 4.8 humans.

top 10 **PET DOG** POPULATIONS

COUNTRY / ESTIMATED PET DOG POPULATION, 2003*

1. **US** 61,340,000
2. **Brazil** 27,000,000
3. **China** 23,366,000
4. **Mexico** 16,111,000
5. **Japan** 9,523,000
6. **France** 8,100,000
7. **Poland** 7,525,000
8. **Italy** 6,950,000
9. **UK** 6,500,000
10. **Germany** 4,800,000

* In those countries for which data available
Source: Euromonitor

Dog ownership in the US has become increasingly humanized: not only are dogs given human names and often considered "one of the family," but a huge industry has grown up to cater to their nutrition and welfare to a standard that rivals that of many people. Second only to the US for its dog population, Brazil claims dogs as its most popular pet, accounting for almost 43 percent of the country's total pet population and—despite widespread economic hardship—77 percent of pet food sales, while pet megastores, dog gyms, and massage therapy centers have been established in major cities.

top 10 PET CAT POPULATIONS

	COUNTRY	ESTIMATED PET CAT POPULATION, 2003*
1	US	78,350,000
2	China	54,161,000
3	Brazil	11,000,000
4	France	9,800,000
5	UK	7,700,000
6	Italy	7,500,000
7	Japan	7,119,000
8	Germany	7,100,000
9	Canada	6,961,000
10	Mexico	6,101,000

* In those countries for which data available

Source: Euromonitor

Estimates of the numbers of domestic cats in the 20 leading cat-owning countries show a total population of 216,132,000, with the biggest increase in Mexico (up 31.2 percent since 1998), and the greatest decline in Australia (down 16.4 percent).

⊕ Goldfish
Bred in East Asia for 3,000 years, goldfish have been popular in the West since the late 17th century.

top 10 TYPES OF PET IN THE US

	PET	ESTIMATED NUMBER
1	Cat	78,350,000
2	Dog	61,340,000
3	Small animal pets*	12,740,000
4	Parakeet	11,000,000
5	Freshwater fish	10,800,000[#]
6	Reptile	7,540,000
7	Finch	7,350,000
8	Cockatiel	6,320,000
9	Canary	2,580,000
10	Parrot	1,550,000

* Includes small rodents—rabbits, ferrets, hamsters, guinea pigs, and gerbils

[#] Number of households owning, rather than individual specimens

With an average of more than two cats per cat-owning household, the relatively independent cat is the pet of choice in US homes in greater numbers than dogs, who tend to require more care, costly veterinary treatment, and daily walks.

top 10 CAT NAMES IN THE US

1 Tiger
2 Smokey
3 Tigger
4 Max
5 Oreo
6 Kitty
7 Shadow
8 Princess
9 Oliver
10 Sam

Source: American Pet Classics

These names are based on a survey of names provided for identification tags for cats. Beyond the Top 10, popular names include both terms of endearment, such as Angel, and further human names, including Jack, Charlie, and Simon.

Livestock & Crops

top 10 TYPES OF **LIVESTOCK**

ANIMAL / WORLD STOCKS, 2004*

1 Chickens 16,194,925,000   **2 Cattle** 1,334,501,290   **3 Sheep** 1,038,765,370   **4 Ducks** 1,019,479,000   **5 Pigs** 951,771,892
6 Goats 780,099,948   **7 Rabbits** 511,591,000   **8 Turkeys** 276,225,000   **9 Geese** 262,232,000   **10 Buffaloes** 172,719,487

* Provisional figures

Source: Food and Agriculture Organization of the United Nations

First Fact The auroch is the ancestor of all European breeds of cattle. Aurochs are depicted in cave paintings, and their remains show that they were bigger than today's cattle, with longer horns. Roman writers, including Julius Caesar, described Gaulish auroch hunts. As a result of overhunting, aurochs died out in Britain in the Bronze Age and in France by the 16th century, but continued to roam elsewhere in Europe. Although their hunting was restricted to royalty, poaching caused a further decline until only a small herd survived in Poland's Jaktorów Forest. The last cow died there in 1627 and the aurochs became extinct.

top 10 **CHICKEN** COUNTRIES

COUNTRY	CHICKENS, 2001*
1 China	3,974,748,000
2 US	1,970,000,000
3 Indonesia	1,200,000,000
4 Brazil	1,100,000,000
5 Mexico	540,000,000
6 India	425,000,000
7 Russia	340,000,000
8 Japan	286,000,000
9 Iran	280,000,000
10 Turkey	250,000,000
World	*16,194,925,000*

* Provisional figures

Source: Food and Agriculture Organization
of the United Nations

top 10 **SHEEP** COUNTRIES

COUNTRY	SHEEP, 2004*
1 China	157,330,415
2 Australia	94,500,000
3 India	62,500,000
4 Iran	54,000,000
5 Sudan	47,000,000
6 New Zealand	40,065,000
7 UK	35,500,000
8 South Africa	29,100,000
9 Turkey	25,000,000
10 Pakistan	24,700,000
World	*1,038,765,370*
US	*6,090,000*

* Provisional figures

Source: Food and Agriculture Organization
of the United Nations

→ Watermelons

Watermelons were recorded in Egypt 5,000 years ago and introduced into North America in 1629. Although now cultivated worldwide, some 73 percent of the world's watermelons are grown in China, where they are an important part of national cuisine and culture, often presented as gifts and decoratively carved like Halloween pumpkins in the West.

top 10 **PIG** COUNTRIES

	COUNTRY	PIGS, 2004*
1	China	472,895,791
2	US	60,388,700
3	Brazil	33,000,000
4	Germany	26,495,000
5	Spain	23,990,000
6	Vietnam	23,500,000
7	= Mexico	18,100,000
	= Poland	18,100,000
9	Russia	15,979,600
10	France	15,189,000
	World	*909,486,000*

* Provisional figures

Source: Food and Agricultural Organization of the United Nations

The distribution of the world's pig population is determined by cultural, religious, and dietary factors—few pigs are found in African and Islamic countries, for example—with the result that there is a disproportionate concentration of pigs in those countries that do not have such prohibitions.

top 10 **VEGETABLE** CROPS

	CROP*	PRODUCTION, 2004# (TONS)
1	Sugarcane	1,449,995,877
2	Potatoes	361,752,530
3	Sugar beets	261,643,648
4	Soybeans	227,050,478
5	Sweet potatoes	140,288,508
6	Cabbages	75,228,552
7	Onions (dry)	59,346,411
8	Yams	44,720,359
9	Pickles	44,209,114
10	Eggplants	32,894,381

* Excluding cereals

Provisional figures

Source: Food and Agriculture Organization of the United Nations

This includes only vegetables grown for human and animal consumption. Among non-food vegetable crops, cotton has a total annual production approaching 77 million tons, while rubber, tobacco, jute, and other fibers are also economically significant.

top 10 **FRUIT** CROPS

	CROP	PRODUCTION, 2004* (TONS)
1	Tomatoes	127,545,936
2	Watermelons	102,829,393
3	Bananas	77,691,951
4	Grapes	72,034,858
5	Oranges	69,343,709
6	Apples	64,965,056
7	Coconuts	59,117,942
8	Plantains	35,935,155
9	Cantaloupes and other melons	34,935,155
10	Mangoes	28,914,880

* Provisional figures

Source: Food and Agriculture Organization of the United Nations

Over 500 million tonnes of fruit are grown worldwide every year. The status of the tomato is controversial: botanically, it is a fruit, but—based on its use in cooking—for legal and import duty purposes, some countries consider it a vegetable.

Tree Tops

top 10 **MOST FORESTED** COUNTRIES

COUNTRY	PERCENTAGE OF FOREST COVER, 2000
1 Surinam	90.5
2 Solomon Islands	88.8
3 Gabon	84.7
4 Brunei	83.9
5 Guyana	78.5
6 Palau	76.1
7 Finland	72.0
8 North Korea	68.2
9 Papua New Guinea	67.6
10 Seychelles	66.7

Source: Food and Agriculture Organization of the United Nations, *State of the World's Forests*, 2005

These are the 10 countries with the greatest area of forest and woodland as a percentage of their total land area. With increasing deforestation, the world average has fallen from about 32 percent in 1972 to its present 29.6 percent. The least forested large countries in the world are the desert lands of the Middle East and North Africa, such as Oman, which has none, and Egypt and Qatar, each with just 0.1 percent.

top 10 **TIMBER-PRODUCING** COUNTRIES

COUNTRY	ROUNDWOOD PRODUCTION, 2003 (CU FT)	(CU M)
1 US	15,823,055,440	448,058,992
2 India	11,336,966,340	321,027,107
3 China	10,103,757,060	286,106,512
4 Brazil	8,423,836,933	238,536,476
5 Canada	6,876,702,088	194,726,500
6 Russia	5,950,521,895	168,500,000
7 Indonesia	3,955,392,633	112,004,236
8 Ethiopia	3,321,747,018	94,061,392
9 Dem. Rep. of Congo	2,548,669,057	72,170,264
10 Nigeria	2,467,337,677	69,867,216
World total	*118,030,295,100*	*3,342,245,450*

Source: Food and Agriculture Organization of the United Nations

If all the world's annual timber production were made into 1-x-12-in (2.5-x-30-cm) planks, laid end to end they would stretch 100 times around the world at the equator.

⬆ **Tree trunk**
Although elephants are still used in the Indian logging industry, forestry has increasingly become a highly mechanized business and is an important component of the economies of many developing countries.

top 10 MOST COMMON TREES IN THE US

1 Silver maple
2 Black cherry
3 Box elder
4 Eastern cottonwood
5 Black willow
6 Northern red oak
7 Flowering dogwood
8 Black oak
9 Ponderosa pine
10 Coast Douglas fir

Source: American Forests

Hardwood trees native to the Eastern and Southern states prevail in this list, while the Ponderosa pine and Douglas fir are softwoods most typical of the Northwest coast forests.

top 10 TALLEST TREES IN THE US

	SPECIES*	LOCATION	HEIGHT (FT)	(M)
1	**Coast redwood**, *Sequoia sempervirens*	Jedediah Smith Redwoods State Park, CA	321	97.8
2	**Coast Douglas fir**, *Pseudotsuga menziesii* var. *menziesii*	Jedediah Smith Redwoods State Park, CA	301	91.7
3	**Giant sequoia**, *Sequoiadendron giganteum*	Sequoia National Park, CA	274	83.5
4	**Noble fir**, *Abies procera*	Mount St. Helens National Monument, WA	272	82.9
5	**Grand fir**, *Abies grandis*	Redwood National Park, CA	257	78.3
6	**Western hemlock**, *Tsuga heterophylla*	Olympic National Park, WA	241	73.5
7	**Port Orford cedar**, *Chamaecyparis lawsoniana*	Siskiyou National Forest, OR	229	69.8
8	**Ponderosa pine**, *Pinus ponderosa* var. *ponderosa*	Plumas County, CA	227	69.2
9	**Pacific silver fir**, *Abies amabilis*	Olympic National Park, WA	218	66.4
10	**California white fir**, *Abies concolor* var. *lowiana*	Yosemite National Park, CA	217	66.1

* Tallest example of each species only

A Coast redwood that formerly topped this list fell during the winter of 1992. The General Sherman giant sequoia in 3rd place is thought to be the planet's most colossal living thing, with a volume of 52,508 cubic ft (1,486.9 cubic meters) and weighing as much as nine blue whales or 360 elephants.

Chapter

23456

the 10 worst gun massacres: page 73

top 10 longest reigning monarchs: page 68

789101

The Human World

top 10 countries with the highest marriage rate: page 60

Human Body

BONE / AVERAGE LENGTH (IN / CM)

These are average dimensions of the bones of an adult male measured from their extremities (ribs are measured along the curve, and the pelvis measurement is taken diagonally). The same bones in the female skeleton are usually 6 to 13 percent smaller, with the exception of the sternum, which is virtually identical.

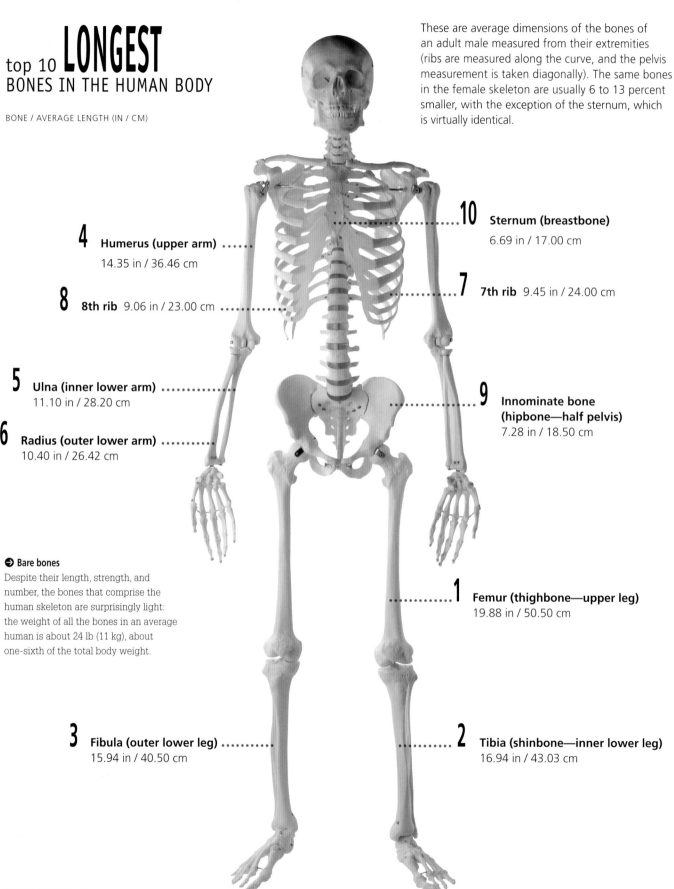

4 Humerus (upper arm) ......
14.35 in / 36.46 cm

8 8th rib 9.06 in / 23.00 cm ....

5 Ulna (inner lower arm) ....
11.10 in / 28.20 cm

6 Radius (outer lower arm) ....
10.40 in / 26.42 cm

10 Sternum (breastbone)
6.69 in / 17.00 cm

7 7th rib 9.45 in / 24.00 cm

9 Innominate bone
(hipbone—half pelvis)
7.28 in / 18.50 cm

1 Femur (thighbone—upper leg)
19.88 in / 50.50 cm

3 Fibula (outer lower leg) ....
15.94 in / 40.50 cm

2 Tibia (shinbone—inner lower leg)
16.94 in / 43.03 cm

➲ Bare bones
Despite their length, strength, and number, the bones that comprise the human skeleton are surprisingly light: the weight of all the bones in an average human is about 24 lb (11 kg), about one-sixth of the total body weight.

the 10 STATES IN THE US WITH THE **MOST OBESE** PEOPLE

STATE	PERCENTAGE OBESE, 2003*
1 **Alabama**	28.4
2 **Mississippi**	28.1
3 **West Virginia**	27.7
4 **Indiana**	26.0
5 **Kentucky**	25.6
6 **Arkansas**	25.2
7 **Michigan**	25.2
8 **Georgia**	25.1
9 **Tennessee**	25.0
10 **Ohio**	24.9
National average	*22.8*

* Percentage of adults that are obese

Source: National Center for Chronic Disease Prevention and Health Promotion

top 10 **LARGEST** HUMAN ORGANS

ORGAN		AVERAGE WEIGHT (OZ)	(G)
1 **Skin**		384.0	10,886
2 **Liver**		55.0	1,560
3 **Brain**	male	49.7	1,408
	female	44.6	1,263
4 **Lungs**	total	38.5	1,090
	right	*20.5*	*580*
	left	*18.0*	*510*
5 **Heart**	male	11.1	315
	female	9.3	265
6 **Kidneys**	total	10.2	290
	right	*4.9*	*140*
	left	*5.3*	*150*
7 **Spleen**		6.0	170
8 **Pancreas**		3.5	98
9 **Thyroid**		1.2	35
10 **Prostate**	male only	0.7	20

This list is based on average immediate postmortem weights, as recorded by St. Bartholemew's Hospital, London, UK, and other sources during a 10-year period. Various instances of organs far in excess of the average have been recorded, including male brains of over 4.4 lb (2 kg).

➡ **Face value**
Once the preserve of the wealthy and celebrities, cosmetic surgery has become a global industry valued at over $20 billion.

top 10 **COSMETIC SURGERY** PROCEDURES PERFORMED IN THE US

PROCEDURE	NUMBER PERFORMED, 2004
1 **Liposuction**	478,251
2 **Breast augmentation**	334,052
3 **Cosmetic eyelid surgery**	290,343
4 **Nose reshaping**	166,187
5 **Facelift**	157,061
6 **Tummy tuck**	150,987
7 **Breast reduction** (women)	144,374
8 **Breast lift**	98,351
9 **Forehead lift**	95,212
10 **Chin augmentation**	32,039

Source: American Society for Aesthetic Plastic Surgery

Plastic surgery to rebuild damaged parts of the human body was performed in India in ancient times. It was later developed to aid disfigured service personnel during World War I, and in recent times has spawned cosmetic surgery techniques, whereby individuals elect to have various parts of their bodies reshaped in the interests of aesthetic appeal.

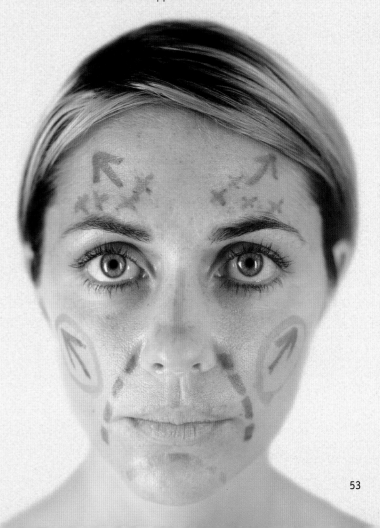

Disease & Illness

the 10 WORST EPIDEMICS

	EPIDEMIC / LOCATION	DATE	ESTIMATED NO. OF DEATHS
1	Black Death Europe/Asia	1347–80s	75,000,000
2	AIDS Worldwide	1981–	27,800,000*
3	Influenza Worldwide	1918–20	21,640,000
4	Bubonic plague India	1896–1948	12,000,000
5	Typhus Eastern Europe	1914–15	3,000,000
6 =	"Plague of Justinian" Europe/Asia	541–90	millions[#]
=	Cholera Europe	1826–37	millions[#]
=	Cholera Worldwide	1846–60	millions[#]
=	Cholera Worldwide	1893–94	millions[#]
10	Smallpox Mexico	1530–45	>1,000,000

* Up to 2005

[#] No precise figures available

Precise figures for deaths during the disruptions of epidemics are inevitably unreliable, but the Black Death or bubonic plague—which was probably transmitted by fleas from infected rats—swept across Asia and Europe in the 14th century, destroying entire populations, including more than half the inhabitants of London, some 25 million in Europe, and 50 million in Asia.

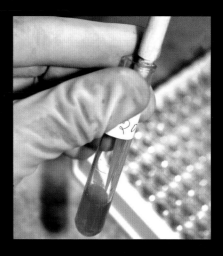

← AIDS test
It is commonly accepted that AIDS (Acquired Immunodeficiency Syndrome) results from the HIV (Human Immunodeficiency Virus) infection. In the past 25 years it has become one of the biggest killers worldwide, with total deaths second only to those of the Black Death and still gaining.

the 10 MOST COMMON CAUSES OF DEATH BY INFECTIOUS AND PARASITIC DISEASES

CAUSE	APPROXIMATE NO. OF DEATHS, 2002
1 Lower respiratory infections	3,884,000
2 HIV/AIDS	2,777,000
3 Diarrheal diseases	1,798,000
4 Tuberculosis	1,566,000
5 Malaria	1,272,000
6 Measles	611,000
7 Whooping cough (pertussis)	294,000
8 Neonatal tetanus	214,000
9 Meningitis	173,000
10 Syphilis	157,000

Source: World Health Organization, *World Health Report 2004*

In 2002, infectious and parasitic diseases accounted for some 10,904,000 of the 57,029,000 deaths worldwide. After declining, certain childhood diseases, including measles and whooping cough, showed an increase in this year.

the 10 COUNTRIES WITH THE **MOST** CASES OF **MALARIA**

COUNTRY	MALARIA CASES PER 100,000 PEOPLE*, 2000
1 Guinea	75,386
2 Botswana	48,704
3 Burundi	48,098
4 Zambia	34,204
5 Malawi	25,948
6 Mozambique	18,115
7 Gambia	17,340
8 Ghana	15,344
9 Solomon Islands	15,172
10 Yemen	15,160

* Data refers to malaria cases reported to the World Health Organization (WHO) and may represent only a fraction of the true number in a country

Source: United Nations, *Human Development Report 2004*

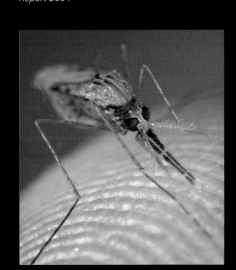

G Small but deadly
The *Anopheles* mosquito carries the parasite that causes malaria, a disease of tropical countries and one of the world's foremost killers.

the 10 COUNTRIES WITH THE **MOST** DEATHS FROM **CANCER**

COUNTRY	DEATH RATE PER 100,000* (FEMALE)	(MALE)
1 Hungary	269.1	386.7
2 Croatia	216.9	330.9
3 Italy	227.8	328.0
4 Belgium	227.1	323.2
5 Czech Republic	243.1	321.8
6 France	187.9	303.2
7 Spain	168.7	298.5
8 Estonia	213.3	297.6
9 Denmark	283.2	296.9
10 Japan	181.4	291.3
US	*186.2*	*207.2*

* Ranked by incidence in male population, in latest year for which data available

Source: International Agency for Research on Cancer at http://www-dep.iarc.fr

Cancer has become the leading cause of death in many Western countries, with such factors as diet, obesity, and smoking cited among those that predispose individuals to its various forms. Improved methods of treatment, however, mean that in many cases a cancer diagnosis no longer equates to a death sentence.

↑ Bad habit
The world's annual consumption of 5.5 trillion cigarettes affects the health of one in six of its inhabitants.

the 10 COUNTRIES WITH THE **MOST** DEATHS FROM **HEART DISEASE**

COUNTRY	DEATH RATE PER 100,000*
1 Ukraine	935.8
2 Bulgaria	887.8
3 Russia	746.6
4 Latvia	734.7
5 Estonia	715.6
6 Romania	701.6
7 Hungary	687.1
8 Moldova	632.0
9 Croatia	609.6
10 Czech Republic	566.5

* In those countries/latest year for which data available

Source: United Nations

High-risk factors including diet and smoking have contributed to the former Soviet states having rates of coronary heart disease that are seven or eight times greater than those of France and Italy.

Birth & Death

the 10 COUNTRIES WITH THE **HIGHEST BIRTH RATE**

	COUNTRY	EST. BIRTH RATE, 2006*
1	Niger	47.64
2	Uganda	47.35
3	Afghanistan	46.60
4	Mali	46.18
5	Chad	45.41
6	Somalia	45.13
7	Angola	44.18
8	Dem. Rep. of Congo	43.97
9	Burkina Faso	43.83
10	Liberia	43.55
	Canada	*10.78*
	US	*14.14*
	World	*20.10*

* The estimated number of live births per 1,000 people in the population

Source: US Census Bureau, International Data Base

The countries with the highest birth rates are among the poorest countries in the world. In these countries, people often deliberately have large families so that the children can help to earn income for the family when they are older. The 10 countries with the highest birth rate therefore correspond very closely with the 10 countries with the highest fertility rate—the average number of children born to each woman in the country.

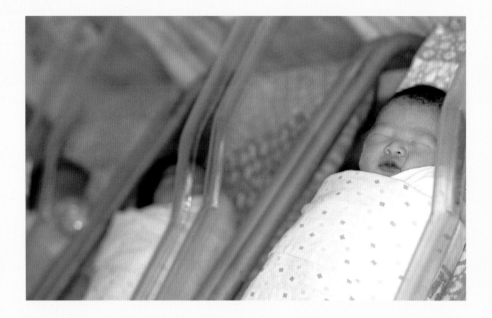

the 10 COUNTRIES WITH THE **LOWEST BIRTH RATE**

	COUNTRY	EST. BIRTH RATE, 2006*
1	Hong Kong	7.29
2	Germany	8.25
3	Andorra	8.71
4	Italy	8.72
5	Austria	8.74
6	Lithuania	8.75
7	Slovenia	8.98
8	Czech Republic	9.02
9	Latvia	9.24
10	Monaco	9.19

* The estimated number of live births per 1,000 people in the population

Source: US Census Bureau, International Data Base

Improvements in birth control, the cost of raising children, and the decision of many to limit the size of their families are among a range of reasons why the birth rate in many countries has steadily declined in modern times: in 2003, the US birth rate was reported as having fallen to the lowest ever recorded, at 13.9 per 1,000. If counted as an independent country, the Vatican—with a birth rate of zero—would head this list.

⬆ New arrivals
For many reasons, including the cost of bringing up children and the effect on the ability of mothers to continue to work, the fertility rate of most developed countries is considerably lower than that of the less developed regions of the world.

top 10 COUNTRIES WITH THE **MOST BIRTHS**

	COUNTRY	EST. BIRTHS, 2006
1	India	24,108,697
2	China	17,410,152
3	Nigeria	5,331,353
4	Indonesia	4,992,509
5	Pakistan	4,930,998
6	Bangladesh	4,391,487
7	US	4,220,001
8	Brazil	3,114,575
9	Ethiopia	2,840,068
10	Dem. Rep. of Congo	2,721,565
	Canada	*356,806*
	World	*130,712,621*

Source: US Census Bureau, International Data Base

As India's birth rate is maintained and China's subject to curbs, the population of India is set to overtake that of China by 2030.

top 10 YEARS WITH THE MOST BIRTHS IN THE US

YEAR	BIRTHS
1957	4,308,000
1961	4,268,000
1960	4,258,000
1958	4,255,000
1959	4,245,000
1956	4,218,000
1962	4,167,000
1990	4,158,000
1991	4,111,000
1955	4,104,000

This statistic first exceeded 3 million in 1921, but then remained lower than this in the 1920s and 1930s, until 1943 when it hit 3,104,000. The first year in which births topped 4 million was 1954. There was a postwar low of 3,137,000 in 1973, but by 2000 the figures once again exceeded the 4-million mark.

⊕ Africa's tragedy

The world's highest death rates are suffered disproportionately in African countries, where the AIDS epidemic in particular has more than doubled the rates recorded in the 1990s.

top 10 COUNTRIES WITH THE LOWEST DEATH RATE

	COUNTRY	EST. DEATH RATE, 2006*
1	**Kuwait**	2.41
2	**Saudi Arabia**	2.58
3	**Jordan**	2.65
4	**Brunei**	3.45
5	**Libya**	3.48
6	**Oman**	3.81
7	**Solomon Islands**	3.92
8	**Bahrain**	4.14
9	**Ecuador**	4.23
10	**Costa Rica**	4.36

* The estimated number of deaths per 1,000 people in the population

Source: US Census Bureau, International Data Base

The crude death rate is derived by dividing the total number of deaths in a given year by the total population and multiplying by 1,000. These tend to mean that countries with young populations have low death rates and older populations high rates, so statisticians also use age-standardized death rates, which factor in the age structure.

the 10 COUNTRIES WITH THE HIGHEST DEATH RATE

	COUNTRY	EST. DEATH RATE, 2006*
1	**Botswana**	29.50
2	**Angola**	26.04
3	**Swaziland**	25.88
4	**Lesotho**	25.17
5	**Zimbabwe**	25.16
6	**Malawi**	23.30
7	**South Africa**	22.00
8	**Mozambique**	21.35
9	**Niger**	21.21
10	**Sierra Leone**	20.56
	Canada	*7.80*
	US	*8.26*
	World	*8.80*

* The estimated number of deaths per 1,000 people in the population

Source: US Census Bureau, International Data Base

All 10 of the countries with the highest death rate are in sub-Saharan Africa. A decade ago, South Africa had a rate of just 9.8, but the AIDS toll has severely affected the demographic pattern, with a high proportion of young people falling victim. The societies affected by this imbalance and its repercussions face decades of hardship.

Life Spans

top 10 COUNTRIES WITH THE **HIGHEST** LIFE EXPECTANCY

	COUNTRY	LIFE EXPECTANCY AT BIRTH, 2006
1	Andorra	83.51
2	= San Marino	81.71
	= Singapore	81.71
4	Hong Kong	81.59
5	Japan	81.25
6	= Sweden	80.51
	= Switzerland	80.51
8	Australia	80.50
9	Iceland	80.31
10	Canada	80.22
	US	*77.85*
	World	*64.60*

Source: US Census Bureau, International Data Base

the 10 COUNTRIES WITH THE **LOWEST** LIFE EXPECTANCY

	COUNTRY	LIFE EXPECTANCY AT BIRTH, 2006
1	Botswana	33.74
2	Swaziland	35.12
3	Zimbabwe	36.26
4	Angola	36.32
5	Lesotho	36.65
6	Malawi	36.96
7	Mozambique	39.82
8	Zambia	40.03
9	Central African Republic	41.03
10	Niger	42.02

Source: US Census Bureau, International Data Base

➲ Brief lives

The average life expectancies of many African countries are worse than those of Europe over 100 years ago, and less than half those of most developed countries today.

the 10 COUNTRIES WITH THE **SMALLEST DISPARITY** BETWEEN MALE AND FEMALE LIFE EXPECTANCIES

	COUNTRY	ESTIMATED LIFE EXPECTANCY, 2006 (MALE)	(FEMALE)	GAP*
1	Bangladesh	62.47	62.45	0.02
2	Lesotho	36.80	36.50	0.30
3	Botswana	33.90	33.56	0.34
4	Afghanistan	43.16	43.53	0.37
5	Bhutan	55.02	54.53	0.49
6	Nepal	60.43	59.91	0.52
7	Malawi	36.69	37.23	0.54
8 =	Niger	42.29	41.74	0.55
=	Zambia	39.76	40.31	0.55
10	Mozambique	39.53	40.13	0.60
	US	*75.02*	*80.82*	*5.80*

* Number of years by which male and female life expectancies differ

Source: US Census Bureau, International Data Base

➔ **Sex equality**
Except in a few cases, female life expectancy exceeds that of male, but Bangladesh is unusual in that its inhabitants can expect virtually identical lifespans.

the 10 COUNTRIES WHERE **MALE LIFE EXPECTANCY MOST EXCEEDS** FEMALE LIFE EXPECTANCY

	COUNTRY	ESTIMATED LIFE EXPECTANCY, 2006 (MALE)	(FEMALE)	GAP*
1	Swaziland	36.51	33.69	2.82
2	Namibia	44.46	42.29	2.17
3	Kenya	49.78	48.07	1.71
4	Zimbabwe	39.76	40.31	1.20
5	South Africa	43.25	42.19	1.06
6	Martinique	79.50	78.85	0.65
7	Niger	42.29	41.74	0.55
8	Nepal	60.43	59.91	0.52
9	Bhutan	55.02	54.53	0.49
10	Botswana	33.90	33.56	0.34

* Number of years by which male life expectancy exceeds female life expectancy

Source: US Census Bureau, International Data Base

the 10 COUNTRIES WHERE **FEMALE LIFE EXPECTANCY MOST EXCEEDS** MALE LIFE EXPECTANCY

	COUNTRY	ESTIMATED LIFE EXPECTANCY, 2006 (MALE)	(FEMALE)	GAP*
1	Russia	60.45	74.10	13.65
2	Belarus	63.47	74.98	11.51
3	Estonia	66.58	77.83	11.25
4	Kazakhstan	61.56	72.52	10.96
5	Seychelles	66.69	77.63	10.94
6	Latvia	66.08	76.85	10.77
7	Ukraine	61.92	72.68	10.76
8	Lithuania	69.20	79.49	10.29
9	Hungary	68.45	77.14	8.69
10	Azerbaijan	59.78	68.13	8.35

* Number of years by which female life expectancy exceeds male life expectancy

Source: US Census Bureau, International Data Base

Marriage & Divorce

top 10 COUNTRIES WITH THE **HIGHEST MARRIAGE** RATE

COUNTRY / MARRIAGES PER 1,000 PER ANNUM*

1 **China** 35.9

2 **Cyprus** 13.4

3 **Barbados** 13.1

4 **Liechtenstein** 12.6

5 **Jamaica** 10.4

6 **Ethiopia** 10.2

7 **Fiji** 10.1

8 **Seychelles** 9.7

9 **Bangladesh** 9.5

10 **Jordan** 9.1

US 8.5

* In those countries/latest year for which data available

Source: United Nations

High marriage rates may be distorted by the numbers of visitors to a country. Jamaica, for example, has a low marriage rate among Jamaican nationals but a high number of visitors who marry on the island and spend their honeymoon there. The highest marriage rates in the world are actually recorded in places that are not independent countries. Gibraltar, for example, a British dependency, has a marriage rate of 24.9 per 1,000.

⊕ **Afghan teen bride**
A young woman prepares for marriage in Afghanistan, where local tradition determines that many girls wed at an age when those in developed countries are still in school.

top 10 COUNTRIES WHERE **WOMEN MARRY** THE YOUNGEST

	COUNTRY	AVERAGE AGE AT FIRST MARRIAGE
1	Dem. Rep. of Congo	16.6
2	Niger	17.6
3	= Afghanistan	17.8
	= São Tomé and Príncipe	17.8
5	= Chad	18.0
	= Mozambique	18.0
7	Bangladesh	18.1
8	Uganda	18.2
9	= Congo	18.4
	= Mali	18.4

Source: United Nations

top 10 COUNTRIES WHERE **MEN MARRY** THE YOUNGEST

	COUNTRY	AVERAGE AGE AT FIRST MARRIAGE
1	Nepal	22.0
2	San Marino	22.2
3	Uganda	22.5
4	Mozambique	22.6
5	São Tomé and Príncipe	23.0
6	Tajikistan	23.1
7	Maldives	23.2
8	Uzbekistan	23.3
9	= Cuba	23.5
	= Malawi	23.5

Source: United Nations

the 10 COUNTRIES WITH THE **LOWEST MARRIAGE** RATE

	COUNTRY	MARRIAGES PER 1,000 PER ANNUM*
1	El Salvador	2.1
2	Peru	2.4
3	United Arab Emirates	2.5
4	Georgia	2.7
5	Dominican Republic	2.9
6	= Andorra	3.2
	= Armenia	3.2
	= Saudi Arabia	3.2
9	Venezuela	3.3
10	= Panama	3.4
	= Qatar	3.4

* In those countries/latest year for which data available

Source: United Nations

the 10 COUNTRIES WITH THE **HIGHEST DIVORCE** RATE

	COUNTRY	DIVORCE RATE PER 1,000*
1	Russia	5.30
2	Belarus	4.35
3	US	4.19
4	Ukraine	3.70
5	Aruba	3.61
6	Cuba	3.32
7	= Estonia	3.17
	= Lithuania	3.17
9	Czech Republic	3.09
10	Belgium	2.85

* In those countries/latest year for which data available

Source: United Nations

top 10 COUNTRIES WITH THE **LOWEST DIVORCE** RATE

	COUNTRY	DIVORCE RATE PER 1,000*
1	Guatemala	0.12
2	Mongolia	0.27
3	Libya	0.31
4	Georgia	0.40
5	= Chile	0.42
	= El Salvador	0.42
7	Jamaica	0.44
8	Armenia	0.47
9	Turkey	0.49
10	Bosnia & Herzegovina	0.54

* In those countries/latest year for which data available

Source: United Nations

The countries that figure among those with the lowest rates represent a range of cultures and religions, which either condone or condemn divorce to varying extents, thus affecting its prevalence or otherwise. In Libya, for example, it has long been relatively easy for men to divorce women, but not the other way round, while in many countries the status of a divorced woman is extremely low and her withdrawal from a marriage ends her economic support. In Jamaica, partners often separate without the formality of divorce.

First Fact The first divorce in the New World was granted on January 5, 1643 by the Colony of the Massachusetts Bay to Anne Clarke, wife of Denis Clarke, who had deserted her. The court record declared, "She is garunted to bee divorced." By 1975, the number of divorces in the US had exceeded one million a year, a level it has maintained ever since.

➲ D-I-V-O-R-C-E
Once unmentionable, prohibited, or rare, divorce is now so common in many countries that almost half of all marriages end in divorce.

Name Game

top 10 FIRST NAMES IN ENGLAND & WALES

GIRLS (2004)	(2003)	BOYS (2004)	(2003)
1 Emily	Emily	Jack	Jack
2 Ellie	Ellie	Joshua	Joshua
3 Jessica	Chloe	Thomas	Thomas
4 Sophie	Jessica	James	James
5 Chloe	Sophie	Daniel	Daniel
6 Lucy	Megan	Samuel	Oliver
7 Olivia	Lucy	Oliver	Benjamin
8 Charlotte	Olivia	William	Samuel
9 Katie	Charlotte	Benjamin	William
10 Megan	Hannah	Joseph	Joseph

Source: Office for National Statistics

top 10 FIRST NAMES IN AUSTRALIA*

GIRLS (2004)	(2000–2003)	BOYS (2004)	(2000–2003)
1 Emily	Emily	Jack	Jack
2 Olivia	Jessica	Joshua	Joshua
3 Chloe	Olivia	Lachlan	Lachlan
4 Jessica	Sarah	Thomas	Thomas
5 Charlotte	Georgia	William	Daniel
6 Ella	Isabella	James	James
7 Isabella	Chloe	Ethan	William
8 Sophie	Hannah	Samuel	Benjamin
9 Emma	Emma	Daniel	Nicholas
10 Grace	Sophie	Benjamin	Matthew

* Since 2000

* Based on figures from New South Wales and Victoria

Source: New South Wales Registry of Births, Deaths and Marriages in Australia/Victorian Registry of Births, Deaths and Marriages in Australia

◀ Jack Black
Born Thomas Black in 1969, when Thomas was one of the US's most popular names, comedy actor Jack Black adopted the name Jack, currently both England and Australia's most popular boy's name.

Olivia Newton-John ▶
Born in 1948 when the name Olivia was distinctly unfashionable, British-born Australian actress Olivia Newton-John now sees her first name among the favorites in English-speaking countries.

top 10 FIRST NAMES IN THE US

GIRLS (2003)	(2002)	BOYS (2003)	(2002)
1 Emily	Emily	Jacob	Jacob
2 Emma	Madison	Michael	Michael
3 Madison	Hannah	Joshua	Joshua
4 Hannah	Emma	Matthew	Matthew
5 Olivia	Alexis	Andrew	Ethan
6 Abigail	Ashley	Joseph	Joseph
7 Alexis	Abigail	Ethan	Andrew
8 Ashley	Sarah	Daniel	Christopher
9 Elizabeth	Samantha	Christopher	Daniel
10 Samantha	Olivia	Anthony	Nicholas

Source: Social Security Administration

These rankings are based on a cross-country sampling of US Social Security Number applications. They indicate that within the Top 10 in the course of a single year the name Olivia gained the greatest popularity, rising from 10th to 5th place.

top 10 **LAST NAMES** IN THE UK

	SURNAME	NUMBER
1	Smith	652,563
2	Jones	538,874
3	Williams	380,379
4	Taylor	306,296
5	Brown	291,872
6	Davies*	279,647
7	Evans	225,580
8	Thomas	202,773
9	Wilson	201,224
10	Johnson	193,260

* There are also 97,349 people bearing the surname Davis

This survey of British surnames is based on an analysis of 54.4 million appearing in the British electoral rolls—hence enumerating only those over age 18 and eligible to vote. Some 12 people out of every thousand in the UK are now called Smith, compared with 14.55 per thousand of names appearing in a sample from the 1851 Census.

top 10 **LAST NAMES** IN THE US

	NAME	PERCENTAGE OF ALL US NAMES
1	Smith	1.006
2	Johnson	0.810
3	Williams	0.699
4	= Brown	0.621
	= Jones	0.621
6	Davis	0.480
7	Miller	0.424
8	Wilson	0.339
9	Moore	0.312
10	= Anderson	0.311
	= Taylor	0.311
	= Thomas	0.311

The Top 10 US surnames together make up over six percent of the entire US population—in other words, one American in every 16 bears one of these names. Extending the list, some 28 different names comprise 10 percent of the whole population.

First Fact

The longest sustained popularity of any female first name in England and Wales, the US, and Australia was that of Mary. It was the most common name among the first settlers in America in the 17th century and up to 1962, when it lost out to Lisa. In post-Reformation England, Mary was briefly unfashionable for its Catholic associations, but was the No. 1 female name from 1700 until about 1924, when it was overtaken by Margaret, and in Australia throughout the 19th century and up to 1970, when it was replaced at the top spot by Jennifer.

Accident & Injury

the 10 MOST COMMON CAUSES OF **INJURY** IN THE US

CAUSE OF INJURY / NUMBER OF EMERGENCY ROOM VISITS, 2002

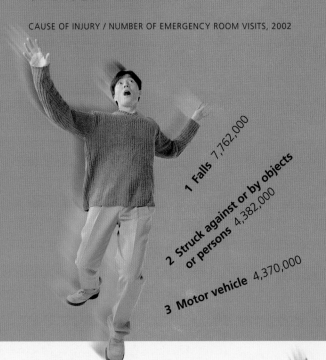

1 Falls 7,762,000

2 Struck against or by objects or persons 4,382,000

3 Motor vehicle 4,370,000

4 Cutting or piercing 2,974,000

5 Overexertion and strenuous movements 1,699,000

6 Natural/environmental 1,496,000

7 Adverse effects of medical treatment 1,445,000

8 Assault 1,387,000

9 Poisoning 720,000

10 Burning 502,000

Source: National Center for Health Statistics

the 10 MOST COMMON CAUSES OF **ACCIDENTAL DEATH** IN THE US

TYPE OF ACCIDENT	ACCIDENTAL DEATHS*, 2002 (TOTAL)	(PERCENTAGE OF TOTAL)
1 Motor vehicle	43,910	41.5
2 Poisoning	17,515	16.6
3 Falling	16,240	15.4
4 Suffocation	4,881	4.6
5 Drowning	3,364	3.2
6 Fire/burning	3,218	3.0
7 Transportation (except motor vehicles)	2,402	2.1
8 Natural/environmental	1,524	1.4
9 Pedestrian	1,236	1.2
10 Striking by/against	888	0.8
Total unintentional fatal injuries	*105,711*	*100.0*

* Excluding deaths of those under one year old

Source: National Center for Injury Prevention and Control

⬆ Accidents will happen
Unintentional injuries result in large numbers of visits to doctors and hospital emergency rooms.

the 10 MOST COMMON CAUSES OF **DEATH AT WORK** IN THE US

CAUSE OF DEATH	FATALITIES, 2003
1 **Highway transportation: collision between moving vehicles**	648
2 **Homicide** (includes 487 shootings)	631
3 **Fall to lower level**	601
4 **Transportation on farm/industrial premises**	347
5 **Highway transportation: vehicle struck stationary object or equipment**	341
6 **Worker struck by a vehicle**	336
7 **Struck by falling object**	322
8 **Highway transportation: jackknifed/overturned**	252
9 **Contact with electric current**	246
10 **Caught in or compressed by equipment/machinery**	237
Total work fatalities in 2003	*5,559*

Source: US Bureau of Labor Statistics, *National Census of Fatal Occupational Injuries, 2003*

Although a small increase from the previous year's 5,534 fatal work injuries was recorded in 2003, overall figures have moved steadily down in the past 10 years: workplace homicides, for example, hit a high of 1,080 in 1994 and highway fatalities in all categories totaled 1,496 in 1999, compared with the figure of 1,350 in 2003.

⊕ Danger, workers present
Some 20 percent of all work fatalities in the US occur in the construction industry, with agriculture, forestry, fishing, and hunting accounting for a further 13 percent.

the 10 MOST **ACCIDENT-PRONE** COUNTRIES

	COUNTRY	ACCIDENT DEATH RATE PER 100,000*
1	**Estonia**	102.8
2	**Latvia**	101.4
3	**Russia**	100.2
4	**Ukraine**	83.0
5	**Lithuania**	75.2
6	**Hungary**	58.6
7	**Moldova**	56.7
8	= **Finland**	52.8
	= **France**	52.8
10	**Belarus**	51.7
	US	*36.2*

* In those countries/latest year for which data available

Source: *UN Demographic Yearbook*

the 10 MOST COMMON CAUSES OF **WORK INJURIES** IN THE US

CAUSE OF INJURY	NONFATAL CASES, 2003*
1 **Overexertion when lifting**	1,850,600
2 **Fall on same level**	1,745,700
3 **Struck by object**	1,664,400
4 **Overexertion** (except lifting)	1,566,900
5 **Struck against object**	914,400
6 **Fall to lower level**	826,700
7 **Transportation accidents**	576,700
8 **Repetitive motion**	574,200
9 **Caught in equipment or object**	570,300
10 **Exposure to harmful substances**	557,800

* Requiring days away from work; private industry only

Source: Bureau of Labor Statistics

Rulers & Leaders

top 10 **IN LINE** TO THE BRITISH THRONE

HRH The Prince of Wales

(Prince Charles Philip
Arthur George)
b. November 14, 1948

then his elder son:

HRH The Duke of York

(Prince Andrew Albert
Christian Edward)
b. February 19, 1960

then his elder daughter:

HRH Prince Edward

(Prince Edward Antony
Richard Louis)
b. March 10, 1964

then his daughter:

HRH The Princess Royal

(Princess Anne Elizabeth
Alice Louise)
b. August 15, 1950

then her son:

**HRH Prince William
of Wales**

(Prince William Arthur
Philip Louis)
b. June 21, 1982

then his younger brother:

**HRH Princess Beatrice
of York**

(Princess Beatrice
Elizabeth Mary)
b. August 8, 1988

then her younger sister:

**Lady Louise Alice
Elizabeth Mary
Mountbatten Windsor**

b. November 8, 2003

then her aunt:
HRH The Princess Royal

**Master Peter Mark
Andrew Phillips**

b. November 15, 1977

**HRH Prince Henry
of Wales**

(Prince Henry Charles
Albert David)
b. September 15, 1984

then his uncle:
HRH The Duke of York

**HRH Princess Eugenie
of York**

(Princess Eugenie
Victoria Helena)
b. March 23, 1990

then her uncle:
HRH Prince Edward

➲ **Prime time**
The daughter of Jawaharal
Nehru, India's first prime
minister following the country's
independence, Indira Gandhi
became the world's second
female prime minister. Both
she and her son Rajiv, who
succeeded her to the office,
were assassinated.

The birth in 1988 of Princess Beatrice altered the order of
succession, ousting David Albert Charles Armstrong-Jones,
Viscount Linley (the son of Princess Margaret), from the No. 10
position. The birth of Princess Beatrice's sister, Princess Eugenie,
in 1990 evicted HRH Princess Margaret (the sister of the Queen),
who died in 2002. The recent birth of Lady Louise Windsor
means that Zara Phillips (the daughter of Princess Anne) has
fallen out of the Top 10.

➔ **Presidential popularity**
Father and son George H. W. and George W. Bush rank alongside each other for popular votes received in their first elections, with George W. achieving a record number in his 2004 reelection.

top 10 LONGEST-SERVING PRESIDENTS TODAY

	PRESIDENT	COUNTRY	TOOK OFFICE
1	General Gnassingbé Eyadéma	Togo	Apr. 14, 1967
2	El Hadj Omar Bongo	Gabon	Dec. 2, 1967
3	Colonel Mu'ammar Gadhafi*	Libya	Sept. 1, 1969
4	Zayid ibn Sultan al-Nuhayyan	United Arab Emirates	Dec. 2, 1971
5	Fidel Castro	Cuba	Nov. 2, 1976
6	Ali Abdullah Saleh	Yemen	July 17, 1978
7	Maumoon Abdul Gayoom	Maldives	Nov. 11, 1978
8	Teodoro Obiang Nguema Mbasogo	Equatorial Guinea	Aug. 3, 1979
9	José Eduardo Dos Santos	Angola	Sept. 21, 1979
10	Hosni Mubarak	Egypt	Oct. 6, 1981

* Since a reorganization in 1979, Colonel Gadhafi has held no formal position, but continues to rule under the ceremonial title of "Leader of the Revolution"

All the presidents in this list have been in power for more than 20—some for over 30—years. Fidel Castro was prime minister of Cuba from February 1959. Since he was also chief of the army, and there was no opposition party, he effectively ruled as dictator from then, but he was not technically president until the Cuban constitution was revised in 1976. Similarly, Robert Mugabe has ruled Zimbabwe since April 18, 1980, but only became president in 1987 (prior to this, he held the title of prime minister).

the 10 US PRESIDENTS WITH THE GREATEST NUMBER OF POPULAR VOTES

	PRESIDENT	YEAR	VOTES
1	George W. Bush	2004	59,459,765
2	Ronald Reagan	1984	54,281,858
3	George W. Bush	2000	50,459,211
4	George H. W. Bush	1988	48,881,221
5	Bill Clinton	1996	47,401,185
6	Richard Nixon	1972	47,165,234
7	Bill Clinton	1992	44,908,254
8	Ronald Reagan	1980	43,899,248
9	Lyndon Johnson	1964	43,126,506
10	Jimmy Carter	1976	40,828,929

There are 538 Electoral College members in total, but they are obliged to vote for the candidate who wins the popular vote in only 38 of the 50 US states. On occasions, presidents have won with fewer popular votes than their opponents.

the 10 FIRST FEMALE PRIME MINISTERS AND PRESIDENTS

	PRIME MINISTER OR PRESIDENT	COUNTRY	FIRST PERIOD IN OFFICE
1	Sirimavo Bandaranaike (PM)	Sri Lanka	July 1960–Mar. 1965
2	Indira Gandhi (PM)	India	Jan.1966–Mar. 1977
3	Golda Meir (PM)	Israel	Mar. 1969–June 1974
4	Maria Estela Perón (President)	Argentina	July 1974–Mar. 1976
5	Elisabeth Domitien (PM)	Central African Republic	Jan. 1975–Apr. 1976
6	Margaret Thatcher (PM)	UK	May 1979–Nov. 1990
7	Dr. Maria Lurdes Pintasilgo (PM)	Portugal	Aug. 1979–Jan. 1980
8	Mary Eugenia Charles (PM)	Dominica	July 1980–June 1995
9	Vigdís Finnbogadóttir (President)	Iceland	Aug. 1980–Aug. 1996
10	Gro Harlem Brundtland (PM)	Norway	Feb.–Oct. 1981

First Fact
Following the assassination of her husband Solomon West Ridgeway Dias Bandaranaike, Sirimavo Ratwatte Dias Bandaranaike (1916–2000) took over as leader of the Ceylon (later Sri Lanka) Freedom Party, won the election, and thereby became the world's first female prime minister. She was to serve in this office three times (1960–65, 1970–77, and 1994–2000), while her daughter Chandrika Kumaratunga became the country's first female president in 1994.

top 10 **LONGEST REIGNING MONARCHS**

	MONARCH	COUNTRY	REIGN	AGE AT ACCESSION	REIGN (YEARS)
1	King Louis XIV	France	1643–1715	5	72
2	King John II	Liechtenstein	1858–1929	18	71
3	Emperor Franz-Josef	Austria-Hungary	1848–1916	18	67
4	Queen Victoria	UK	1837–1901	18	63
5	Emperor Hirohito	Japan	1926–89	25	62
6	Emperor K'ang Hsi	China	1661–1722	7	61
7	King Sobhuza II*	Swaziland	1921–82	22	60#
8	Emperor Ch'ien Lung	China	1735–96	25	60#
9	King Christian IV	Denmark	1588–1648	11	59#
10	King George III	UK	1760–1820	22	59#

* Paramount chief until 1967, when Great Britain recognized him as king with the granting of internal self-government

Precise differences between reign days distinguish between those of identical duration in years

King Harald I of Norway is said to have ruled for 70 years from 870–940, and the even longer reigns of 95 and 94 years are credited respectively to King Mihti of Arakan (Myanmar) around 1279–1374, and Pharaoh Phiops (Pepi) II of Egypt (Neferkare) around 2269–2175 BC, but there is inadequate historical evidence to substantiate any of these claims.

◆ Long reigns
Clockwise, from top left: Christian IV, Hirohito, Franz-Josef, and Queen Victoria. Acceding to a throne in their youth, a long life, and the avoidance of the risks that traditionally threaten monarchs, allowed each of these people to reign for 60 or more years. Queen Victoria survived no fewer than eight attempts on her life: had the first, by Edward Oxford on June 10, 1840, succeeded, her reign would have lasted less than three years.

The First To...

the 10 FIRST PEOPLE TO **CROSS NIAGARA FALLS** BY TIGHTROPE

	TIGHTROPE WALKER	DATE
1	**Blondin** (Jean François Gravelet)	June 30, 1859
2	**Signor Guillermo Antonio Farini** (William Leonard Hunt)	Aug. 15, 1860
3	**Harry Leslie**	June 15, 1865
4	**J. F. "Professor" Jenkins**	Aug. 25, 1869
5	**Signor Henri Belleni**	Aug. 25, 1873
6	**Stephen Peer**	Sept. 10, 1873
7	**Maria Spelterini**	July 8, 1876
8	**Samuel Dixon**	Sept. 6, 1890
9	**Clifford Caverley**	Oct. 12, 1892
10	**James Hardy**	July 1, 1896

Several of these funambulists were members of the making-things-as-difficult-as-possible school: on one of his crossings, Blondin pushed a wheelbarrow, Farini strapped a washing machine on to his back, and Professor Jenkins rode a bicycle, while Maria Spelterini had her ankles and wrists manacled and wore peach baskets on her feet. Most walkers made more than one crossing.

the 10 FIRST MOUNTAINEERS TO **CLIMB EVEREST**

	MOUNTAINEER / NATIONALITY	DATE
1	**Edmund Hillary**, New Zealander	May 29, 1953
2	**Tenzing Norgay**, Nepalese	May 29, 1953
3	**Jürg Marmet**, Swiss	May 23, 1956
4	**Ernst Schmied**, Swiss	May 23, 1956
5	**Hans-Rudolf von Gunten**, Swiss	May 24, 1956
6	**Adolf Reist**, Swiss	May 24, 1956
7	**Wang Fu-chou**, Chinese	May 25, 1960
8	**Chu Ying-hua**, Chinese	May 25, 1960
9	**Konbu**, Tibetan	May 25, 1960
10 =	**Nawang Gombu**, Indian	May 1, 1963
=	**James Whittaker**, American	May 1, 1963

Some 15 reconnaissance expeditions and attempts on Everest—several resulting in the deaths of the mountaineers—preceded the first successful conquest of the world's tallest peak. Nawang Gombu and James Whittaker are 10th equal because, neither wishing to deny the other the privilege of being first, they ascended the last steps to the summit side by side.

⬆ **Rope trick**
French tightrope walker Blondin is dwarfed by Niagara Falls as he makes the first of his 21 crossings on June 30, 1859.

the 10 FIRST EXPEDITIONS TO **REACH THE NORTH POLE OVERLAND**

EXPEDITION LEADER OR CO-LEADER / NATIONALITY / DATE

1 Ralph S. Plaisted, American, Apr. 19, 1968   **2 Wally W. Herbert**, British, Apr. 5, 1969   **3 Naomi Uemura**, Japanese, May 1, 1978

4 Dmitri Shparo, Soviet, May 31, 1979   **5 Sir Ranulph Fiennes/Charles Burton**, Apr. 11, 1982

6 Will Steger/Paul Schurke, American, May 1, 1986   **7 Jean-Louis Etienne**, French, May 11, 1986

8 Fukashi Kazami, Japanese, Apr. 20, 1987   **9 Helen Thayer**, American*, Apr. 20, 1988   **10 Robert Swan**, British, May 14, 1989

* New Zealand-born

the 10 FIRST PEOPLE TO **REACH THE SOUTH POLE**

Just 33 days separated the first two expeditions to reach the South Pole. Scott's British Antarctic Expedition was organized with its avowed goal "to reach the South Pole and to secure for the British Empire the honor of this achievement." Meanwhile, Norwegian explorer Roald Amundsen also set out on an expedition to the Pole. When Scott eventually reached his goal, he discovered that the Norwegians had beaten them. Demoralized, Scott's team began the arduous return journey, but, plagued by illness, hunger, bad weather, and exhaustion, the entire expedition died just as Amundsen's triumph was being reported to the world.

➲ Pole position
Roald Amundsen records his conquest of the South Pole a month ahead of Captain Scott's expedition, which ended in disaster.

December 14, 1911

EXPLORER / NATIONALITY

1

= **Roald Amundsen***, Norwegian
= **Olav Olavsen Bjaaland**, Norwegian
= **Helmer Julius Hanssen**, Norwegian
= **Helge Sverre Hassel**, Norwegian
= **Oscar Wisting**, Norwegian

* Expedition leader

January 17, 1912

EXPLORER / NATIONALITY

6

= **Robert Falcon Scott***, British
= **Henry Robertson Bowers**, British
= **Edgar Evans**, British
= **Lawrence Edward Grace Oates**, British
= **Edward Adrian Wilson**, British

* Expedition leader

SOUTH POLE

SCOTT'S ROUTE ⎯⎯⎯

AMUNDSEN'S ROUTE ⎯⎯⎯

Crime & Punishment

the 10 COUNTRIES WITH THE HIGHEST MURDER RATES

	COUNTRY	REPORTED MURDERS PER 100,000 POPULATION, 2002*
1	Honduras	154.02
2	South Africa	114.84
3	Colombia	69.98
4	Lesotho	50.41
5	Rwanda	45.08
6	Jamaica	43.71
7	El Salvador	34.33
8	Venezuela	33.20
9	Bolivia	31.98
10	Namibia	26.32
	US	*5.61*

* Or latest year for which data available

Source: Interpol

the 10 MOST COMMON MURDER WEAPONS AND METHODS IN THE US

	WEAPON OR METHOD	VICTIMS, 2003
1	Firearms	9,638
2	Knives or cutting instruments	1,816
3	"Personal weapons" (hands, feet, fists, etc.)	946
4	Blunt objects (hammers, clubs, etc.)	651
5	Strangulation	184
6	Fire	163
7	Asphyxiation	128
8	Narcotics	41
9	Poison	9
10	Explosives	4
	Total	*14,408*

Source: *FBI Uniform Crime Reports*

the 10 COUNTRIES WITH THE HIGHEST REPORTED CRIME RATES

	COUNTRY	CRIMES PER 100,000, 2002*
1	Finland	14,525.74
2	Sweden	13,350.27
3	Guyana	12,933.18
4	New Zealand	12,586.64
5	England and Wales	11,326.60
6	Grenada	10,177.89
7	Norway	9,822.91
8	Denmark	9,005.77
9	Belgium	8,597.66
10	Canada	8,572.50
	US	*4,160.51*

* Or latest year for which data available

Source: Interpol

An appearance in this list does not necessarily confirm these as the most crime-ridden countries, since the rate of reporting relates closely to such factors as confidence in local law enforcement authorities. However, a rate of approximately 1,000 per 100,000 may be considered average, so those in the Top 10 are well above it.

the 10 COUNTRIES WITH THE HIGHEST PRISON POPULATION RATE

	COUNTRY	PRISONERS PER 100,000*
1	US	701
2	Russia	606
3	Kazakhstan	522
4	Turkmenistan	489
5	= Belarus	459
	= Belize	459
7	Suriname	437
8	Dominica	420
9	Ukraine	415
10	Maldives	414

* Most figures relate to the period 1999–2003

Source: British Home Office, *World Prison Population List*, 5th edition

the 10 COUNTRIES WITH THE MOST EXECUTIONS

	COUNTRY	EXECUTIONS*, 2003
1	China	726
2	Iran	108
3	US	65
4	Vietnam	64
5	Saudi Arabia	53
6	Chad	9
7	Singapore	8
8	Jordan	7
9	= Botswana	4
	= Thailand	4
	= Zimbabwe	4

* Verifiable reported executions

Some 118 countries have abolished the death penalty in law or practice, while 78 retain it. According to Amnesty International, in 2003 a total of at least 1,146 people were executed in 28 countries.

the 10 WORST GUN MASSACRES*

PERPETRATOR / LOCATION /
DATE / CIRCUMSTANCES

KILLED 57

1

Woo Bum Kong
Sang-Namdo, South Korea
April 28, 1982

Off-duty policeman Woo Bum Kong (or Wou Bom-Kon), 27, went on a drunken rampage with rifles and hand grenades, killing 57 and injuring 38 before blowing himself up with a grenade.

KILLED 35

2

Martin Bryant
Port Arthur, Tasmania, Australia
April 28, 1996

Bryant, a 28-year-old Hobart resident, used a rifle in a horrific spree that began in a restaurant and ended with a siege in a guesthouse in which he held hostages and set it on fire before being captured by police.

KILLED 29

3

Baruch Goldstein
Hebron, occupied West Bank, Israel
February 25, 1994

Goldstein, a 42-year-old US immigrant doctor, carried out a gun massacre of Palestinians at prayer at the Tomb of the Patriarchs before being beaten to death by the crowd.

KILLED 28

4

Campo Elias Delgado
Bogota, Colombia
December 4, 1986

Delgado, a Vietnamese war veteran and electronics engineer, stabbed two and shot a further 26 people before being killed by police.

KILLED 22

5=

= George Jo Hennard
Killeen, Texas
October 16, 1991

Hennard drove his pickup truck through the window of Luby's Cafeteria and, in 11 minutes, killed 22 with semiautomatic pistols before shooting himself.

KILLED 22

= James Oliver Huberty
San Ysidro, California
July 18, 1984

Huberty, age 41, opened fire in a McDonald's restaurant, killing 21 before being shot dead by a SWAT marksman. A further 19 were wounded, including a victim who died the following day.

KILLED 17

7=

= Thomas Hamilton
Dunblane, Stirling, Scotland
March 13, 1996

Hamilton, 43, shot 16 children and a teacher in Dunblane Primary School before killing himself in the UK's worst-ever shooting incident.

KILLED 17

= Robert Steinhäuser
Erfurt, Germany
April 26, 2002

Former student Steinhäuser returned to Johann Gutenberg Secondary School and killed 14 teachers, two students, and a police officer with a handgun before shooting himself.

KILLED 16

9=

= Michael Ryan
Hungerford, Berkshire, England
August 19, 1987

Ryan, 26, shot 14 dead and wounded 16 others (two of whom died later) before shooting himself.

KILLED 16

= Ronald Gene Simmons
Russellville, Arkansas
December 28, 1987

Simmons, 47, killed 16, including 14 members of his own family, by shooting or strangling. He was caught and, on February 10, 1989, sentenced to death.

KILLED 16

= Charles Joseph Whitman
Austin, Texas
July 31–August 1, 1966

Ex-Marine marksman Whitman, 25, killed his mother and wife and the following day took the elevator to the 27th floor of the campus tower and ascended to the observation deck at the University of Texas at Austin, from where he shot 14 and wounded 34 before being shot dead by police officer Romero Martinez.

* By individuals, excluding terrorist and military actions; totals exclude perpetrator

World War II

the 10 WORST MILITARY SHIP LOSSES OF WORLD WAR II

	SHIP*	COUNTRY	DATE	APPROX. NO. KILLED
1	**Wilhelm Gustloff**	Germany	Jan. 30, 1945	7,800
2	**Goya**	Germany	Apr. 16, 1945	6,202
3	**Cap Arcona**	Germany	Apr. 26, 1945	6,000
4	**Junyo Maru**	Japan	Sept. 18, 1944	5,620
5	**Toyama Maru**	Japan	June 29, 1944	5,400
6	**Arcona**	Germany	May 3, 1945	5,000
7	**Lancastria**	UK	June 17, 1940	3,050
8	**Steuben**	Germany	Feb. 9, 1945	3,000
9	**Thielbeck**	Germany	May 3, 1945	2,750
10	**Yamato**	Japan	Apr. 7, 1945	2,498

* Includes warships and passenger vessels used for troop and refugee transport

The German liner *Wilhelm Gustloff*, laden with civilian refugees and wounded German soldiers and sailors, was torpedoed off the coast of Poland by a Soviet submarine, *S-13*. Although imprecise, some sources even suggest a figure as high as 9,400; the probable death toll is some five times as great as that of the *Titanic*.

⊙ Scramble!
Fighter pilots race for their planes during the Battle of Britain. The UK's aircraft losses were less than one-third those of Germany or the USSR.

the 10 COUNTRIES SUFFERING THE GREATEST AIRCRAFT LOSSES IN WORLD WAR II

	COUNTRY	AIRCRAFT LOST
1	**Germany**	116,584
2	**USSR**	106,652
3	**US**	59,296
4	**Japan**	49,485
5	**UK**	33,090
6	**Australia**	7,160
7	**Italy**	5,272
8	**Canada**	2,389
9	**France**	2,100
10	**New Zealand**	684

Reports of aircraft losses vary considerably from country to country, some of them including aircraft damaged, lost due to accidents, or scrapped, as well as those destroyed during combat. The Japanese figure for combat-only losses, for example, is sometimes reported as 38,105. The huge Soviet losses, which were undisclosed at the time, are believed to include aircraft withdrawn from frontlines as well as those destroyed. Very precise combat loss figures exist for the Battle of Britain—during the period July 10 to October 31, 1940, 1,065 RAF aircraft were destroyed, compared with 1,922 Luftwaffe fighters, bombers, and other aircraft.

the 10 COUNTRIES SUFFERING THE **GREATEST MILITARY LOSSES** IN WORLD WAR II

COUNTRY / APPROX. NO. KILLED

1 **USSR** 13,600,000*
2 **Germany** 3,300,000
3 **China** 1,324,516
4 **Japan** 1,140,429
5 **British Empire**# 357,116
   (UK 264,000)
6 **Romania** 350,000
7 **Poland** 320,000
8 **Yugoslavia** 305,000
9 **US** 292,131
10 **Italy** 279,800
   Total 21,268,992

* Total, of which 7.8 million battlefield deaths

\# Including Australia, Canada, India, New Zealand, etc.

The actual numbers killed in World War II have been the subject of intense argument. The immense military casualty rate of the USSR in particular is hard to comprehend. Most authorities now think that of the 30 million Soviets who bore arms, there were 13.6 million military deaths, but it should also be borne in mind that these were military losses—to these should be added many millions of civilian war deaths, while recent estimates have suggested an additional figure of up to 25 million civilian deaths as a result of Stalinist purges that began just before the war.

the 10 COUNTRIES SUFFERING THE **GREATEST CIVILIAN LOSSES** IN WORLD WAR II

COUNTRY / APPROX. NO. KILLED*

1 **China** 8,000,000
2 **USSR** 6,500,000
3 **Poland** 5,300,000
4 **Germany** 2,350,000
5 **Yugoslavia** 1,500,000
6 **France** 470,000
7 **Greece** 415,000
8 **Japan** 393,400
9 **Romania** 340,000
10 **Hungary** 300,000

* During World War II, many deaths among civilians—especially in China and the USSR—resulted from famine and internal purges. For political and propaganda reasons, totals are less well-documented than military losses.

the 10 **NAZI WAR CRIMINALS** HANGED AT NUREMBERG

NAME / AGE / DETAILS

1 **Joachim Von Ribbentrop**, 53, former ambassador to Great Britain and Hitler's last foreign minister (the first to be hanged, at 1:02 am on Oct. 16, 1946)
2 **Field Marshal Wilhelm Von Keitel**, 64, who had ordered the killing of 50 Allied air force officers after the Great Escape
3 **General Ernst Kaltenbrunner**, 44, SS and Gestapo leader
4 **Reichminister Alfred Rosenberg**, 53, ex-Minister of Occupied Eastern Territories
5 **Reichminister Hans Frank**, 46, ex-governor of Poland
6 **Reichminister Wilhelm Frick**, 69, former Minister of the Interior
7 **Gauleiter Julius Streicher**, 61, editor of anti-Semitic magazine *Die Stürmer*
8 **Reichminister Fritz Sauckel**, 52, ex-General Plenipotentiary for the Utilization of Labor (the slave-labor program)
9 **Colonel-General Alfred Jodl**, 56, former Chief of the General Staff
10 **Gauleiter Artur Von Seyss-Inquart**, 53, governor of Austria and later Commissioner for Occupied Holland

During the International Military Tribunal trials from November 20, 1945 to August 31, 1946, 24 Nazi war criminals stood trial. Of them, 12 were found guilty and sentenced to death (including Martin Bormann, who had escaped, and was tried *in absentia*, and Herman Goering, who cheated the gallows by committing suicide with a capsule of cyanide at 10:50 pm the previous day. The remaining 10 were hanged on October 16, 1946.

⊙ **War graves**
A US military cemetery in France shows the scale of the losses sustained by one country in a single campaign.

Military Might

⊙ Balance of power China and the US represent the greatest military strengths today in a world facing the threats of global terrorism and rogue states.

top 10 **LARGEST** ARMED FORCES

COUNTRY	ESTIMATED TOTAL ACTIVE FORCES			
	(ARMY	NAVY	AIR FORCE)	TOTAL
1 China	1,600,000	255,000	400,000	2,255,000
2 United States	502,000	400,000	379,500	1,456,850*
3 India	1,100,000	55,000	170,000	1,325,000
4 North Korea	1,106,000	46,000	110,000	1,262,000
5 Russia	360,000	155,000	184,600	1,058,700#
6 South Korea	560,000	63,000	64,700	687,700
7 Pakistan	550,000	25,000	45,000	620,000
8 Iran	350,000	18,000	52,000	540,000†
9 Turkey	402,000	52,750	60,100	514,850
10 Vietnam	412,000	42,000	30,000	484,000

* Includes 175,350 Marine Corps

\# Includes Strategic Deterrent Forces, Paramilitary, National Guard, etc.

† Includes 120,000 Revolutionary Guards

In addition to the active forces listed here, many of the world's foremost countries have substantial reserves on standby; South Korea's has been estimated at some 4.5 million, Vietnam's at three to four million, and China's 800,000. China is also notable for having a massive arsenal of military equipment at its disposal, including some 7,850 tanks and 3,000 combat aircraft. North Korea has the world's highest military/civilian ratio: 558 out of every 10,000 of the population serve in its forces, compared with South Korea's 144 per 10,000. The US ratio is 50 per 10,000.

top 10 **SMALLEST** ARMED FORCES*

COUNTRY	ESTIMATED TOTAL ACTIVE FORCES
1 Antigua and Barbuda	170
2 Seychelles	450
3 Barbados	610
4 Gambia	800
5 Bahamas	860
6 Luxembourg	900
7 Belize	1,050
8 Cape Verde	1,200
9 Equatorial Guinea	1,320
10 Guyana	1,600

* Includes only those countries that declare a defense budget

A number of small countries maintain military forces for ceremonial purposes, national prestige, or reasons other than national defense, and would clearly be inadequate to resist an invasion by their much larger neighbors. Luxembourg's army, however, took an active part in peacekeeping duties in former Yugoslavia.

⊙ **Soaring costs** The US and India, both notable for their multi-billon dollar and ever-increasing defense budgets, join forces in an aerial military exercise.

top 10 COUNTRIES WITH THE
LARGEST DEFENSE BUDGETS

COUNTRY	BUDGET ($)
1 US	404,920,000,000
2 Russia	62,200,000,000
3 China	55,948,000,000
4 France	45,695,000,000
5 Japan	42,835,000,000
6 UK	42,782,000,000
7 Germany	35,145,000,000
8 Italy	27,751,000,000
9 Saudi Arabia	18,747,000,000
10 India	15,508,000,000

The so-called "peace dividend"—the reduction in defense expenditure since the end of the Cold War between the West and the former Soviet Union—was short-lived. In response to the threats of international terrorism and "rogue states," such as Iraq, the budgets of the US (which stood at $305,500,000 in 2001) and its allies have increased to record levels. Globally, the total defense expenditure is now almost $1 trillion, of which over $600 billion is by NATO countries. The budget of North Korea, an impoverished country with a population of just 22 million, is a remarkable $5.5 billion.

top 10 COUNTRIES WITH THE
SMALLEST DEFENSE BUDGETS

COUNTRY*	BUDGET ($)
1 Gambia	2,000,000
2 Antigua and Barbuda	4,000,000
3 = Cape Verde	5,000,000
= Guyana	5,000,000
5 Equatorial Guinea	6,000,000
6 Surinam	8,000,000
7 Guinea-Bissau	9,000,000
8 Malawi	11,000,000
9 Seychelles	12,000,000
10 = Barbados	13,000,000
= Mauritius	13,000,000

* Includes only those countries that declare defense budgets

Compared with the multi-billion-dollar defense budgets of the world's biggest military spenders, those of these countries are minute. However, if expressed as a proportion of their gross domestic product, with expenditure amounting to more than one percent, several of these countries are actually on a par with many larger and wealthier nations. Gambia's minuscule $2 million budget supports an army of 800 and a marine unit of 70, plus a tiny UN peacekeeping force.

Religions

top 10 LARGEST CHRISTIAN POPULATIONS

COUNTRY	CHRISTIAN POPULATION, 2006 EST.
1 US	254,696,000
2 Brazil	168,498,000
3 China	113,786,000
4 Mexico	103,222,000
5 Russia	84,417,000
6 Philippines	75,177,000
7 India	69,663,000
8 Nigeria	63,046,000
9 Germany	61,662,000
10 Dem. Rep. of Congo	54,936,000

Source: Center for the Study of Global Christianity, Gordon-Conwell Theological Seminary

The Christian populations of these 10 countries make up almost 50 percent of the world total. Although Christian communities are found in virtually every country in the world, it is difficult to put a precise figure on nominal membership (a declared religious persuasion) rather than regular attendance.

⊙ **Growth rate**
With one of the fastest growth rates of any religion, it is predicted that the number of Muslims could reach 1.89 billion by 2025.

top 10 LARGEST JEWISH POPULATIONS

COUNTRY	JEWISH POPULATION, 2006 EST.
1 US	5,771,000
2 Israel	4,845,000
3 France	608,000
4 Argentina	511,000
5 Palestine	459,000
6 Canada	416,000
7 Brazil	386,000
8 UK	308,000
9 Russia	242,000
10 Germany	228,000

Source: Center for the Study of Global Christianity, Gordon-Conwell Theological Seminary

The Diaspora, or scattering of Jewish people, has been in progress for nearly 2,000 years, and as a result Jewish communities are found in virtually every country in the world. In 1939 it was estimated that the total world Jewish population was 17 million. Some 6 million fell victim to Nazi persecution, reducing the figure to about 11 million, but it is now estimated to have grown to exceed 13 million.

top 10 LARGEST HINDU POPULATIONS

COUNTRY	HINDU POPULATION, 2006 EST.
1 India	816,677,000
2 Nepal	19,431,000
3 Bangladesh	17,044,000
4 Indonesia	7,759,000
5 Sri Lanka	2,186,000
6 Pakistan	2,150,000
7 Malaysia	1,888,000
8 US	1,163,000
9 South Africa	1,079,000
10 Myanmar	1,025,000

Source: Center for the Study of Global Christianity, Gordon-Conwell Theological Seminary

Hindus constitute some 74 percent of the population of India and 72 percent of that of Nepal, but only 13 percent of that of Bangladesh and as little as three percent of Indonesia's.

top 10 LARGEST MUSLIM POPULATIONS

COUNTRY	MUSLIM POPULATION, 2006 EST.
1 Pakistan	158,312,000
2 India	139,820,000
3 Bangladesh	135,620,000
4 Indonesia	122,811,000*
5 Turkey	72,211,000
6 Iran	68,623,000
7 Egypt	64,769,000
8 Nigeria	55,863,000
9 Algeria	32,341,000
10 Morocco	31,476,000

* An additional 46 million people are considered Muslim by the Indonesian government but are more properly categorized as New Religionists (Islamicized syncretistic religions).

Source: Center for the Study of Global Christianity, Gordon-Conwell Theological Seminary

→ Cross road
Christianity is predicted to maintain its status as the world's foremost religion, with some estimates forecasting a total global population of around 3 billion Christians by 2025.

top 10 RELIGIOUS BELIEFS IN THE US

	RELIGION	FOLLOWERS, 2006 EST.
1	Christianity	254,696,000
2	Agnosticism	28,099,000
3	Judaism	5,771,000
4	Islam	4,752,000
5	Buddhism	2,828,000
6	New religions	1,527,000
7	Atheism	1,444,000
8	Ethnic religions	1,174,000
9	Hinduism	1,163,000
10	Baha'ism	843,000

Source: Center for the Study of Global Christianity, Gordon-Conwell Theological Seminary

Since it is against US law for people to be questioned about their religious beliefs as part of the decennial national Census, statistical information must be gathered by other methods. The US religious data collected by the Center for the Study of Global Christianity at the Gordon-Conwell Theological Seminary is considered the most authoritative source. It includes statistics on all Christian denominations and world religions, and provides the most reliable available snapshot of the current numbers of people claiming affiliation to each religious group—including agnosticism (the belief that the existence of a god or gods cannot be known with certainty) and atheism (the denial of the existence of a god).

top 10 RELIGIOUS BELIEFS

	RELIGION	FOLLOWERS, 2006 EST.
1	Christianity	2,159,841,000
2	Islam	1,342,394,000
3	Hinduism	877,126,000
4	Agnosticism	772,177,000
5	Chinese folk religions	406,889,000
6	Buddhism	382,155,000
7	Ethnic religions	257,888,000
8	Atheism	152,152,000
9	New religions	108,939,000
10	Sikhism	25,731,000

Source: Center for the Study of Global Christianity, Gordon-Conwell Theological Seminary

These authoritative estimates imply that almost one-third of the world's population are nominally (self-declared), if not practicing, Christians, and one-fifth followers of Islam. Alongside the growth of some religious groups, mainstream religions have seen a decline in formal attendance as increasing numbers of people describe themselves as "spiritual" rather than "religious," while it is thought that at least 15 percent of the world population professes no religious beliefs of any kind.

top 10 countries with the longest coastlines: page 82

Chapter

3 **4** **5** **6** **7** **8**

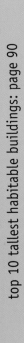

top 10 tallest habitable buildings: page 90

top 10 most populated countries: page 84

top 10 countries with most neighbors: page 83

891012

Town & Country

top 10 largest US states: page 88

Countries of the World

top 10 LARGEST COUNTRIES

COUNTRY	AREA (SQ MILES)	(SQ KM)	PERCENTAGE OF WORLD TOTAL
1 Russia	6,592,850	17,075,400	13.0
2 Canada	3,855,103	9,984,670	7.6
3 China	3,600,948	9,326,411	7.1
4 US	3,539,245	9,166,601	6.9
5 Brazil	3,265,077	8,456,511	6.4
6 Australia	2,941,300	7,617,931	5.8
7 India	1,148,148	2,973,190	2.2
8 Argentina	1,056,642	2,736,690	2.1
9 Kazakhstan	1,049,155	2,717,300	2.0
10 Algeria	919,595	2,381,741	1.8
World total	*50,580,568*	*131,003,055*	*100.0*

Source: US Census Bureau, International Data Base/Statistics Canada

top 10 SMALLEST COUNTRIES

COUNTRY	AREA (SQ MILES)	(SQ KM)
1 Vatican City	0.2	0.44
2 Monaco	0.7	2
3 Nauru	8	21
4 Tuvalu	10	26
5 San Marino	23	60
6 Liechtenstein	62	161
7 Marshall Islands	70	181
8 Maldives	115	300
9 Malta	124	321
10 Grenada	130	339

Source: US Census Bureau, International Data Base

The "country" status of the Vatican is questionable, since its government and other features are intricately linked with those of Italy. The Vatican did become part of unified Italy in the 19th century, but its identity as an independent state was recognized by a treaty on February 11, 1929.

top 10 COUNTRIES WITH THE LONGEST COASTLINES

COUNTRY / TOTAL COASTLINE LENGTH (MILES / KM)

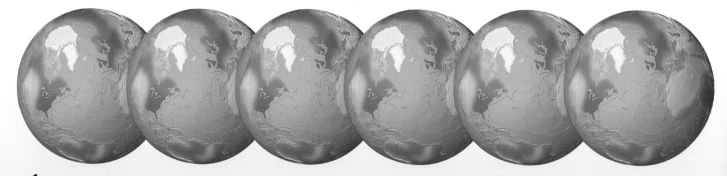

1 Canada 125,566 miles / 202,080 km

2 Indonesia 33,999 miles / 54,716 km **3 Russia** 23,396 miles / 37,653 km **4 Philippines** 22,559 miles / 36,289 km

5 Japan 18,486 miles / 29,751 km **6 Australia** 16,007 miles / 25,760 km **7 Norway** 13,624 miles / 21,925 km

8 US 12,380 miles / 19,924 km **9 New Zealand** 9,404 miles / 15,134 km **10 China** 9,010 miles / 14,500 km

Including all its islands, the coastline of Canada is more than six times as long as the distance around the Earth at the equator (24,902 miles/40,076 km). The coastline of the UK (7,723 miles/ 12,429 km) is longer than the distance from London to Honolulu, which puts it in 13th place after Greece's 8,498-mile (13,676-km) coastline. Greenland (27,394 miles/44,087 km) is a self-governed Danish territory. If it were a country in its own right, it would rank in third place in this list.

⊕ **From one extreme to the other** China has frontiers with 14 other countries, its neighbors representing landscapes as diverse as Nepal's Himalayas and Mongolia's Gobi Desert.

top 10 COUNTRIES WITH **MOST** NEIGHBORS

COUNTRY / NEIGHBORS	NO. OF NEIGHBORS
1 = China	14
Afghanistan, Bhutan, India, Kazakhstan, Kyrgyzstan, Laos, Mongolia, Myanmar, Nepal, North Korea, Pakistan, Russia, Tajikistan, Vietnam	
= Russia	14
Azerbaijan, Belarus, China, Estonia, Finland, Georgia, Kazakhstan, Latvia, Lithuania, Mongolia, North Korea, Norway, Poland, Ukraine	
3 Brazil	10
Argentina, Bolivia, Colombia, French Guiana, Guyana, Paraguay, Peru, Suriname, Uruguay, Venezuela	
4 = Dem. Rep. of Congo	9
Angola, Burundi, Central African Republic, Congo, Rwanda, Sudan, Tanzania, Uganda, Zambia	
= Germany	9
Austria, Belgium, Czech Republic, Denmark, France, Luxembourg, Netherlands, Poland, Switzerland	
= Sudan	9
Central African Republic, Chad, Dem. Rep. of Congo, Egypt, Eritrea, Ethiopia, Kenya, Libya, Uganda	
7 = Austria	8
Czech Republic, Germany, Hungary, Italy, Liechtenstein, Slovakia, Slovenia, Switzerland	

COUNTRY / NEIGHBORS	NO. OF NEIGHBORS
= France	8
Andorra, Belgium, Germany, Italy, Luxembourg, Monaco, Spain, Switzerland	
= Turkey	8
Armenia, Azerbaijan, Bulgaria, Georgia, Greece, Iran, Iraq, Syria	
10 = Mali	7
Algeria, Burkina Faso, Côte d'Ivoire, Guinea, Mauritania, Niger, Senegal	
= Niger	7
Algeria, Benin, Burkina Faso, Chad, Libya, Mali, Nigeria	
= Saudi Arabia	7
Iraq, Jordan, Kuwait, Oman, Qatar, United Arab Emirates, Yemen	
= Tanzania	7
Burundi, Kenya, Malawi, Mozambique, Rwanda, Uganda, Zambia	
= Ukraine	7
Belarus, Hungary, Moldova, Poland, Romania, Russia, Slovakia	
= Zambia	7
Angola, Dem. Rep. of Congo, Malawi, Mozambique, Namibia, Tanzania, Zimbabwe	

It should be noted that some countries have more than one discontinuous border with the same country; this has been counted only once.

Country Populations

top 10 MOST POPULATED COUNTRIES

	COUNTRY	POPULATION, EST. 2006
1	China	1,313,973,713
2	India	1,095,351,995
3	US	298,444,215
4	Indonesia	245,452,739
5	Brazil	188,078,227
6	Pakistan	165,803,560
7	Bangladesh	147,365,352
8	Russia	142,893,540
9	Nigeria	131,866,254
10	Japan	127,463,611
	World	*6,529,645,083*

Source: US Census Bureau, International Data Base

top 10 MOST POPULATED COUNTRIES IN 2050

	COUNTRY	POPULATION, EST. 2050
1	India	1,601,004,572
2	China	1,424,161,948
3	US	420,080,587
4	Nigeria	356,544,098
5	Indonesia	336,247,428
6	Pakistan	294,995,104
7	Bangladesh	279,955,405
8	Brazil	228,426,737
9	Dem. Rep. of Congo	181,260,098
10	Mexico	147,907,650
	World	*9,190,252,532*

Source: US Census Bureau, International Data Base

➔ Most populated

China has been the world's most populated country since ancient times: even 2,000 years ago it contained a quarter of the world's inhabitants, a figure that is destined to be eclipsed by India.

top 10 COUNTRIES WITH THE **HIGHEST PROPORTION** OF IMMIGRANTS

COUNTRY / EST. NET NO. OF IMMIGRANTS
PER 1,000 POPULATION, 2006

1 **Kuwait** 15.7

2 **Qatar** 14.1

3 **San Marino** 10.7

4 **Singapore** 9.1

5 **Luxembourg** 8.8

6 **Monaco** 7.7

7 **Andorra** 6.5

8 **Jordan** 6.3

9 **Botswana** 6.1

10 **Canada** 5.8

US 3.2

Source: US Census Bureau, International Data Base

A number of island territories would figure strongly in this list if they had country status: Cayman Islands with an estimated net migration of 17.8 per 1,000 in 2006, Turks and Caicos with 10.5, and British Virgin Islands with 9.2.

top 10 COUNTRIES WITH THE **HIGHEST PROPORTION** OF EMIGRANTS

COUNTRY / EST. NET NO. OF EMIGRANTS
PER 1,000 POPULATION, 2006

1 **Micronesia** 21.0

2 **Grenada** 12.6

3 **Cape Verde** 11.9

4 **Samoa** 11.8

5 **Trinidad and Tobago** 10.9

6 **Dominica** 9.3

7 **Surinam** 8.8

8 **St. Vincent and the Grenadines** 7.6

9 **Guyana** 7.5

10 **Antigua and Barbuda** 6.1

Source: US Census Bureau, International Data Base

Economic migration from small island communities is especially prevalent: few have industries other than tourism, and many inhabitants opt to leave in search of the attractions of work and life offered by neighboring mainlands.

top 10 **COUNTRIES OF BIRTH** OF IMMIGRANTS TO THE US

COUNTRY OF BIRTH / IMMIGRANTS ADMITTED, 2003

1 Mexico 115,864   **2 India** 50,372   **3 Philippines** 45,372   **4 China** 40,659

5 El Salvador 28,296   **6 Dominican Republic** 26,205   **7 Vietnam** 22,133

8 Colombia 14,177   **9 Guatemala** 14,415   **10 Russia** 13,951

Total all countries 705,827

Source: Office of Immigration Statistics, *2003 Yearbook of Immigration Statistics*

World Cities

top 10 LARGEST CAPITAL CITIES

CITY / COUNTRY	ESTIMATED POPULATION*
1 **Tokyo** (including Yokohama and Kawasaki), Japan	34,000,000
2 **Mexico City** (including Nezahualcóyotl, Ecatepec, and Naucalpan), Mexico	22,350,000
3 **Seoul** (including Bucheon, Goyang, Incheon, Seongnam, and Suweon), South Korea	22,050,000
4 **Delhi** (including Faridabad and Ghaziabad), India	19,000,000
5 **Jakarta** (including Bekasi, Bogor, Depok, and Tangerang), Indonesia	16,850,000
6 **Cairo** (including Al-Jizah and Shubra al-Khaymah), Egypt	15,250,000
7 **Manila** (including Kalookan and Quezon City), Philippines	14,550,000
8 **Moscow**, Russia	13,650,000
9 **Buenos Aires** (including San Justo and La Plata), Argentina	13,350,000
10 **Dhaka**, Bangladesh	12,750,000

* As of Jan. 30, 2005

Source: Th. Brinkhoff: *The Principal Agglomerations of the World*, http://www.citypopulation.de

These populations are of "urban agglomerations"—city centers and their densely populated outlying suburbs, with the strict definition taking account of population density in determining the boundaries of the agglomeration. They often encompass other neighboring cities and their suburbs, the resulting totals inevitably exceeding those of the city proper.

top 10 LARGEST NON-CAPITAL CITIES

CITY / COUNTRY	ESTIMATED POPULATION*
1 **New York** (including Newark and Paterson, NJ), US	21,800,000
2 **São Paulo** (including Guarulhos), Brazil	20,000,000
3 **Mumbai** (including Kalyan, Thane, and Ulhasnagar), India	19,400,000
4 **Los Angeles** (including Riverside and Anaheim), US	17,750,000
5 **Osaka** (including Kobe and Kyoto), Japan	16,750,000
6 **Calcutta**[#] (including Haora), India	15,350,000
7 **Karachi**[#], Pakistan	13,800,000
8 **Shanghai**, China	13,400,000
9 **Rio de Janeiro**[#] (including Nova Iguaçu and São Gonçalo), Brazil	12,000,000
10 **Istanbul**[#], Turkey	11,250,000

* As of Jan. 30, 2005

[#] Former capital

Source: Th. Brinkhoff: *The Principal Agglomerations of the World*, http://www.citypopulation.de

top 10 **FASTEST-GROWING** CITIES

CITY / COUNTRY	AVERAGE ANNUAL POPULATION GROWTH RATE* (PERCENTAGE), 2000–05
1 Ansan, South Korea	9.15
2 Toluca, Mexico	6.15
3 Sana'a, Yemen	5.83
4 Niamey, Niger	5.70
5 Songnam, South Korea	5.47
6 P'ohang, South Korea	5.43
7 Rajshahi, Bangladesh	5.29
8 Kabul, Afghanistan	5.10
9 =Antananarivo, Madagascar	5.05
=Campo Grande, Brazil	5.05
Calgary, Canada	*2.32*
Norfolk/Virginia Beach/Newport News, VA, US	*1.73*

* Of urban agglomerations with 750,000 inhabitants or more

Source: United Nations Population Division, *World Urbanization Report: The 2001 Revision*

These cities, which include several capitals (Sana'a, Naimey, Kabul, and Antananarivo) have experienced recent population increases for a variety of reasons: in the case of Naimey, for example, as a result of droughts elsewhere in the country.

top 10 CITIES THAT ARE HOME TO THE **LARGEST PROPORTIONS** OF THEIR COUNTRIES' POPULATIONS

CITY / COUNTRY	POPULATION, 2003 (TOTAL)	(PERCENTAGE OF COUNTRY)
1 =Hong Kong, China	7,000,000	100.0
=Singapore, Singapore	4,300,000	100.0
3 San Juan, Puerto Rico	2,300,000	60.1
4 Beirut, Lebanon	1,800,000	49.1
5 Kuwait City, Kuwait	1,200,000	48.5
6 Tel Aviv, Israel	2,900,000	45.3
7 Montevideo, Uruguay	1,300,000	39.3
8 Tripoli, Libya	2,000,000	36.1
9 Yerevan, Armenia	1,100,000	35.3
10 Santiago, Chile	5,500,000	34.7
New York, NY	*18,300,000*	*6.2*

Source: United Nations Population Division, *Urban Agglomerations 2003*

City of angels
In 1900, the population of the city of Los Angeles was just 102,479. By the 2000 Census, the population of central LA had reached 3,694,820, while the expanding conurbation is home to five times that number.

US States

top 10 LARGEST US STATES

STATE	LAND AREA* (SQ MILES)	(SQ KM)
1 Alaska	571,951	1,481,347
2 Texas	261,797	678,051
3 California	155,959	403,933
4 Montana	145,552	376,979
5 New Mexico	121,356	314,309
6 Arizona	113,635	294,312
7 Nevada	109,826	284,448
8 Colorado	103,718	268,627
9 Wyoming	97,100	251,489
10 Oregon	95,997	248,631

* Excluding water

The total land area of the US has grown progressively—in 1800 it was 867,980 sq miles (2,248,058 sq km), and by 1900 it had grown to 2,974,159 sq miles (7,703,036 sq km). The admission of Alaska into the Union on January 3 and Hawaii on August 20, 1959 increased the land area by almost 20 percent, bringing the total to its present 3,540,999 sq miles (9,171,146 sq km).

top 10 SMALLEST US STATES

STATE	LAND AREA* (SQ MILES)	(SQ KM)
1 Rhode Island	1,045	2,706
2 Delaware	1,955	5,063
3 Connecticut	4,845	12,548
4 Hawaii	6,423	16,635
5 New Jersey	7,419	19,215
6 Massachusetts	7,838	20,300
7 New Hampshire	8,969	23,229
8 Vermont	9,249	23,955
9 Maryland	9,775	25,317
10 West Virginia	24,087	62,385

* Excluding water

The smallest state, Rhode Island, has the longest official name—"State of Rhode Island and Providence Plantations." A total of 546 Rhode Islands—which also includes some 500 sq miles (1,295 sq km) of inland water—could fit into the land area of the largest state, Alaska.

top 10 US STATES WITH THE HIGHEST ELEVATIONS

STATE	PEAK	HIGHEST ELEVATION* (FT)	(M)
1 Alaska	Mount McKinley	20,320	6,194
2 California	Mount Whitney	14,494	4,418
3 Colorado	Mount Elbert	14,433	4,399
4 Washington	Mount Rainier	14,410	4,392
5 Wyoming	Gannett Peak	13,804	4,207
6 Hawaii	Mauna Kea	13,796	4,205
7 Utah	Kings Peak	13,528	4,123
8 New Mexico	Wheeler Peak	13,161	4,011
9 Nevada	Boundary Peak	13,140	4,005
10 Montana	Granite Peak	12,799	3,901

* Only the highest elevation in each state is included; many states have further peaks of lesser height

Alaska has not only the tallest US mountain, but a further 12 that are taller than the next highest, California's Mount Whitney. All of them are in Denali National Park with Mount McKinley, or in Wrangel-St. Elias National Park, with the single exception of Fairweather, which is in Glacier Bay National Park.

⊙ American high
Mount McKinley (also known as Denali)—the tallest US peak—was first climbed on June 7, 1912 by a party led by Hudson Stuck, the British-born Archdeacon of the Yukon.

top 10 **LEAST** POPULATED US STATES

	STATE	POPULATION, 2004
1	Wyoming	506,529
2	Vermont	621,394
3	North Dakota	634,366
4	Alaska	655,435
5	South Dakota	770,883
6	Delaware	830,364
7	Montana	926,865
8	Rhode Island	1,080,632
9	Hawaii	1,262,840
10	New Hampshire	1,299,500

Source: US Census Bureau

With a high proportion of its area devoted to agriculture and almost half the land area of Wyoming federally owned, the low population density of the state is likely to be maintained.

top 10 **MOST** DENSELY POPULATED US STATES

	STATE	POPULATION* PER (SQ MILE)	(SQ KM)
1	New Jersey	1,172.7	452.7
2	Rhode Island	1,075.3	415.1
3	Massachusetts	818.4	315.9
4	Connecticut	723.1	279.1
5	Maryland	568.6	219.5
6	Delaware	425.0	164.0
7	New York	407.2	157.2
8	Florida	322.6	124.5
9	Ohio	279.8	108.0
10	Pennsylvania	276.8	106.8

* Of land area as at 2004

Source: US Census Bureau

The population densities of the states have increased dramatically over the past 200 years: that of New Jersey, for example, was 250.7 per sq mile (96.8 per sq km) in 1900, and just 28.1 per sq mile (10.8 per sq km) in 1800.

top 10 US STATES WITH THE **LONGEST** COASTLINES

	STATE	COASTLINE (MILES)	(KM)
1	Alaska	33,904	54,563
2	Florida	8,426	13,560
3	Louisiana	7,721	12,426
4	Maine	3,478	5,597
5	California	3,427	5,515
6	North Carolina	3,375	5,432
7	Texas	3,359	5,406
8	Virginia	3,315	5,335
9	Maryland	3,190	5,134
10	Washington	3,026	4,870

Pennsylvania's 89-mile (143-km) coastline is the shortest among the states that have one—26 states, plus Washington D.C., have no coastline at all.

⊘ Soaring symbol
The bald eagle has been a symbol of the US since 1782, when the design of the Great Seal depicted it clutching an olive branch and 13 arrows in its talons, representing peace and war.

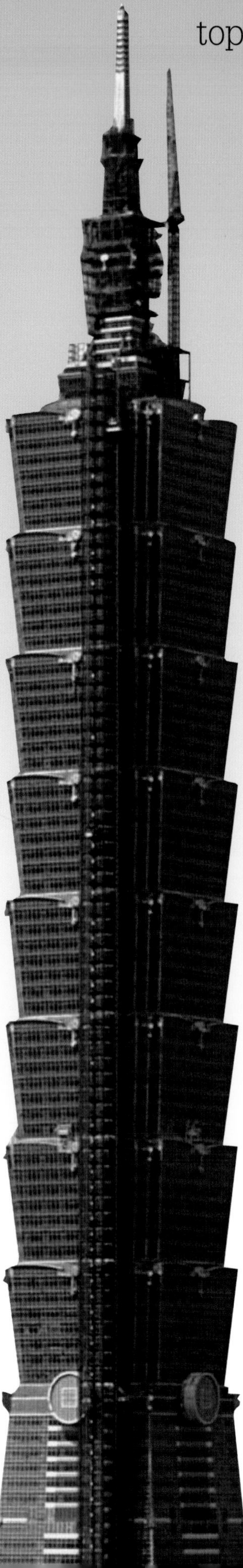

top 10 **TALLEST HABITABLE BUILDINGS**

BUILDING / LOCATION / YEAR COMPLETED	STORIES	HEIGHT (FT)	HEIGHT (M)
1 Taipei 101, Taipei, Taiwan, 2004	101	1,669	509
2 Petronas Towers, Kuala Lumpur, Malaysia, 1998	88	1,482	452
3 Sears Tower, Chicago, IL, 1974	108	1,450	442
4 Jin Mao Building, Shanghai, China, 1998	88	1,381	421
5 Two International Finance Center, Hong Kong, China, 2003	90	1,361	415
6 CITIC Plaza, Guangzhou, China, 1997	80	1,282	391
7 Shun Hing Square, Shenzen, China, 1996	69	1,259	384
8 Empire State Building, New York, NY, 1931	102	1,250	381
9 Central Plaza, Hong Kong, China, 1992	78	1,227	374
10 Bank of China Tower, Hong Kong, China, 1990	72	1,204	367

According to rules established by the Council on Tall Buildings and Urban Habitat, the height of a building is taken from street level to the structural top of the building. This includes spires, but not subterranean floors or nonstructural additions such as masts, antennae, or flagpoles.

← Taipei 101

So named because it has 101 storeys above ground level, Taipei 101 is the world's tallest building (according to the definition that allows certain architectural structures).Taipei 101 has a spire which contributes to its total height.

→ Petronas Towers

Once the record-holder and still the tallest twin towers, the Petronas Towers are connected by a sky bridge between the 41st and 42nd floors. The building was featured in the Sean Connery/Catherine Zeta-Jones movie *Entrapment* (1999).

Super Structures

top 10 **LONGEST** BRIDGES

BRIDGE* / LOCATION / YEAR COMPLETED / LENGTH OF MAIN SPAN

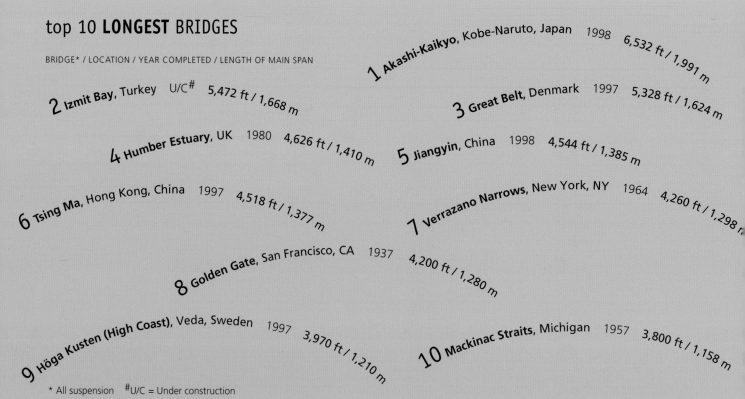

1 Akashi-Kaikyo, Kobe-Naruto, Japan   1998   6,532 ft / 1,991 m

2 Izmit Bay, Turkey   U/C#   5,472 ft / 1,668 m

3 Great Belt, Denmark   1997   5,328 ft / 1,624 m

4 Humber Estuary, UK   1980   4,626 ft / 1,410 m

5 Jiangyin, China   1998   4,544 ft / 1,385 m

6 Tsing Ma, Hong Kong, China   1997   4,518 ft / 1,377 m

7 Verrazano Narrows, New York, NY   1964   4,260 ft / 1,298 m

8 Golden Gate, San Francisco, CA   1937   4,200 ft / 1,280 m

9 Höga Kusten (High Coast), Veda, Sweden   1997   3,970 ft / 1,210 m

10 Mackinac Straits, Michigan   1957   3,800 ft / 1,158 m

* All suspension   #U/C = Under construction

The Messina Strait Bridge between Sicily and Calabria, Italy, received the go-ahead in June 2002, with work to begin in 2005; it will take six years and cost $5.9 billion. Designed to carry road and rail traffic on a 197-ft (60-m) deck, it will have by far the longest center span of any bridge, at 10,827 ft (3,300 m), although at 12,828 ft (3,910 m), Japan's Akashi-Kaikyo bridge is the world's longest overall.

top 10 **LONGEST** TUNNELS*

TUNNEL# / COUNTRY / YEAR COMPLETED / LENGTH (MILES / KM)

Several of the tunnels listed presented the additional challenge of being bored beneath the sea: the Channel Tunnel, one of the most ambitious tunneling projects of all time, defeated engineers for almost 200 years before finally being realized.

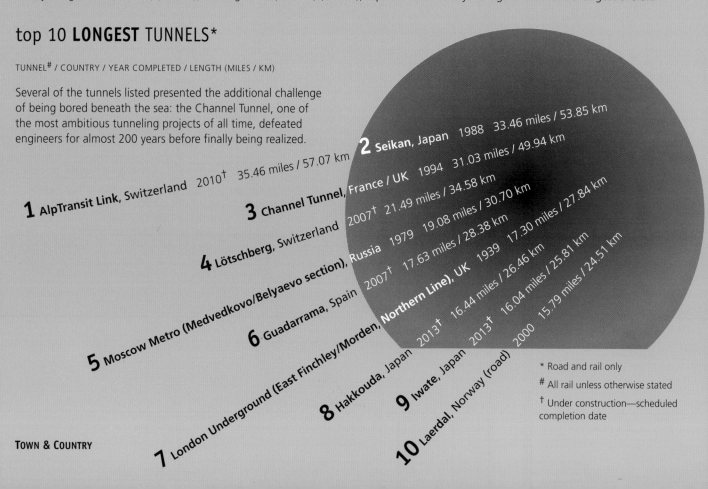

1 AlpTransit Link, Switzerland   2010†   35.46 miles / 57.07 km

2 Seikan, Japan   1988   33.46 miles / 53.85 km

3 Channel Tunnel, France / UK   1994   31.03 miles / 49.94 km

4 Lötschberg, Switzerland   2007†   21.49 miles / 34.58 km

5 Moscow Metro (Medvedkovo/Belyaevo section), Russia   1979   19.08 miles / 30.70 km

6 Guadarrama, Spain   2007†   17.63 miles / 28.38 km

7 London Underground (East Finchley/Morden, Northern Line), UK   1939   17.30 miles / 27.84 km

8 Hakkouda, Japan   2013†   16.44 miles / 26.46 km

9 Iwate, Japan   2013†   16.04 miles / 25.81 km

10 Laerdal, Norway (road)   2000   15.79 miles / 24.51 km

* Road and rail only

All rail unless otherwise stated

† Under construction—scheduled completion date

top 10 **TALLEST** TELECOMMUNICATIONS TOWERS

TOWER / LOCATION	COMPLETED	HEIGHT (FT)	(M)
1 **CN Tower**, Toronto, Canada	1975	1,821	555
2 **Ostankino Tower***, Moscow, Russia	1967	1,762	537
3 **Oriental Pearl Broadcasting Tower**, Shanghai, China	1995	1,535	468
4 **Borj-e Milad Telecommunications Tower**, Tehran, Iran	2003	1,426	435
5 **Menara Telecom Tower**, Kuala Lumpur, Malaysia	1996	1,381	421
6 **Tianjin TV and Radio Tower**, Tianjin, China	1991	1,362	415
7 **Central Radio and TV Tower**, Beijing, China	1994	1,328	405
8 **Kiev TV Tower**, Kiev, Ukraine	1973	1,263	385
9 **TV Tower**, Tashkent, Uzbekistan	1983	1,230	375
10 **Liberation Tower**, Kuwait City, Kuwait	1998	1,220	372

* Severely damaged by fire, Aug. 2000

All the towers listed are self-supporting, rather than masts braced with guy wires, and all have observation facilities, the highest being that in the CN Tower, Toronto (the world's tallest self-supporting structure of any kind) at 1,467 ft (447 m). The proposed Jakarta TV Tower, scheduled for completion in 2009, will top this list at 1,831 ft (558 m).

top 10 **LARGEST VOLUME** DAMS*

DAM	LOCATION	COMPLETED	VOLUME (CU YD)	VOLUME (CU M)
1 **Syncrude Tailings**	Alberta, Canada	1992	706,293,000	540,000,000
2 **Chapetón**	Paraná, Argentina	U/C#	387,415,000	296,200,000
3 **Pati**	Paraná, Argentina	1990	301,064,000	230,180,000
4 **New Cornelia Tailings**	Ten Mile Wash, Arizona	1973	274,016,000	209,500,000
5 **Tarbela**	Indus, Pakistan	1976	159,210,000	121,720,000
6 **Kambaratinsk**	Naryn, Kyrgyzstan	U/C#	146,752,000	112,200,000
7 **Fort Peck**	Missouri/Montana	1937	125,629,000	96,050,000
8 **Lower Usuma**	Usuma, Nigeria	1990	121,703,000	93,049,000
9 **Cipasang**	Cimanuk, Indonesia	U/C#	117,716,000	90,000,000
10 **Atatürk**	Euphrates, Turkey	1990	110,522,000	84,500,000

* Volume of material used in construction (earth, rocks, concrete, etc.)

U/C = Under construction

◆ EnviroMission Solar Tower
The progressive increase in height of the world's tallest structure, from the Great Pyramid to the EnviroMission Solar Tower, is graphically depicted in this artist's impression.

RMIT University, Melbourne Australia and EnviroMission Limited.

"

Chapter

No. 27

64 PAGES OF ACTION!

MAY, 1939

Detective COMICS 10¢

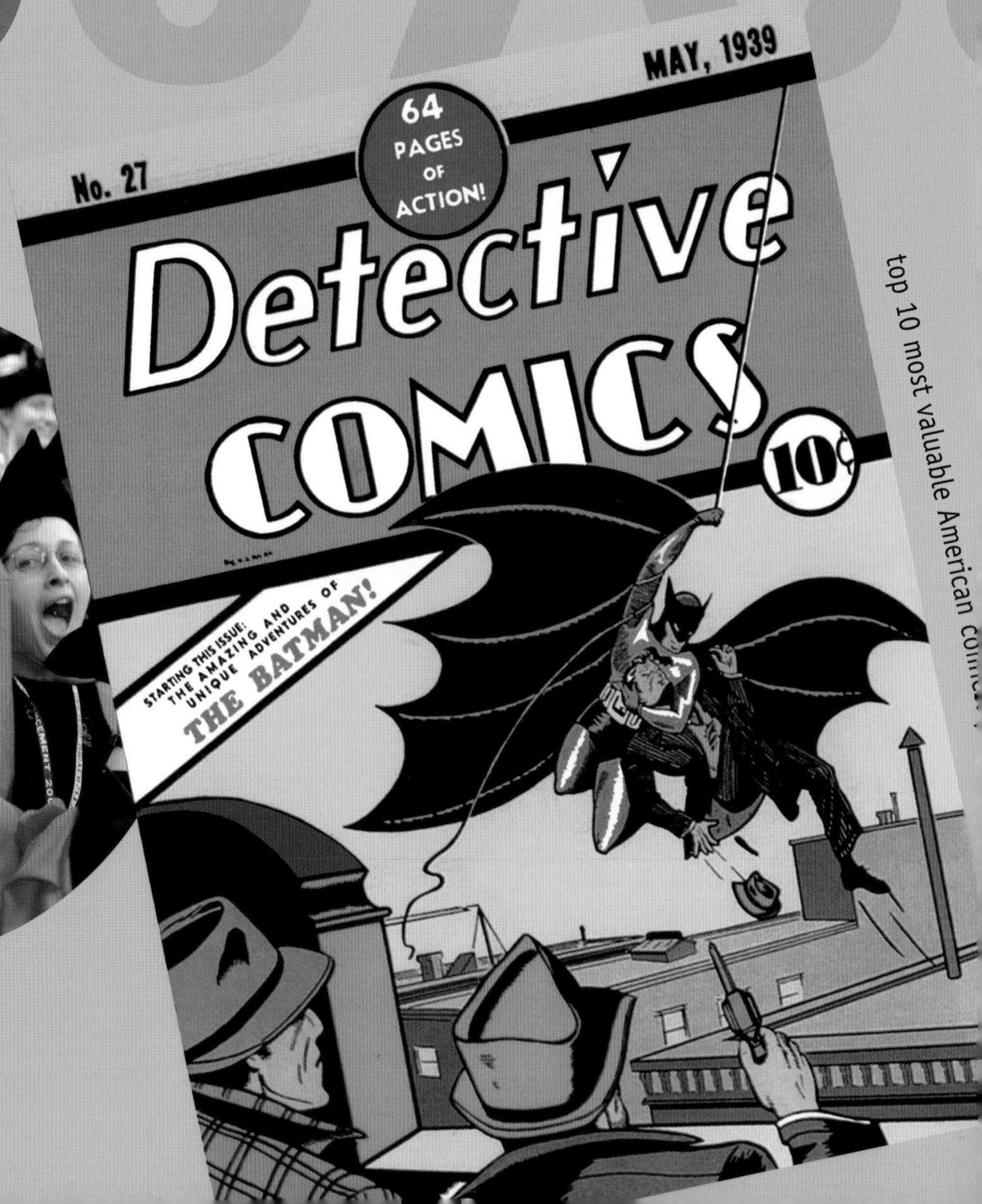

STARTING THIS ISSUE: AND THE AMAZING AND UNIQUE ADVENTURES OF THE BATMAN!

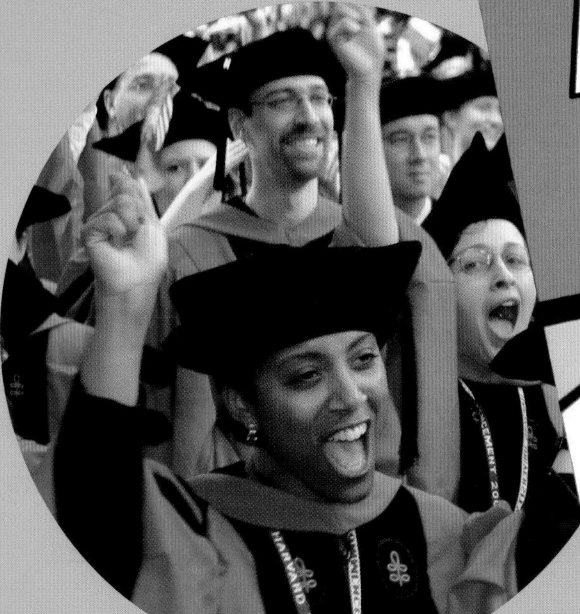

top 10 largest libraries: page 99

top 10 countries with the most English language speakers: page 96

Culture & Learning

top 10 most stolen painters: page 107

World Wide Words

top 10 COUNTRIES WITH THE **MOST ENGLISH LANGUAGE** SPEAKERS

	COUNTRY	APPROXIMATE NO. OF SPEAKERS*
1	USA	215,423,557
2	UK	58,190,000
3	Canada	20,000,000
4	Australia	14,987,000
5	Ireland	3,750,000
6	= New Zealand	3,700,000
	= South Africa	3,700,000
8	Jamaica#	2,600,000
9	Trinidad and Tobago#	1,145,000
10	Guyana#	650,000

* People for whom English is their mother-tongue

\# Includes English Creole

The Top 10 represents the countries with the greatest numbers of inhabitants who speak English as their mother-tongue. After the 10th entry, the figures dive to 260,000 or fewer in the case of the Bahamas, Barbados, and Zimbabwe. These and other countries comprise a world total of over 500 million, with perhaps one billion speaking English as a second language: a large proportion of the population of the Philippines, for example, speaks English, and there are many countries where English is either an official language or is widely understood and used in conducting legal affairs, in government, and business.

⬇ Strong character
While Chinese remains the world's most spoken language, English is increasingly considered the *lingua franca* of the world's youth.

top 10 **EUROPEAN COUNTRIES** SPEAKING ENGLISH AS A FOREIGN LANGUAGE

	COUNTRY*	PERCENTAGE SPEAKING ENGLISH AS A FOREIGN LANGUAGE
1	Malta	84
2	Denmark	79
3	Sweden	76
4	Netherlands	75
5	Cyprus	67
6	Austria	55
7	Finland	50
8	= Luxembourg	46
	= Slovenia	46
10	Germany	44

* EU member states

While Maltese is the first language of most of Malta's inhabitants, English is a second official language spoken by the majority of the population. Malta was liberated by the British from occupation by Napoleon and was a British colony for 150 years from 1814, becoming an important naval base with long-standing links with the UK. Its role during World War II resulted in the entire island's uniquely receiving the George Cross, Britain's highest award for bravery.

top 10 LANGUAGES THAT WILL BE **SPOKEN BY THE YOUTH** OF 2050

	LANGUAGE	ESTIMATED NO. OF 15–24-YEAR-OLD SPEAKERS (1995)	(2050)
1	Chinese	201,600,000	166,000,000
2	Hindu/Urdu	59,800,000	73,700,000
3	Arabic	39,500,000	72,200,000
4	English	51,700,000	65,000,000
5	Spanish	58,000,000	62,800,000
6	Portuguese	32,200,000	32,500,000
7	Bengali	25,200,000	31,600,000
8	Russian	14,800,000	22,500,000
9	Japanese	11,300,000	18,200,000
10	Malay	9,500,000	10,500,000

Source: David Graddol, *The Future of English?*, British Council

By 2050, it is estimated that German and French, which ranked 10 and 11 in the 1995 Top 10, will be pushed further down the scale by the rise in young people speaking Malay.

top 10 MOST COMMONLY **MISSPELLED** WORDS IN ENGLISH

MISSPELLING	CORRECT SPELLING
1 suppose to	supposed to
2 caffiene	caffeine
3 recieve	receive
4 seperate	separate
5 adress	address
6 occured	occurred
7 definately	definitely
8 therefor	therefore
9 usefull	useful
10 transfered	transferred

Source: *Bloomsbury English Dictionary*, 2nd edition, 2004

top 10 **MOST SPOKEN** LANGUAGES

	LANGUAGE	APPROXIMATE NO. OF SPEAKERS
1	Chinese (Mandarin)	1,120,000,000
2	English	480,000,000
3	Spanish	320,000,000
4	Russian	285,000,000
5	French	265,000,000
6	Hindustani*	250,000,000
7	Arabic#	221,000,000
8	Portuguese	188,000,000
9	Bengali	185,000,000
10	Japanese	133,000,000

* Hindi and Urdu are essentially the same language, Hindustani. As the official language of Pakistan it is written in modified Arabic script and called Urdu. As the official language of India it is written in the Devanagari script and called Hindi.

Includes 16 variants of the Arabic language

There are 11 further languages that are spoken by between 60 and 100 million people, including Korean, French, Chinese, Javanese, Chinese (Yue), Telugu, Marathi, Vietnamese, Tamil, Italian, and Turkish.

⊙ Sign of the times
Although understood only by some 25 million inhabitants of Thailand, the Thai script is almost redundant, such is the graphic and universal impact of a stop sign.

top 10 **ONLINE** LANGUAGES

	LANGUAGE	INTERNET USERS*
1	English	286,642,757
2	Chinese	105,736,236
3	Japanese	66,763,838
4	Spanish	55,887,063
5	German	54,234,545
6	French	36,412,050
7	Korean	30,670,000
8	Italian	28,610,000
9	Portuguese	23,058,254
10	Dutch	13,657,170
	World total	814,931,592

* Latest figures at 3 Dec 2004

Source: Nielsen//NetRatings/International Telecommunications Union/Internet World Stats

⊙ Multi-lingual
Mandarin and Arabic co-exist on a shop sign in the Chinese city of Urumqi, Xinjiang Province.

Education & Learning

top 10 UNIVERSITIES

	UNIVERSITY / LOCATION	POINTS*
1	**Harvard University**, Massachusetts	1,000
2	**University of California, Berkeley**	880.2
3	**Massachusetts Institute of Technology**	788.9
4	**California Institute of Technology**	738.9
5 =	**Cambridge University**, UK	731.8
=	**Oxford University**, UK	731.8
7	**Stanford University**, California	688.0
8	**Yale University**, Connecticut	582.8
9	**Princeton University**, New Jersey	557.5
10	**ETH Zurich**, Switzerland	553.7

* Scaled by awarding the top university 1,000 points and ranking all others proportionately

Source: Times University Guides, *Times Higher Education Supplement* (*THES*)

⬆ Reason to cheer at Harvard
Graduates of Harvard—ranked as the world's leading university—celebrate the completion of their degree courses.

This Top 10 has been taken from a table of 50 universities ranked in accordance with the findings of a survey undertaken by the *THES*, in which 1,300 academics across 88 countries were asked which universities they thought were the best in their fields of expertise. Also taken into account in the ranking were data on cited research of faculty members; ratios of faculty/student numbers; and success in attracting foreign students and internationally renowned academics.

Harvard, which came out at the top of this survey, was founded in 1636 as the "New College," but was renamed three years later in honor of British-born clergyman John Harvard (1607–38), who endowed the college with half of his estate and his collection of 400 books. Five US presidents attended Harvard, along with innumerable celebrities, from billionaire Bill Gates (who did not graduate) to actress Natalie Portman.

top 10 **LARGEST** LIBRARIES

	LIBRARY / LOCATION	YEAR FOUNDED	NO. OF VOLUMES
1	**Russian State Library***, Moscow, Russia	1862	43,000,000
2	**National Library of Russia**, St. Petersburg, Russia	1795	32,064,000
3	**Library of Congress**, Washington, DC	1800	29,000,000
4	**National Library of China**, Beijing, China	1909	22,000,000
5	**Library of the Russian Academy of Sciences**, St. Petersburg, Russia	1714	20,000,000
6	**National Library of Canada**, Ottawa, Canada	1953	19,500,000
5	**Deutsche Bibliothek#**, Frankfurt, Germany	1990	19,133,986
6	**British Library†**, London, UK	1753	16,000,000
7	**Vernadsky National Scientific Library of Ukraine**, Kiev, Ukraine	1919	14,000,000
8	**Institute for Scientific Information on Social Sciences of the Russian Academy of Sciences**, Moscow, Russia	1969	13,500,000
9	**Harvard University Library**, Cambridge, Massachusetts	1638	13,143,330
10	**Library for Natural Sciences of the Russian the Russian Academy of Sciences**, Moscow, Russia	1973	12,549,000

* Founded 1862 as Rumyantsev Library, formerly State V.I. Lenin Library

Formed in 1990 through the unification of the Deutsche Bibliothek, Frankfurt (founded 1947) and the Deutsche Bucherei, Leipzig

† Founded as part of the British Museum, 1753; became an independent body in 1973

top 10 **OLDEST** UNIVERSITIES AND COLLEGES IN THE US

	UNIVERSITY / LOCATION	YEAR CHARTERED
1	**Harvard University**, Massachusetts	1636
2	**College of William & Mary**, Virginia	1692
3	**Yale University**, Connecticut	1701
4	**University of Pennsylvania**	1740
5	**Moravian College**, Pennsylvania	1742
6	**Princeton University**, New Jersey	1746
7	**Washington & Lee University**, Virginia	1749
8	**Columbia University**, New York	1754
9	**Brown University**, Rhode Island	1764
10	**Rutgers**, New Jersey	1766

Source: National Center for Education Statistics

top 10 COUNTRIES WITH THE **FEWEST** ELEMENTARY SCHOOL PUPILS PER TEACHER

	COUNTRY	PUPIL / TEACHER RATIO IN ELEMENTARY SCHOOLS, 2001–02*
1	**San Marino**	5
2	**Libya**	8
3	=**Denmark**	10
	=**Hungary**	10
	=**Netherlands**	10
6	=**Iceland**	11
	=**Italy**	11
	=**Sweden**	11
9	=**Belgium**	12
	=**Israel**	12
	=**Luxembourg**	12
	=**Qatar**	12
	=**Saudi Arabia**	12
	US	*15*

* Or latest year for which data available

Source: UNESCO

top 10 COUNTRIES **SPENDING THE MOST** ON EDUCATION

	COUNTRY	PUBLIC EXPENDITURE AS PERCENTAGE OF GNP*, 2001–02#
1	**Lesotho**	13.0
2	**Zimbabwe**	11.1
3	**Yemen**	10.6
4	**St. Vincent and the Grenadines**	8.9
5	**Cuba**	8.7
6	=**Palau**	8.6
	=**Vanuatu**	8.6
8	**Malay sia**	8.5
9	**Denmark**	8.4
10	**Saudi Arabia**	8.3
	Canada	*5.5*
	US	*5.0*

* GNP = Gross National Product

Or latest year available; in those countries for which data available

Source: UNESCO

If the Marshall Islands were a country, it would top the list, with 2001–02 public expenditure on education at 16.4 percent of this US territory's GNP.

Books

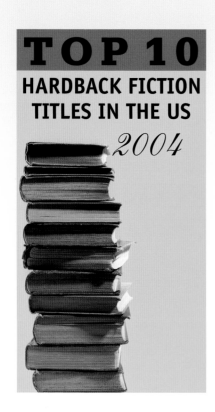

TOP 10 HARDBACK FICTION TITLES IN THE US *2004*

	TITLE	AUTHOR	SALES
1	The Da Vinci Code	Dan Brown	4,290,000
2	The Five People You Meet in Heaven	Mitch Albom	3,287,722
3	The Last Juror	John Grisham	2,290,000
4	Glorious Appearing	Tim LaHaye and Jerry B. Jenkins	1,600,318
5	Angels & Demons	Dan Brown	1,285,000
6	State of Fear	Michael Crichton	1,249,277
7	London Bridges	James Patterson	1,064,378
8	Trace	Patricia Cornwell	1,033,573
9	The Rule of Four	Ian Caldwell and Dustin Thomason	945,000
10	The Da Vinci Code—Special Illustrated Collector's Edition	Dan Brown	905,000

Source: *Publishers Weekly*

Dan Brown's remarkable success story was the worldwide publishing sensation of 2004. His *The Da Vinci Code* had already amassed an exceptional 5,724,750 hardback sales the previous year, while although not issued until November, the illustrated version also entered the year's Top 10. Worldwide, sales of *The Da Vinci Code* in various editions have topped 25 million in 44 languages. The controversy and publicity surrounding *Code* also benefited its predecessors, *Digital Fortress* (1997), *Angels & Demons* (2000), and *Deception Point* (2001), prompting readers avidly to consume the entire Brown oeuvre.

the 10 LATEST WINNERS OF THE PULITZER PRIZE FOR FICTION

YEAR	TITLE	AUTHOR
2005	Gilead	Marilynne Robinson
2004	The Known World	Edward P. Jones
2003	Middlesex	Jeffrey Eugenides
2002	Empire Falls	Richard Russo
2001	The Amazing Adventures of Kavalier & Clay	Michael Chabon
2000	Interpreter of Maladies	Jhumpa Lhiri
1999	The Hours	Michael Cunningham
1998	American Pastoral	Philip Roth
1997	Martin Dressler: The Tale of an American Dreamer	Steven Millhauser
1996	Independence Day	Richard Ford

top 10 US HARDBACK **NONFICTION** BESTSELLERS, 2004

	TITLE / AUTHOR	SALES
1	**The Purpose-Driven Life**, Rick Warren	7,340,000
2	**The South Beach Diet**, Arthur Agatston, M.D.	3,002,597
3	**My Life,** Bill Clinton	2,000,000
4	**America (The Book),** Jon Stewart and the Daily Show Writers	1,519,027
5	**The South Beach Diet Cookbook**, Arthur Agatston, M.D.	1,490,898
6	**Family First**, Dr. Phil McGraw	1,355,000
7	**He's Just Not That Into You**, Greg Behrendt and Liz Tuccillo	1,261,055
8	**Eats, Shoots & Leaves**, Lynne Truss	1,092,128
9	**Your Best Life Now**, Joel Osteen	974,645
10	**Guinness World Records 2005**	970,000

Source: *Publishers Weekly*

top 10
BESTSELLING
BOOKS OF ALL TIME

	TITLE / AUTHOR / FIRST PUBLISHED	APPROXIMATE SALES*
1	**The Bible**, c.1451–55	over 6,000,000,000
2	**Quotations from the Works of Mao Tse-tung**, 1966	900,000,000
3	**The Lord of the Rings**, J. R. R. Tolkien, 1954–55	over 100,000,000
4	**American Spelling Book**, Noah Webster, 1783	up to 100,000,000
5	**The Guinness Book of Records** (now Guinness World Records), 1955	over 95,000,000#
6	**World Almanac**, 1868	over 80,000,000#
7	**The McGuffey Readers**, William Holmes McGuffey, 1836	60,000,000
8	**The Common Sense Book of Baby and Child Care**, Benjamin Spock, 1946	over 50,000,000
9	**A Message to Garcia**, Elbert Hubbard, 1899	over 40,000,000
10 =	**In His Steps: "What Would Jesus Do?"**, Rev. Charles Monroe Sheldon, 1896	over 30,000,000
=	**Valley of the Dolls**, Jacqueline Susann, 1966	over 30,000,000

* Including translations

Aggregate sales of annual publication

The publication of multiple editions, translations, and pirated copies—and often exaggerated sales claims—make it notoriously problematic to establish precise sales of many recently published books. It is even more difficult with books published before sales figures were recorded. Globally, the Bible tops this list (the Koran may rival it, but sales estimates are speculative). Chairman Mao's "Little Red Book" could hardly fail to become a bestseller, since in the years 1966–71 it was compulsory for every Chinese adult to own a copy. The *American Spelling Book* and *The McGuffey Readers* were long-standing school textbooks, while *A Message to Garcia* was bought in bulk and distributed to employees in vast numbers. Many standard works, from *Roget's Thesaurus* and translations of books by Karl Marx to the *Complete Works of Shakespeare* and Conan Doyle's *Sherlock Holmes* stories, have been sold in countless editions of unknown magnitude. There may be other single novels with a valid claim to a place in the Top 10, including Margaret Mitchell's *Gone With the Wind* (1936) and Harper Lee's *To Kill a Mockingbird* (1960), which may each have sold over 30 million copies. In the realm of nonfiction, Boy Scouts founder Robert Baden-Powell's manual *Scouting for Boys* (1908) could be one of the 20th century's bestselling books, since almost every boy in the world who became a Scout once owned a copy.

top 10 **MOST VALUABLE** **AMERICAN COMICS**

COMIC	VALUE ($)*
1 **Action Comics No. 1** Published in June 1938, the first issue of *Action Comics* marked the original appearance of Superman.	440,000
2 **Detective Comics No. 27** Issued in May 1939, it is prized as the first comic book to feature Batman.	375,000
3 **Marvel Comics No. 1** The Human Torch and other heroes were first introduced in the issue dated October 1939.	330,000
4 **Superman No. 1** The first comic book devoted to Superman, reprinting the original *Action Comics* story, was published in summer 1939.	270,000
5 **All-American Comics No. 16** The Green Lantern made his debut in the issue dated July 1940.	160,000
6= **Batman No. 1** Published in spring 1940, this was the first comic book devoted to Batman.	125,000
Captain America Comics No. 1 Published in March 1941, this was the original comic book in which Captain America appeared.	125,000
8 **Flash Comics No. 1** Dated January 1940, and featuring The Flash, it is rare because it was produced in small numbers for promotional purposes, and was unique as Issue No. 2 was retitled *Whiz Comics*.	97,000
9= **More Fun Comics No. 52** The Spectre made his debut in the issue dated February 1940.	84,000
Whiz Comics No. 1 Published in February 1940—and confusingly numbered "2"—it was the first comic book to feature Captain Marvel.	84,000

* For example, in "Near Mint" condition

Source: *The Overstreet Comic Book Price Guide, #34, 2004.* © 2004 Gemstone Publishing, Inc. All rights reserved

POW!

64 PAGES OF ACTION

No. 27

Detec COM

STARTING THIS ISSUE; THE AMAZING AND UNIQUE ADVENTURES OF THE BATMAN!

➔ **Caped crusader**
Following the success of Superman, artist Bob Kane created Batman, whose debut appearance is among the most prized comics of the "Golden Age."

↑ All-American hero
First published at the height of World War II, Captain America appealed to the anti-Nazi sentiments of the period.

Top 10 English-Language Daily Newspapers

Newspaper / Country	Average daily circulation, 2004
1 The Sun, UK	3,332,831
2 USA Today, US	2,617,000
3 The Daily Mail, UK	2,412,261
4 The Wall Street Journal, US	2,091,000
5 The Mirror, UK	1,828,938
6 The New York Times, US	1,677,000
7 Los Angeles Times, US	1,379,000
8 The Times of India, India	1,284,000
9 The Washington Post, US	1,030,000
10 Chicago Tribune, US	1,002,000

Source: World Association of Newspapers, *World Press Trends 2004*, www.wan-press.org/Audit Bureau of Circulations Ltd.

The world's bestselling English language dailies represent both long-established publications and relative newcomers: the *Daily Herald*, the first paper to ever sell two million copies, was launched in 1911, became *The Sun* in 1964, and was relaunched as a tabloid in 1969. *The Daily Mail* started in 1896, absorbing the *News Chronicle* in 1960 and *Daily Sketch* in 1971. *USA Today*, launched in 1982, was one of the first newspapers to use computers and to transmit editions for simultaneous publication around the world. *The Times of India* began in 1838 as *The Bombay Times and Journal of Commerce*, changing to its present name in 1861.

⬅ Press ahead

Despite the inexorable growth of other sources of news, from television to the Internet, daily newspapers have maintained their role as the medium of choice for a high proportion of the English-speaking public.

Top 10 Daily Newspapers

Newspaper / Country	Average daily circulation, 2004
1 **Yomiuri Shimbun**, Japan	14,081,000
2 **The Asahi Shimbun**, Japan	12,235,000
3 **Nihon Keizai Shimbun**, Japan	4,643,000
4 **Chunichi Shimbun**, Japan	4,542,000
5 **Bild**, Germany	3,989,000
6 **Mainichi Shimbun**, Japan	3,957,000
7 **The Sun**, UK	3,332,831
8 **Sankei Shimbun**, Japan	2,723,000
9 **Canako Xiaoxi (Beijing)**, China	2,670,000
10 **USA Today**, US	2,617,000

Source: World Association of Newspapers, *World Press Trends 2004*, www.wan-press.org

Top 10 Daily Newspapers in the US

Newspaper	Average daily US circulation*
1 **USA Today**	2,220,863
2 **The Wall Street Journal**	2,106,774
3 **The New York Times**	1,121,057
4 **Los Angeles Times**	902,164
5 **Daily News (New York)**	715,052
6 **The Washington Post**	707,690
7 **New York Post**	686,207
8 **Chicago Tribune**	600,988
9 **Houston Chronicle**	554,783
10 **San Francisco Chronicle**	505,022

* During six-month period to end of Sept. 2004

Source: Audit Bureau of Circulations

Top 10 Newspaper-Reading Countries

Country	Daily copies per 1,000 people, 2004
1 **Iceland**	705.9
2 **Norway**	684.0
3 **Japan**	646.9
4 **Sweden**	590.0
5 **Finland**	524.2
6 **Bulgaria**	472.7
7 **Macau**	448.9
8 **Denmark**	436.6
9 **Switzerland**	419.6
10 **UK**	393.4
US	*263.2*

Source: World Association of Newspapers, *World Press Trends 2004*, www.wan-press.org

⊙ Avid readers

With a large, loyal, and highly literate readership among its population of 127 million, six of the world's Top 10 bestselling daily newspapers are Japanese.

Top 10 Magazines in the US

Magazine / Issues per year	Average paid circulation*
1 **AARP The Magazine**[#], 6	22,720,073
2 **AARP Bulletin**[#], 10	22,038,673
3 **Reader's Digest**, 12	10,228,531
4 **TV Guide**, 52	9,016,188
5 **Better Homes and Gardens**, 12	7,628,424
6 **National Geographic Magazine**, 12	5,468,471
7 **Good Housekeeping**, 12	4,623,113
8 **Family Circle**, 17	4,372,813
9 **Ladies' Home Journal**, 36	4,108,619
10 **Woman's Day**, 17	4,060,619

* During 2004, first six months

[#] High proportion of circulation attributed to membership benefits

Source: Magazine Publishers of America

Art

top 10 BEST-ATTENDED ART EXHIBITIONS, 2004

EXHIBITION / VENUE / CITY / DATES	TOTAL ATTENDANCE / DAILY ATTENDANCE*
1 MoMA Museum of Modern Art, Neue Nationalgalerie, Berlin, Feb. 20–Sept. 19	**1,200,000**
	6,568
2 Pre-Raphaelites in Florence, Galleria degli Uffizi, Florence, Apr. 6–Aug. 31	**693,847**
	5,507
3 Art in the Age of Dante, Gallerie dell'Accademia, Florence, June 1–Sept. 26	**512,498**
	4,343
4 James Rosenquist: A Retrospective, Guggenheim Museum, Bilbao, May 13–Oct. 17	**487,582**
	3,596
5 Joan Miró 1917–34: the Birth of the World, Centre Georges Pompidou, Paris, Mar. 3–June 28	**475,601**
	4,742
6 Mark Rothko: Walls of Light, Guggenheim Museum, Bilbao, June 8–Oct. 24	**451,275**
	3,783
7 Henri Matisse: Process/Variation, National Museum of Western Art, Tokyo, Sept.10–Dec. 12	**451,105**
	5,389
8 Edward Hopper, Tate Modern, London, May 27–Sept. 5	**429,909**
	4,215
9 Fashion and Furniture in the 18th Century, Metropolitan Museum of Art, New York, Apr. 29–Sept. 6	**420,234**
	3,738
10 Edouard Manet: Impressions of the Sea, Van Gogh Museum, Amsterdam, June 18–Sept. 26	**400,000**
	3,960

* Approximate totals provided by museums; excludes exhibitions that began in 2003   Source: *The Art Newspaper*

top 10 MOST EXPENSIVE PAINTINGS

PAINTING / ARTIST / SALE / DATE	PRICE
1 Garçon à la Pipe, Pablo Picasso (Spanish, 1881–1973), Sotheby's, New York, May 5, 2004	$93,000,000
2 Portrait du Dr. Gachet, Vincent van Gogh (Dutch, 1853–90), Christie's, New York, May 15, 1990	$75,000,000
3 Au Moulin de la Galette, Pierre-Auguste Renoir (French, 1841–1919), Sotheby's, New York, May 17, 1990	$71,000,000
4 Massacre of the Innocents, Sir Peter Paul Rubens (Flemish, 1577–1640), Sotheby's, London, July 10, 2002	$68,400,000 (£45,000,000)
5 Portrait de l'Artiste Sans Barbe, Vincent van Gogh, Christie's, New York, Nov. 19, 1998	$65,000,000
6 Rideau, Cruchon et Compôtier, Paul Cézanne (French, 1839–1906), Sotheby's, New York, May 10, 1999	$55,000,000
7 Les Noces de Pierrette, Pablo Picasso, Binoche et Godeau, Paris, Nov. 30, 1989	$51,671,920 (F.Fr315,000,000)
8 Femme aux Bras Croises, Pablo Picasso, Christie's Rockefeller, New York, Nov. 8, 2000	$50,000,000
9 Irises, Vincent van Gogh, Sotheby's, New York, Nov. 11, 1987	$49,000,000
10 Femme Assise Dans un Jardin, Pablo Picasso, Sotheby's, New York, Nov. 10, 1999	$45,000,000

❶ Doctor in the auction house
In the final months of his troubled life, Vincent van Gogh was cared for by Doctor Paul Gachet (1828–1909) and painted this distinctive portrait of him. It was sold at auction to Japanese collector Ryoei Saito for a record price in 1990, but—following Saito's death in 1996—has mysteriously disappeared.

top 10 MOST STOLEN PAINTERS

ARTIST / NO. OF WORKS STOLEN   Source: Art Loss Register

1 Pablo Picasso
551

356
2 Joan Miró

3 Marc Chagall
309

4 Salvador Dalí
231

5 Pierre-Auguste Renoir
209

6 Albrecht Dürer
203

7 Rembrandt van Rijn
174

159
8 Andy Warhol

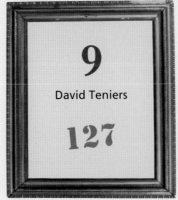

9 David Teniers
127

10 Henri Matisse
108

* Approximate totals provided by museums; excludes exhibitions that began in 2003

Source: *The Art Newspaper*

top 10 BEST-ATTENDED ART EXHIBITIONS IN THE US, 2004

EXHIBITION / VENUE	TOTAL ATTENDANCE*
1 **Fashion and Furniture in the 18th Century**, Metropolitan Museum of Art	420,234
2 **Andy Goldsworthy on the Roof**, Metropolitan Museum of Art	383,481
3 **Byzantium: Faith and Power, 1261–1557**, Metropolitan Museum of Art	301,339
4 **Modern Art from the Kröller Müller Museum**, Seattle Art Museum	288,228
5 =Constantin Brancusi: The Essence of Things, Guggenheim Museum	278,101
=Photographs from the Buhl Collection, Guggenheim Museum	278,101
7 **Gauguin Tahiti**, Museum of Fine Arts	241,124
8 **Whitney Biennial**, Whitney Museum of American Art	228,164
9 **Masterpieces from the Rau Collection**, Portland Art Museum	225,000
10 **Seurat and the Making of "La Grand Jatte,"** Art Institute of Chicago	213,672

top 10 albums of all time: page 114

Chapter

5 6 7 8 9

top 10 singles of all time in the US: page 110

top 10 singles of all time: page 112

top 10 most popular tracks by female solo singers, 2004: page 118

Music

Single Stars

top 10 SINGLES OF **ALL TIME** IN THE US

	TITLE / ARTIST OR GROUP	ESTIMATED US SALES
1	Candle in the Wind (1997)/Something About the Way You Look Tonight, Elton John	11,000,000
2	White Christmas, Bing Crosby	8,000,000
3 =	Hey Jude, The Beatles	4,000,000
=	Hound Dog/Don't Be Cruel, Elvis Presley	4,000,000
=	I Will Always Love You, Whitney Houston	4,000,000
=	We Are the World, USA for Africa	4,000,000
=	Whoomp! (There It Is), Tag Team	4,000,000
8 =	(Every Thing I Do) I Do It For You, Bryan Adams	3,000,000
=	How Do I Live, LeAnn Rimes	3,000,000
=	I'll Be Missing You, Puff Daddy and Faith Evans (featuring 112)	3,000,000
=	Love Me Tender/Any Way You Want Me, Elvis Presley	3,000,000
=	Macarena (Bayside Boys Mix), Los Del Rio	3,000,000

Source: RIAA

Taken from the movie *Holiday Inn* (1942), Bing Crosby's "White Christmas" sold more than 30 million copies worldwide, making it the bestselling single ever. In the US, it took 55 years and the death of Princess Diana to generate sales capable of overtaking it, as Elton John's specially penned tribute did, and by a considerable margin. Resting comfortably below these two mega-sellers is a group certified by the RIAA in the élite four-million league. It spans the period from Presley's "Hound Dog/Don't be Cruel" (1956), through the Beatles' "Hey Jude" (1968) and USA for Africa's charity single (1985), to the singles by Bryan Adams (1991) and Whitney Houston (1992), both of which—like "White Christmas" 50 years earlier—were derived from blockbuster movies.

the 10 FIRST **MILLION-SELLING** ROCK 'N' ROLL SINGLES IN THE US

	TITLE / ARTIST OR GROUP	YEAR
1	Rock Around the Clock, Bill Haley & His Comets	1954
2	Shake Rattle and Roll, Bill Haley & His Comets	1954
3	Maybellene, Chuck Berry	1955
4	Ain't that a Shame, Fats Domino	1955
5	Ain't that a Shame, Pat Boone	1955
6	Seventeen, Boyd Bennett	1955
7	I Hear You Knocking, Gale Storm	1955
8	See You Later Alligator, Bill Haley & His Comets	1955
9	Tutti Frutti, Little Richard	1955
10	Heartbreak Hotel, Elvis Presley	1956

"Rock Around the Clock" and "Shake Rattle and Roll" were both recorded on the same day, April 12, 1954. The first, which topped the US chart for seven weeks, is considered the disc that launched the rock era, selling all over the world and receiving a further impetus when it was featured in the 1955 movie *Blackboard Jungle*. With innumerable cover versions in many languages, one authoritative estimate calculated that cumulative global sales of "Rock Around the Clock" have exceeded 100 million.

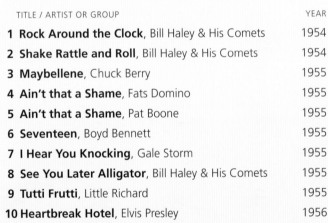

← Elton John

With sales of almost 11 million in the US, five million in the UK, and 37 million worldwide, Elton John's "Candle in the Wind" (1997) is the bestselling single ever.

top 10 SINGLES THAT STAYED LONGEST AT NO. 1 IN THE US*

	TITLE / ARTIST OR GROUP / YEAR OF RELEASE	WEEKS AT NO. 1
1	**One Sweet Day**, Mariah Carey and Boyz II Men, 1995	16
2 =	**Candle in the Wind (1997)/Something About the Way You Look Tonight**, Elton John, 1997	14
=	**I'll Make Love to You**, Boyz II Men, 1994	14
=	**I Will Always Love You**, Whitney Houston, 1992	14
=	**Macarena (Bayside Boys Mix)**, Los Del Rio, 1995	14
6 =	**End of the Road**, Boyz II Men, 1992	13
=	**The Boy is Mine**, Brandy and Monica, 1998	13
8 =	**Lose Yourself**, Eminem, 2002	12
=	**Yeah**, Usher featuring Lil Jon and Ludacris, 2004	12
10 =	**Don't be Cruel/Hound Dog**, Elvis Presley, 1956	11
=	**I Swear**, All-4-One, 1994	11
=	**Independent Women Part 1**, Destiny's Child, 2000	11
=	**Un-Break My Heart**, Toni Braxton, 1996	11

* Based on *Billboard* charts

Source: Music Information Database

This listing covers the period from 1955, when *Billboard*'s US Top 100 was inaugurated for singles. Long No. 1 runs were actually more commonplace in the pre-rock 'n' roll days of the 1940s and early 1950s, when the market was generally slower-moving. Oddly enough, 1981 holds the record for the greatest number of singles (three) having runs of two months or more.

🔊 **Usher into the charts**
In the 10 years since the release of his first album, Usher (Raymond) has achieved phenomenal success, with *Yeah* topping the US, UK, and other charts around the world.

top 10 DIGITAL TRACKS IN THE US, 2004

	TITLE	ARTIST OR GROUP
1	**The Reason**	Hoobastank
2	**This Love**	Maroon 5
3	**Let's Get It Started**	Black Eyed Peas
4	**Hey Ya!**	OutKast
5	**Yeah**	Usher featuring Lil Jon and Ludacris
6	**She Will Be loved**	Maroon 5
7	**1985**	Bowling For Soup
8	**Toxic**	Britney Spears
9	**Drop It Like It's Hot**	Snoop Dogg
10	**Lose My Breath**	Destiny's Child

Source: Nielsen SoundScan

In 2003, sales of digital tracks totaled 19.2 million. In 2004, that figure rose to 140,902,000.

top 10 SINGLES IN THE US, 2004

	TITLE	ARTIST OR GROUP
1	**I Believe**	Fantasia
2	**Solitaire/The Way Dreams**	Clay Aiken
3	**Dreams**	Diana DeGarmo
4	**F**k It (I Don't Want You Back)**	Eamon
5	**Me, Myself And I**	Beyoncé
6	**8th World Wonder**	Kimberley Locke
7	**Leave (Get Out)**	JoJo
8	**Naughty Girl**	Beyoncé
9	**The Way You Move/ Hey Ya!**	OutKast featuring Sleepy Brown
10	**Milkshake**	Kelis

Source: *Billboard*

top 10 **SINGLES OF ALL TIME**

	TITLE / ARTIST OR GROUP	RELEASED	SALES EXCEED
1	**Candle in the Wind (1997)/Something About the Way You Look Tonight.,** Elton John	1997	37,000,000
2	**White Christmas,** Bing Crosby	1942	30,000,000
3	**Rock Around the Clock,** Bill Haley and His Comets	1954	17,000,000
4	**I Want to Hold Your Hand,** The Beatles	1963	12,000,000
5	= **It's Now or Never,** Elvis Presley	1960	10,000,000
	= **Hey Jude,** The Beatles	1968	10,000,000
	= **I Will Always Love You,** Whitney Houston	1992	10,000,000
8	= **Diana,** Paul Anka	1957	9,000,000
	= **Hound Dog/Don't Be Cruel,** Elvis Presley	1956	9,000,000
10	= **(Everything I Do) I Do it for You,** Bryan Adams	1991	8,000,000
	= **I'm a Believer,** The Monkees	1966	8,000,000

➔ **Christmas gift**
Originally sung in *Holiday Inn* (1942), the hit song "White Christmas" was reprised by Bing Crosby (left, with Rosemary Clooney, Vera Ellen, and Danny Kaye) in the 1954 movie of the same name.

Global sales are notoriously difficult to calculate, since for many decades, little statistical research on record sales was done in a large part of the world. "Worldwide" is thus usually taken to mean the known minimum "Western world" sales. It took 55 years for a record to overtake Bing Crosby's 1942 *White Christmas*, although the song (also recorded by others and sold as sheet music) has achieved such enormous total sales that it would still appear in first position in any list of bestselling songs.

Beatlemania
Worldwide, over six million copies of the Beatles' "Hey Jude" (1968) were sold within the year of its release.

Record Albums

top 10 ALBUMS **OF ALL TIME**

TITLE / ARTIST OR GROUP	YEAR OF ENTRY
1 **Thriller**, Michael Jackson	1982
2 **Dark Side of the Moon**, Pink Floyd	1973
3 **Their Greatest Hits 1971–1975**, The Eagles	1976
4 **The Bodyguard**, Soundtrack	1992
5 **Rumours**, Fleetwood Mac	1977
6 **Sgt. Pepper's Lonely Hearts Club Band**, The Beatles	1967
7 **Led Zeppelin IV**, Led Zeppelin	1971
8 **Greatest Hits**, Elton John	1974
9 **Come On Over**, Shania Twain	1997
10 **Jagged Little Pill**, Alanis Morissette	1995

Total worldwide sales of albums have traditionally been notoriously hard to gauge, but even with the huge expansion of the album market during the 1980s, and multiple-million sales of many major releases, this Top 10 is still élite territory.

Over the moon
With world sales estimated at some 35 million, Pink Floyd's concept album *Dark Side of the Moon* has maintained its perennial appeal for over 30 years.

top 10 **ALBUMS** THAT **STAYED LONGEST** IN THE US ALBUM CHART

TITLE / ARTIST OR GROUP	TOTAL WEEKS
1 **Dark Side of the Moon**, Pink Floyd	741
2 **Johnny's Greatest Hits**, Johnny Mathis	490
3 **My Fair Lady**, Original Cast	480
4 **Highlights from The Phantom of the Opera**, Original Cast	331
5 **Oklahoma!**, Soundtrack	305
6 **Tapestry**, Carole King	302
7 **Heavenly**, Johnny Mathis	295
8 **MCMXC AD**, Enigma	282
9 **Metallica**, Metallica	281
10 = **Hymns**, Tennessee Ernie Ford	277
= **The King and I**, Soundtrack	277

Source: Music Information Database

top 10 ALBUMS THAT **STAYED LONGEST** AT NO. 1 IN THE US CHARTS

	TITLE / ARTIST OR GROUP / YEAR	WEEKS AT NO. 1
1	**Thriller**, Michael Jackson, 1982	37
2	=**Calypso**, Harry Belafonte, 1956	31
	=**Rumours**, Fleetwood Mac, 1977	31
4	=**Purple Rain**, Soundtrack, Prince, 1984	24*
	=**Saturday Night Fever**, Soundtrack, 1978	24*
6	**Please Hammer Don't Hurt 'Em**, MC Hammer, 1990	21
7	=**Blue Hawaii**, Soundtrack, Elvis Presley, 1962	20*
	=**The Bodyguard**, Soundtrack, Whitney Houston, 1992	20
9	=**Ropin' The Wind**, Garth Brooks, 1991	18
	=**More of the Monkees**, The Monkees, 1967	18*
	=**Dirty Dancing**, Soundtrack, 1988	18

* Continuous runs

Source: Music Information Database

Some sources identify the soundtrack album of *West Side Story* (1962) as the longest No. 1 resident of the *Billboard* chart, but its 57-week stay was in a chart exclusively for stereo albums—then a relatively new phenomenon; the *South Pacific* soundtrack album (1958) similarly enjoyed 31 weeks in this specialist chart. Not all of the albums from the general chart had continuous No. 1 runs: in some cases, their chart-topping sojourns were punctuated by briefer stays by other records. Five of the Top 10 are movie soundtracks, which suggests that a successful movie tie-in may well be an aid to sales' longevity.

top 10 **ALBUMS** IN THE US, 2004

	TITLE	ARTIST OR GROUP
1	**Confessions**	Usher
2	**Feels Like Home**	Norah Jones
3	**Encore**	Eminem
4	**When the Sun Goes Down**	Kenny Chesney
5	**Here For the Party**	Gretchen Wilson
6	**Live Like You Were Dying**	Tim McGraw
7	**Songs About Jane**	Maroon 5
8	**Fallen**	Evanescence
9	**Autobiography**	Ashlee Simpson
10	**Now That's What I Call Music! 16**	Various Artists

Source: Nielsen SoundScan

🔺 **Strong rumors**
Fleetwood Mac's *Rumours* has sold over 26 million copies worldwide. Stevie Nicks (pictured here) wrote "Dreams," a track on the album and the group's only US No.1 single.

top 10 **ALBUMS** OF **ALL TIME** IN THE US

	TITLE / ARTIST OR GROUP / YEAR OF ENTRY	EST. SALES
1	**Their Greatest Hits, 1971–1975**, The Eagles, 1976	28,000,000
2	**Thriller**, Michael Jackson, 1982	26,000,000
3	**Led Zeppelin IV**, Led Zeppelin, 1971	22,000,000
4	=**Back In Black**, AC/DC, 1980	20,000,000
	=**Come On Over**, Shania Twain, 1997	20,000,000
6	**Rumours**, Fleetwood Mac, 1977	19,000,000
7	=**The Bodyguard**, Soundtrack, 1992	17,000,000
	=**Boston**, Boston, 1976	17,000,000
9	=**Cracked Rear View**, Hootie & the Blowfish, 1994	16,000,000
	=**Jagged Little Pill**, Alanis Morissette, 1995	16,000,000
	=**No Fences**, Garth Brooks, 1990	16,000,000
	=**Hotel California**, The Eagles, 1976	16,000,000
	=**Greatest Hits**, Elton John, 1974	16,000,000

Source: RIAA

The Eagles' *Their Greatest Hits, 1971–1975* was the first album ever to be certified platinum (for sales of over one million copies), and long vied with Jackson's *Thriller* as the USA's all-time No. 1.

Male Solo Singers

top 10 ALBUMS BY MALE SOLO SINGERS, 2004

ALBUM / SINGER	EST. GLOBAL SALES, 2004
1 **Confessions**, Usher	11,867,000
2 **Encore**, Eminem	6,013,000
3 **Greatest Hits**, Robbie Williams	4,270,000
4 **Genius Loves Company**, Ray Charles	3,018,000
5 **Musicology**, Prince	2,781,000
6 **Suit**, Nelly	2,676,000
7 **Live Like You Were Dying**, Tim McGraw	2,616,000
8 **The College Dropout**, Kanye West	2,356,000
9 **Patience**, George Michael	2,120,000
10 **Stardust...The Great American Songbook, Vol. III**, Rod Stewart	2,027,000

Source: *United World Chart*, mediatraffic

Usher's *Confessions* topped the charts in the US, UK, and Canada and reached No. 2 in Australia, achieving the greatest first-week sale by any artist for three years and the most ever by an R&B artist.

top 10 SINGLES BY MALE SOLO SINGERS IN THE US

TITLE / SINGER	YEAR
1 **Candle in the Wind (1997)/Something About the Way You Look Tonight**, Elton John	1997
2 **White Christmas**, Bing Crosby	1942
3 **Hound Dog/Don't Be Cruel**, Elvis Presley	1956
4 **Gangsta's Paradise**, Coolio featuring L.V.	1995
5 **(Everything I Do) I Do It For You**, Bryan Adams	1991
6 **Love Me Tender/Any Way You Want Me**, Elvis Presley	1956
7 **All Shook Up**, Elvis Presley	1957
8 **Jailhouse Rock**, Elvis Presley	1957
9 **Heartbreak Hotel/I Was the One**, Elvis Presley	1956
10 **Baby Got Back**, Sir Mix-A-Lot	1992

Source: Music Information Database

◉ Robbie Williams

With the bestselling album by a non-US singer, Robbie Williams consolidated his international success in 2004 with the release of his *Greatest Hits*, which spans the previous seven years of his chart successes.

top 10 MALE SOLO SINGERS WITH THE **MOST US NO. 1** SINGLES

	SINGER	NO. 1 SINGLES
1	Elvis Presley	19
2	Michael Jackson	11
3	Stevie Wonder	8
4	= Phil Collins	6
	= Elton John	6
6	= George Michael	5
	= Prince	5
	= Usher	5
9	= Lionel Richie	4
	= Bobby Vinton	4

Source: Music Information Database

top 10 **YOUNGEST** MALE SOLO SINGERS TO HAVE A **NO. 1 SINGLE** IN THE US

	SINGER / TITLE	YEAR	AGE* (YR)	MTHS	DAYS
1	Stevie Wonder, Fingertips	1963	13	2	28
2	Donny Osmond, Go Away Little Girl	1971	13	9	2
3	Michael Jackson, Ben	1972	14	1	15
4	Laurie London, He's Got the Whole World in His Hands	1958	14	3	0
5	Paul Anka, Diana	1957	16	1	16
6	Brian Hyland, Itsy Bitsy Teenie Weenie Yellow Polkadot Bikini	1960	16	9	1
7	Shaun Cassidy, Da Doo Ron Ron	1977	17	9	19
8	Paul Anka, Lonely Boy	1959	17	11	18
9	Bobby Vee, Take Good Care of My Baby	1961	18	4	24
10	Usher, Nice & Slow	1998	19	4	0

* During first week of debut No.1 US single

Source: Music Information Database

top 10 **MALE SOLO SINGERS** IN THE US

	SINGER	TOTAL CHART HITS
1	Elvis Presley	127
2	James Brown	90
3	Ray Charles	72
4	Fats Domino	61
5	Elton John	59
6	Pat Boone	57
7	Stevie Wonder	56
8	Neil Diamond	55
9	Rick Nelson	52
10	Rod Stewart	49

Source: Music Information Database

A long career inevitably enhances an artist's potential to achieve a high score in this list, but death is not necessarily a barrier to ongoing chart success, as the posthumous hits of Elvis Presley, Ray Charles, and Rick Nelson testify.

➔ **The King rules**
Elvis Presley's remarkable chart hit tally
is unlikely ever to be overtaken.

Female Solo Singers

top 10 MOST POPULAR TRACKS BY FEMALE SOLO SINGERS, 2004

TRACK / SINGER	POINTS*, 2004
1 **Toxic**, Britney Spears	5,355,000
2 **Left Outside Alone**, Anastacia	4,631,000
3 **Everytime**, Britney Spears	4,118,000
4 **My Happy Ending**, Avril Lavigne	3,960,000
5 **Sick and Tired**, Avril Lavigne	3,805,000
6 **Leave (Get Out)**, JoJo	3,271,000
7 **Don't Tell Me**, Avril Lavigne	2,910,000
8 **Trick Me**, Kelis	2,894,000
9 **Superstar**, Jamelia	2,827,000
10 **Naughty Girl**, Beyonce	2,768,000

* Points awarded according to global airplay, single-sales data, paid download, and vote

Source: *United World Chart*, mediatraffic

top 10 ALBUMS BY FEMALE SOLO SINGERS, 2004

ALBUM / SINGER	EST. GLOBAL SALES, 2004
1 **Feels Like Home**, Norah Jones	9,020,000
2 **Under My Skin**, Avril Lavigne	6,390,000
3 **Anastacia**, Anastacia	4,442,000
4 **Life for Rent**, Dido	3,528,000
5 **Greatest Hits**, Shania Twain	3,520,000
6 **The Diary of Alicia Keys**, Alicia Keys	3,362,000
7 **Greatest Hits: My Prerogative**, Britney Spears	2,994,000
8 **In the Zone**, Britney Spears	2,754,000
9 **Come Away with Me**, Norah Jones	2,623,000
10 **Single Collection Vol. 1**, Hikaru Utadu	2,313,000

Source: *United World Chart*, mediatraffic

top 10 FEMALE SOLO SINGERS IN THE US

SINGER / TOTAL CHART HITS

1 Aretha Franklin 70 **2 Connie Francis** 53 **3 Brenda Lee** 50 **4= Madonna** 49 **= Dionne Warwick** 49
6= Diana Ross 34 **= Barbra Streisand** 34 **8 Patti Page** 33 **9= Cher** 32 **= Olivia Newton-John** 32

Source: Music Information Database

Girl power
In 2004 Canadian singer Avril Lavigne, whose *Under My Skin* hit No. 1 in the US, Canada, UK, and Australia, vied with US pop singer Anastacia (Newkirk). Her album *Anastacia* attained substantial sales despite not being released in her homeland.

top 10 **SINGLES** BY FEMALE SOLO SINGERS IN THE US

TITLE / SINGER	YEAR
1 **I Will Always Love You**, Whitney Houston	1992
2 **How Do I Live**, LeAnn Rimes	1997
3 **Fantasy**, Mariah Carey	1995
4 **Vogue**, Madonna	1990
5 **Mr. Big Stuff**, Jean Knight	1971
6 **You Were Meant for Me/Foolish Games**, Jewel	1996
7 **You Light Up My Life**, Debby Boone	1977
8 **The Power of Love**, Celine Dion	1993
9 **Believe**, Cher	1999
10 **Physical**, Olivia Newton-John	1981

Source: Music Information Database

Among these blockbusters, it is fitting that the song from *The Bodyguard Original Soundtrack* that gave Whitney Houston her multiplatinum success was also written by a woman—Dolly Parton, whose original version of the song peaked in 1982 at a lowly No. 53. Jean Knight's "Mr. Big Stuff," an R&B No. 1, took 25 years to reach certified sales of two million copies.

top 10 **YOUNGEST** FEMALE SOLO SINGERS TO HAVE A NO. 1 SINGLE IN THE US

SINGER / TITLE / YEAR	AGE (YRS	MTHS	DAYS)
1 **Little Peggy March**, I Will Follow Him, 1963	15	1	20
2 **Brenda Lee**, I'm Sorry, 1960	15	7	7
3 **Brenda Lee**, I Want to Be Wanted, 1960	15	11	22
4 **Tiffany**, I Think We're Alone, 1987	16	1	5
5 **Tiffany**, Could've Been, 1988	16	4	4
6 **Lesley Gore**, It's My Party, 1963	17	0	30
7 **Little Eva**, The Loco-Motion, 1962	17	1	27
8 **Britney Spears**, ...Baby One More Time, 1999	17	1	29
9 **Monica**, The First Night, 1998	17	11	9
10 **Shelley Fabares**, Johnny Angel, 1962	18	2	19

Source: Music Information Database

The ages shown are those of each artist on the publication date of the chart in which she achieved her first No. 1 single. While Britney Spears and other teen singers have a place in this list, it is notable that more than half the girls in the Top 10 scored their No. 1 hits in the 1960s: Little Peggy March's "I Will Follow Him" was a translation of a French hit song, "Chariot." March's real name was Margaret Annemarie Battivio, her stage name deriving from her diminutive height (4 ft 10 in/147 cm) and birth month.

Groups & Duos

⬆ **Worldbeater** Maroon 5's first album and global smash *Songs About Jane* topped the charts in the US, UK, and Australia.

top 10 **ALBUMS** BY GROUPS AND DUOS, 2004

ALBUM / GROUP OR DUO	EST. GLOBAL SALES, 2004
1 Songs About Jane, Maroon 5	5,795,000
2 Fallen, Evanescence	5,531,000
3 Elephunk, Black Eyed Peas	5,294,000
4 How to Dismantle an Atomic Bomb, U2	5,289,000
5 Greatest Hits, Guns N' Roses	4,661,000
6 American Idiot, Green Day	3,638,000
7 D12 World, D12	3,533,000
8 Destiny Fulfilled, Destiny's Child	3,299,000
9 Speakerboxxx/The Love Below, Outkast*	3,061,000
10 Hopes and Fears, Keane	2,850,000

* Two discs: *Speakerboxxx* features Big Boi, *The Love Below* features Andre 3000

Source: United World Chart, *mediatraffic*

top 10 **MOST POPULAR** TRACKS BY GROUPS AND DUOS, 2004

TRACK / GROUP OR DUO	POINTS*, 2004
1 This Love, Maroon 5	7,791,000
2 Hey Ya!, Outkast	6,167,000
3 The Reason, Hoobastank	6,044,000
4 It's My Life, No Doubt	4,827,000
5 Shut Up, Black Eyed Peas	4,642,000
6 She Will Be Loved, Maroon 5	4,503,000
7 My Immortal, Evanescence	4,635,000
8 Lose My Breath, Destiny's Child	3,970,000
9 Dragostea Din Tei, O-Zone	3,795,000
10 Let's Get It Started, Black Eyed Peas	3,282,000

* Points awarded according to global airplay, single-sales data, paid download, and vote

Source: *United World Chart*, mediatraffic

top 10 GROUPS IN THE US

	GROUP	TOTAL CHART HITS
1	The Beatles	70
2	The Rolling Stones	57
3	The Beach Boys	55
4	The Temptations	50
5	Chicago	49
6 =	The Bee Gees	43
=	Four Tops	43
8	Smokey Robinson & the Miracles	42
9	The Four Seasons	41
10	The Supremes	40

Source: Music Information Database

As well as the Beatles' preeminence in this list, in April 1964 they achieved a feat that has never been repeated when they held all top five places in the *Billboard* chart with No.1 "Can't Buy Me Love," No. 2 "Twist and Shout," No. 3 "She Loves You," No. 4 "I Want to Hold Your Hand," and No. 5 "Please Please Me."

top 10 DUOS IN THE US

	DUO	TOTAL CHART HITS
1	The Everly Brothers	37
2	Daryl Hall and John Oates	34
3	Carpenters	29
4 =	Jan and Dean	24
=	Righteous Brothers	23
6	Ike and Tina Turner	20
7	Sonny and Cher	18
8	Simon and Garfunkel	17
9 =	Brooks and Dunn	16
=	Peaches and Herb	16

Source: Music Information Database

The Everlys had their first million-selling single in 1957 with "Bye Bye Love." This was followed by a series of chart hits during the 1950s and 60s, with "Wake Up Little Susie," "All I Have to Do Is Dream," "Bird Dog," and "Cathy's Clown"—their biggest seller—all reaching No. 1 on the *Billboard* chart.

⬆ **Fallen rise** Amy Lee fronts Evanescence, whose album *Fallen* provided tracks for the movie *Daredevil*.

top 10 SINGLES BY GROUPS IN THE US

	TITLE / GROUP	YEAR
1	**Hey Jude**, The Beatles	1968
2	**Eye of the Tiger**, Survivor	1982
3	**I Wanna Sex You Up**, Color Me Badd	1991
4	**O.P.P.**, Naughty By Nature	1991
6	**Let It Be**, The Beatles	1970
7	**Get Back**, The Beatles with Billy Preston	1969
8	**Come Together/Something**, The Beatles	1969
9	**Too Close**, Next	1999
10	**Wannabe**, The Spice Girls	1997

Source: Music Information Database

The appearance of "Hey Jude" at the head of this list is perhaps surprising. An unusually long track (7 min 12 sec), which disqualified it from airplay on some radio stations, it does not even figure among the Top 100 of all time in the Beatles' home country (although did reach No. 1 in both the UK and US). It nonetheless sold more than 4 million copies in the US.

Classical

the 10 LATEST WINNERS OF THE "BEST CLASSICAL ALBUM" GRAMMY AWARD

YEAR — COMPOSER / TITLE / CONDUCTOR / SOLOIST(S) / ORCHESTRA

2004 **John Adams,** *On the Transmigration of Souls*
Lorin Maazel, Brooklyn Youth Chorus and New Choral Artists, New York Philharmonic

2003 **Gustav Mahler,** *Symphony No. 3; Kindertotenlieder*
Michael Tilson Thomas, Michelle DeYoung, San Francisco Symphony Orchestra

2002 **Vaughan Williams,** *A Sea Symphony (Symphony No. 1)*
Robert Spano, Norman Mackenzie, Brett Polegato, Christine Goerke, Atlanta Symphony Orchestra

2001 **Hector Belioz,** *Les Troyens*
Sir Colin Davis, Ben Heppner, Kenneth Tarver, Michelle De Young, Peter Mattei, Petra Lang, Sara Mingardo, Stephen Milling, London Symphony Orchestra

2000 **Dmitri Shostakovich,** *The String Quartets*
Emerson String Quartet

1999 **Igor Stravinsky,** *Firebird; The Rite of Spring; Perséphone*
Michael Tilson Thomas, Stuart Neill, San Francico Symphony Orchestra

1998 **Samuel Barber,** *Prayers of Kierkegaard* / **Vaughan Williams,** *Dona Nobis Pacem* / **Béla Bartók,** *Cantata Profana*
Robert Shaw, Richard Clement, Nathan Gunn, Carmen Pelton, Atlanta Symphony Orchestra and chorus

1997 **Richard Danielpour, Leon Kirchner, Christopher Rouse,** *Premieres—Cello Concertos*
Yo-Yo Ma, David Zinman, Philadelphia Orchestra

1996 **John Corigliano,** *Of Rage and Remembrance*
Leonard Slatkin, National Symphony Orchestra

1995 **Claude Debussy,** *La Mer*
Pierre Boulez, Cleveland Orchestra

Source: NARAS

top 10 CLASSICAL ALBUMS IN THE US

TITLE / PERFORMER(S) OR ORCHESTRA — YEAR

1 **The Three Tenors In Concert** — 1990
José Carreras, Placido Domingo, Luciano Pavarotti

2 **Romanza** — 1997
Andrea Bocelli

3 **Sogno** — 1999
Andrea Bocelli

4 **Voice of an Angel** — 1999
Charlotte Church

5 **Chant** — 1994
Benedictine Monks of Santo Domingo De Silos

6 **The Three Tenors In Concert 1994** — 1994
José Carreras, Placido Domingo Luciano Pavarotti, Zubin Mehta

7 **Sacred Arias** — 1999
Andrea Bocelli

8 **Tchaikovsky: Piano Concerto No. 1** — 1958
Van Cliburn

9 **Fantasia: 50th Anniversary Edition** (soundtrack) — 1990
Philadelphia Orchestra

10 **Perhaps Love** — 1981
Placido Domingo

Source: Music Information Database

the 10 LATEST WINNERS OF THE "BEST OPERA RECORDING" GRAMMY AWARD

YEAR	COMPOSER / TITLE / PRINCIPAL SOLOIST(S) / ORCHESTRA

2004 **Wolfgang Amadeus Mozart**, *Le Nozze di Figaro*
Patrizia Ciofi, Véronique Gens, Simon Keenlyside, Angelika Kirchschlager, and Lorenzo Regazzo, Concerto Köln

2003 **Leos Janácek**, *Jenufa*
Jerry Hadley, Karita Mattila, Eva Randová, Anja Silja, Jorma Silvasti, Orchestra of the Royal Opera House, Covent Garden

2002 **Richard Wagner**, *Tannhäuser*
Jane Eaglen, Peter Seiffert, Rene Pape, Thomas Hampson, Waltraud Meier, Staatskapelle Berlin

2001 **Hector Berlioz**, *Les Troyens*
Sir Colin Davis, Michelle De Young, Ben Heppner, Petra Lang, Peter Mattei, Stephen Milling, Sara Mingardo, Kenneth Tarver, London Symphony Orchestra

2000 **Ferruccio Busoni**, *Doktor Faust*
Kent Nagano, Kim Begley, Dietrich Fischer-Dieskau, Dietrich Henschel, Markus Hollop, Torsten Kerl, Eva Jenis, Orchestre de l'Opera Nationale de Lyon

1999 **Igor Stravinsky**, *The Rake's Progress*
Ian Bostridge, Bryn Terfel, Anne Sofie von Otter, Deborah York, Monteverdi Choir, London Symphony Orchestra

1998 **Béla Bartók**, *Bluebeard's Castle*
Jessye Norman, Laszlo Polgar, Karl-August Naegler, Chicago Symphony Orchestra

1997 **Richard Wagner**, *Die Meistersinger Von Nürnberg*
Ben Heppner, Herbert Lippert Karita Mattila, Alan Opie, Rene Pape, Jose van Dam, Iris Vermillion, Chicago Symphony Chorus, Chicago Symphony Orchestra

1996 **Benjamin Britten**, *Peter Grimes*
Philip Langridge, Alan Opie, Janice Watson, Opera London, London Symphony Chorus, City of London Sinfonia

1995 **Hector Berlioz**, *Les Troyens*
Charles Dutoit, Orchestra Symphonie de Montreal

Source: NARAS

◉ **Triple triumph**
Selling in numbers comparable to those of rock stars, the recording of the Rome concert by the "Three Tenors" José Carreras, Placido Domingo, and Luciano Pavarotti that opened the 1990 World Cup became the bestselling classical album ever worldwide.

top 10 LARGEST OPERA HOUSES

	THEATRE	LOCATION	CAPACITY*
1	Arena di Verona#	Verona, Italy	15,000
2	Municipal Opera Theatre#	St. Louis, MO	10,000
3	Metropolitan Opera House	New York, NY	3,800
4	NHK Hall	Tokyo, Japan	3,677
5	Civic Opera House	Chicago, IL	3,563
6	Music Hall	Cincinnati, OH	3,516
7	The Hummingbird Centre	Toronto, Canada	3,223
8	War Memorial Opera House	San Francisco, CA	3,146
9	Dorothy Chandler Pavilion	Los Angeles, CA	3,086
10	Halle aux Grains	Toulouse, France	3,000

* Seating capacity only given, although capacity is often larger when standing capacity is included

Open-air venue

Although there are many more venues in the world where opera is regularly performed, the above list is limited to those where the principal performances are opera.

top 10 OPERAS MOST FREQUENTLY PERFORMED AT THE METROPOLITAN OPERA HOUSE, NEW YORK

	OPERA	COMPOSER	PERFORMANCES*
1	La Bohème	Giacomo Puccini	1,154
2	Aïda	Giuseppi Verdi	1,081
3	Carmen	Georges Bizet	923
4	La Traviata	Giuseppi Verdi	897
5	Tosca	Giacomo Puccini	863
6	Madama Butterfly	Giacomo Puccini	790
7	Rigoletto	Giuseppi Verdi	769
8	Faust	Charles Gounod	722
9	Pagliacci	Ruggero Leoncavallo	695
10	Cavalleria Rusticana	Pietro Mascagni	655

* As of end of 2004–2005 season

Source: Metropolitan Opera

The Metropolitan Opera House opened on October 22, 1883, with a performance of Charles Gounod's *Faust*.

Music Awards

the 10 LATEST GRAMMY SONGS OF THE YEAR

YEAR	SONG	SONGWRITER(S)
2004	**Daughters**	John Mayer
2003	**Dance with My Father**	Luther Vandross and Richard Marx
2002	**Don't Know Why**	Jesse Harris
2001	**Fallin'**	Alicia Keys
2000	**Beautiful Day**	U2 (Bono, Adam Clayton, Edge, and Larry Mullen Jr.)
1999	**Smooth**	Itaal Shur and Rob Thomas
1998	**My Heart Will Go On**	James Horner and Will Jennings
1997	**Sunny Came Home**	Shawn Colvin
1996	**Change the World**	Gordon Kennedy, Wayne Kirkpatrick, and Tommy Sims
1995	**Kiss From a Rose**	Seal

the 10 LATEST GRAMMY ALBUMS OF THE YEAR

YEAR	ALBUM	ARTIST(S) OR GROUP
2004	**Genius Loves Company**	Ray Charles and various artists
2003	**Speakerboxxx/The Love Below**	OutKast
2002	**Come Away with Me**	Norah Jones
2001	**O Brother, Where Art Thou?** (Soundtrack)	Various artists
2000	**Two Against Nature**	Steely Dan
1999	**Supernatural**	Santana
1998	**The Miseducation of Lauryn Hill**	Lauryn Hill
1997	**Time Out of Mind**	Bob Dylan
1996	**Falling into You**	Celine Dion
1995	**Jagged Little Pill**	Alanis Morisette

the 10 LATEST GRAMMY NEW ARTISTS OF THE YEAR

YEAR	ARTIST(S)
2004	**Maroon 5**
2003	**Evanescence**
2002	**Norah Jones**
2001	**Alicia Keys**
2000	**Shelby Lynne**
1999	**Christina Aguilera**
1998	**Lauryn Hill**
1997	**Paula Cole**
1996	**LeeAnn Rimes**
1995	**Hootie & The Blowfish**

The "Best New Artist" Grammy was first awarded at the second event in 1960 to Bobby Darin. Subsequent winners represent a catalog of both stars who went on to achieve greatness, such as the Beatles, and those who sank into obscurity (including Milli Vanilli, whose 1990 award was revoked).

the 10 LATEST GRAMMY POP VOCALISTS OF THE YEAR (FEMALE)

YEAR	VOCALIST	SONG
2004	**Norah Jones**	Sunrise
2003	**Christina Aguilera**	Beautiful
2002	**Norah Jones**	Don't Know Why
2001	**Nelly Furtado**	I'm Like a Bird
2000	**Macy Gray**	I Try
1999	**Sarah McLachlan**	I Will Remember You
1998	**Celine Dion**	My Heart Will Go On
1997	**Sarah McLachlan**	Building a Mystery
1996	**Toni Braxon**	Un-Break My Heart
1995	**Annie Lennox**	No More "I Love You's"

Norah Jones has achieved an enviable place among the pantheon of Grammy-winners, having secured eight wins in 2003 (for work in the previous year), including "Best New Artist," "Record of the Year," and "Song of the Year," and three further awards in 2005.

the 10 LATEST GRAMMY POP VOCALISTS OF THE YEAR (MALE)

YEAR	VOCALIST	SONG
2004	**John Mayer**	Daughters
2003	**Justin Timberlake**	Cry Me a River
2002	**John Mayer**	Your Body is a Wonderland
2001	**James Taylor**	Don't Let Me Be Lonely Tonight
2000	**Sting**	She Walks this Earth (Soberana Rosa)
1999	**Sting**	Brand New Day
1998	**Eric Clapton**	My Father's Eyes
1997	**Elton John**	Candle in the Wind 1997
1996	**Eric Clapton**	Change the World
1995	**Seal**	Kiss From a Rose

When John Mayer (b. 1977) gained his second Grammy award, for "Daughters," from his 2003 album *Heavier Things*, it was part of a double win: he also won "Song of the Year" for the same song.

the 10 LATEST GRAMMY
RECORDS OF THE YEAR

YEAR	RECORD / ARTIST(S) OR GROUP
2004	**Here We Go Again** Ray Charles and Norah Jones
2003	**Clocks** Coldplay
2002	**Don't Know Why** Norah Jones
2001	**Walk On** U2
2000	**Beautiful Day** U2
1999	**Smooth** Santana featuring Rob Thomas
1998	**My Heart Will Go On** Celine Dion
1997	**Sunny Came Home** Shawn Colvin
1996	**Change the World** Eric Clapton
1995	**Kiss From a Rose** Seal

The Grammys are awarded retrospectively. Thus, the 47th awards were presented in 2005 in recognition of musical accomplishment during 2004.

⬅ ⬆ Winning team
Norah Jones accepts the award in the category "Best Pop Collaboration with Vocals" at the 47th Grammy Awards ceremony. Her duo with Ray Charles (who died in 2004) also won "Record of the Year."

125

Music Videos

the 10 LATEST RECIPIENTS OF THE MTV VMA "BEST VIDEO OF THE YEAR" AWARD

YEAR	ARTIST OR GROUP	TITLE
2004	**OutKast**	Hey Ya
2003	**Missy "Misdemeanor" Elliott**	Work It
2002	**Eminem**	Without Me
2001	**Christina Aguilera, Lil' Kim, Mya, Pink** (featuring Missy "Misdemeanor" Elliott)	Lady Marmalade
2000	**Eminem**	The Real Slim Shady
1999	**Lauryn Hill**	Doo Wop (That Thing)
1998	**Madonna**	Ray of Light
1997	**Jamiroquai**	Virtual Insanity
1996	**The Smashing Pumpkins**	Tonight, Tonight
1995	**TLC**	Waterfalls

⊕ Missy's hit
Prior to her award-winning "Work It," US rap superstar Missy "Misdemeanor" Elliott (Melissa Arnette Elliott) scored a UK No. 1 in 1998 with her Mel B collaboration "I Want You Back."

the 10 LATEST RECIPIENTS OF THE MTV VMA "BEST FEMALE VIDEO" AWARD

YEAR	ARTIST	TITLE
2004	**Beyoncé**	Naughty Girl
2003	**Beyoncé** (featuring Jay-Z)	Crazy in Love
2002	**Pink**	Get the Party Started
2001	**Eve** (featuring Gwen Stefani)	Let Me Blow Ya Mind
2000	**Aaliyah**	Try Again
1999	**Lauryn Hill**	Doo Wop (That Thing)
1998	**Madonna**	Ray of Light
1997	**Jewel**	You Were Meant for Me
1996	**Alanis Morissette**	Ironic
1995	**Madonna**	Take a Bow

MTV was launched in the US on August 1, 1981. The inaugural MTV Video Music Awards (VMA) took place on September 14, 1984 at Radio City Music Hall, New York. At the debut ceremony, Cyndi Lauper was the winner for "Girls Just Want to Have Fun." Subsequent female winners have included such megastars as Tina Turner, Whitney Houston, and Annie Lennox. To date, and in addition to numerous other MTV awards, Madonna has received the most nominations in this category, a total of 11 from 1985 to 2001, and is the only triple winner (1987, 1995, and 1998).

the 10 LATEST RECIPIENTS OF THE MTV VMA "BEST GROUP VIDEO" AWARD

YEAR	GROUP	TITLE
2004	**No Doubt**	It's My Life
2003	**Coldplay**	The Scientist
2002	**No Doubt** (featuring Bounty Killer)	Hey Baby
2001	***NSYNC**	POP
2000	**Blink 182**	All the Small Things
1999	**TLC**	No Scrubs
1998	**Backstreet Boys**	Everybody (Backstreet's Back)
1997	**No Doubt**	Don't Speak
1996	**Foo Fighters**	Big Me
1995	**TLC**	Waterfalls

No Doubt and TLC, both represented in the Top 10 with double wins, are the only groups to have won twice in this award's 20-year history. It has principally honored US groups, but British bands Dire Straits (1986) and Coldplay (2003), Ireland's U2 (1992), and Australia's INXS (1988) have also won awards in this category.

top 10 BESTSELLING MUSIC VIDEOS IN THE US, 2004

	TITLE	ARTIST OR GROUP
1	**Live in Texas**	Linkin Park
2	**Part II**	Lil Jon & the East Side
3	**Coldplay Live 2003**	Coldplay
4	**Disclaimer II**	Seether
5	**Past, Present & Future**	Rob Zombie
6	**Ready to Die**	Notorious B.I.G.
7	**Live At Donington**	AC/DC
8	**Concert For George**	Various
9	**The Gorge**	Dave Matthews Band
10	**Led Zeppelin**	Led Zeppelin

Source: *Billboard*

As well as US performers, this list includes British newcomers Coldplay, whose Live 2003 set was recorded in Sydney, Australia, and Australian band AC/DC, whose 1991 Castle Donington (UK) concert was not previously released in the US.

the 10 LATEST RECIPIENTS OF THE MTV VMA "BEST MALE VIDEO" AWARD

YEAR	ARTIST OR GROUP	TITLE
2004	**Usher** (featuring Lil Jon and Ludacris)	Yeah
2003	**Justin Timberlake**	Cry Me a River
2002	**Eminem**	Without Me
2001	**Moby** (featuring Gwen Stefani)	South Side
2000	**Eminem**	The Real Slim Shady
1999	**Will Smith**	Miami
1998	**Will Smith**	Just the Two of Us
1997	**Beck**	The Devil's Haircut
1996	**Beck**	Where It's At
1995	**Tom Petty and the Heartbreakers**	You Don't Know How it Feels

the 10 LATEST RECIPIENTS OF THE MTV VMA "BEST BREAKTHROUGH VIDEO" AWARD

YEAR	ARTIST OR GROUP / TITLE
2004	**Franz Ferdinand**, Take Me Out
2003	**Coldplay**, The Scientist
2002	**The White Stripes**, Fell in Love with a Girl
2001	**Fatboy Slim**, Weapon of Choice
2000	**Björk**, All is Full of Love
1999	**Fatboy Slim**, Praise You
1998	**Prodigy**, Smack My Bitch Up
1997	**Jamiroquai**, Virtual Insanity
1996	**Smashing Pumpkins**, Tonight, Tonight
1995	**Weezer**, Buddy Holly

◉ Rap beat
As well as his two MTV "Best Male Video" awards, Eminem has won seven other MTV Video Music Awards and six MTV Europe awards.

Movie Music

top 10 MUSICAL MOVIES

FILM	YEAR
1 Grease	1978
2 Chicago	2002
3 Saturday Night Fever	1977
4 8 Mile	2002
5 Moulin Rouge!	2001
6 The Sound of Music	1965
7 Evita	1996
8 The Rocky Horror Picture Show	1975
9 Staying Alive	1983
10 Mary Poppins	1964

Traditional musicals (movies in which the cast actually sings) and films in which a musical soundtrack is a key component are included here. After suffering a decline in the 1990s, the success of *Chicago* shows that the blockbuster musical retains its appeal almost 80 years after the genre was created.

➜ Sweet success
With global earnings of over $180 million, *Sweet Home Alabama* is one of the top movies named after a song.

top 10 MUSICAL BIOGRAPHIES

FILM	SUBJECT	YEAR
1 The Sound of Music	The von Trapp family	1965
2 Shine	David Hefgott	1996
3 Coal Miner's Daughter	Loretta Lynn	1980
4 Ray	Ray Charles	2004
5 La Bamba	Ritchie Valens	1987
6 Amadeus	Wolfgang Amadeus Mozart	1984
7 What's Love Got to Do With It?	Tina Turner	1993
8 Selena	Selena Pérez	1997
9 The Doors	The Doors	1991
10 Lady Sings the Blues	Billie Holiday	1972

Biopics on the often troubled lives of famous composers and musicians in both classical and popular genres have long inspired Hollywood. Despite having been released over 40 years ago, blockbuster *The Sound of Music* tops the list, having earned almost twice as much as the second-ranked movie, while the recent release of *Ray* indicates the enduring popularity of such subjects. Outside the Top 10, musical biographies have encompassed artists from rock star Buddy Holly (*The Buddy Holly Story*, 1978) to cellist Jacqueline du Pré (*Hilary and Jackie*, 1998) and composer Cole Porter (*De-Lovely*, 2004).

top 10 MOVIES WITH TITLES DERIVED FROM SONG TITLES

FILM	SONG*	FILM
1 American Pie	1972	1999
2 Sweet Home Alabama	1976	2002
3 Bad Boys	1983	1995
4 Sea of Love	1959	1989
5 One Fine Day	1963	1996
6 My Girl	1965	1991
7 Something to Talk About	1991	1995
8 When a Man Loves a Woman	1966	1994
9 The Crying Game	1964	1992
10 Addicted to Love	1986	1997

* Release of first hit version

Remarkably, the history of movies with titles derived from those of songs dates back more than 100 years, beginning with "How Would You Like to Be the Ice Man?," a popular song before being appropriated for a film released on April 21, 1899! "White Christmas," one of the most successful songs of all time, appeared in the movie *Holiday Inn* (1942) before in turn becoming the title of the 1954 movie.

the 10 LATEST "BEST SONG" OSCAR-WINNERS

YEAR	SONG	FILM
2004	Al Otro Lado del Río	The Motorcycle Diaries
2003	Into the West	The Lord of the Rings: The Return of the King
2002	Lose Yourself	8 Mile
2001	If I Didn't Have You	Monsters, Inc.
2000	Things Have Changed	Wonder Boys
1999	You'll Be in My Heart	Tarzan
1998	When You Believe	The Prince of Egypt
1997	My Heart Will Go On	Titanic
1996	You Must Love Me	Evita
1995	Colors of the Wind	Pocahontas

"Al Otro Lado Del Río" is the first-ever Spanish-language song to win an Oscar. It was written and sung by Uruguayan Jorge Drexler, who was sidelined at the awards ceremony in favor of a version sung by Antonio Banderas.

top 10 SOUNDTRACK ALBUMS IN THE US

	TITLE	YEAR OF RELEASE	SALES
1	The Bodyguard	1992	17,000,000
2	Purple Rain	1984	13,000,000
3	Forrest Gump	1994	12,000,000
4 =	Dirty Dancing	1987	11,000,000
=	Titanic	1997	11,000,000
6	The Lion King	1994	10,000,000
7 =	Footloose	1984	9,000,000
=	Top Gun	1986	9,000,000
9	Grease	1978	8,000,000
10	Saturday Night Fever	1977	7,500,000

Source: RIAA

Predominantly a vehicle for the movie's star, Whitney Houston, the all-time bestselling soundtrack album *The Bodyguard* includes her massive Dolly Parton–penned hit "I Will Always Love You."

⏷ Winning track
The Motorcycle Diaries song "Al Otro Lado Del Río (On the Other Side of the River)" won the "Best Song" Oscar in 2004.

Musical Collectibles

top 10 MOST EXPENSIVE GUITARS*

GUITAR / AUCTION / SALE PRICE[#]

1 Eric Clapton's 1956–57 "Blackie" Fender Stratocaster
Christie's, New York, June 25, 2004
$959,500

2 Jerry Garcia's "Tiger" guitar
Guernsey's at Studio 54, New York, May 9, 2002
$957,500

3 Eric Clapton's 1964 Gibson acoustic ES-335
Christie's, New York, June 25, 2004
$847,500

4 Eric Clapton's 1939 Martin acoustic
Christie's, New York, June 25, 2004
$791,500

5 Jerry Garcia's "Wolf" guitar
Guernsey's at Studio 54, New York, May 9, 2002
$789,500

6 Stevie Ray Vaughan's/Eric Clapton's "Lenny" Fender Stratocaster
Christie's, New York, June 25, 2004
$623,500

7 George Harrison's 1964 Gibson SG, played by both Harrison and John Lennon
Christie's, New York, Dec. 17, 2004
$567,500

8 "Brownie," one of Eric Clapton's favorite electric guitars
Christie's, New York, June 24, 1999
$497,500

9 George Harrison's first guitar, a Spanish-style Egmond "Firewood" model
Cooper Owen/Hard Rock Café, London, Nov. 21, 2003
$470,470 (£276,000)

10 Eric Clapton's Fender 1996 50th Anniversary Fender Stratocaster
Christie's, New York, June 25, 2004
$455,500

* Sold at auction

[#] Including buyer's premium where appropriate; price conversion calculated on rate prevailing at time of sale

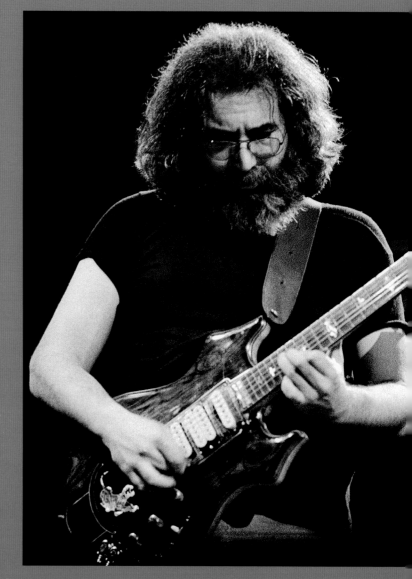

⬆ Jerry's tiger
Named for the inlaid motif on the front, Jerry Garcia's "Tiger" achieved a new world record when it was sold in 2002, along with "Wolf." Both instruments were made by guitar craftsman Doug Irwin, who subsequently inherited them following Garcia's death in 1995.

top 10 MOST EXPENSIVE MUSICAL INSTRUMENTS*

INSTRUMENT# / AUCTION / SALE PRICE†

1 John Lennon's Steinway Model Z upright piano
Fleetwood-Owen online auction, Hard Rock Café,
London and New York, Oct. 17, 2000
$2,150,000

2 "Kreutzer" violin by Antonio Stradivari, 1727
Christie's, London, Apr. 1, 1998
$1,582,847 (£946,000)

3 "Cholmondeley" violincello by Antonio Stradivari
Sotheby's, London, June 22, 1998
$1,141,122 (£682,000)

4 Italian cello by Giovanni Battista Guadagnini, Parma, 1760
Christie's, London, Nov. 3, 2004
$626,194 (£341,250)

5 Steinway grand piano, decorated by Lawrence Alma-Tadema and Edward Poynter for Henry Marquand, 1884–87
Sotheby Parke Bernet, New York, Mar. 26, 1980
$390,000

6 Single-manual harpsichord by Joseph Joannes Couchet, Antwerp, 1679
Sotheby's, London, Nov. 21, 2001
$378,004 (£267,500)

7 Double bass by Domenico Montagnana
Sotheby's, London, Mar. 16, 1999
$250,339 (£155,500)

8 Verne Powell's platinum flute
Christie's, New York, Oct. 18, 1986
$187,000

9 Viola by Giovanni Paolo Maggini
Christie's, London, Nov. 20, 1984
$161,121 (£129,000)

10 Charlie Parker's saxophone
Christie's, London, Sept. 8, 1994
$143,750 (£93,000)

* Sold at auction; excluding guitars

Most expensive example only for each type of instrument

† Including buyer's premium where appropriate; price conversion calculated on rate prevailing at time of sale

top 10 MOST EXPENSIVE POP LYRICS*

ITEM / AUCTION / SALE PRICE#

1 John Lennon's handwritten lyrics for "Nowhere Man" (1965)
Christie's, New York, Nov. 18, 2003
$455,000

2 Bernie Taupin's handwritten lyrics for the rewritten "Candle in the Wind" (1997)
Christie's, Los Angeles, Feb. 11, 1998
$400,000

3 Paul McCartney's handwritten lyrics for "Getting Better" (1967)
Sotheby's, London, Sept. 14, 1995
$249,333 (£161,000)

4 Mal Evans' notebook, compiled 1967–68, which includes a draft by Paul McCartney of the lyrics for "Hey Jude" (1968)
Sotheby's, London, Sept. 15, 1998
$187,287 (£111,500)

5 John Lennon's handwritten lyrics for "If I Fell", written on the back of a Valentine's card (1964)
Christie's, Los Angeles, Sept. 20, 2001
$171,000

6 Page of John Lennon's handwritten lyrics for "I Am the Walrus" (1967)
Christie's, London, Sept. 30, 1999
$129,266 (£78,500)

7 John Lennon's handwritten lyrics for "Being for the Benefit of Mr. Kite" (1967)
Sotheby's, London, Sept. 18, 1996
$103,597 (£66,400)

8 Twelve pages of John Lennon's handwritten lyrics for the *Plastic Ono Band* album, inscribed to his therapist, Dr. Arthur Janov, creator of "primal scream" therapy (1970)
Christie's, Los Angeles, Nov. 15, 2000
$102,800

9 Paul McCartney's handwritten lyrics for "She's Leaving Home" (1967)
Sotheby's, London, Aug. 27, 1992
$89,217 (£45,100)

10 John Lennon's handwritten lyrics for "A Day in the Life" (1967)
Sotheby's, London, Aug. 27, 1992
$87,041 (£44,000)

* Sold at auction

Including buyer's premium where appropriate; price conversion calculated on rate prevailing at time of sale

Chapter

678910

top 10 movies to win the most Oscars: page 145

top 10 superhero movies: page 139

SCENE 24 TAKE

top 10 animated film budgets: page 156

Stage & Screen

Theater

top 10 LONGEST-RUNNING MUSICALS ON BROADWAY

SHOW / YEARS RUNNING	PERFORMANCES
1 **Cats**, 1982–2000	7,485
2 **The Phantom of the Opera**, 1988–	7,061*
3 **Les Misérables**, 1987–2003	6,680
4 **A Chorus Line**, 1975–90	6,137
5 **Beauty and the Beast**, 1994–	4,386*
6 **Miss Saigon**, 1991–2001	4,092
7 **Rent**, 1996–	3,614*
8 **42nd Street**, 1980–89	3,486
9 **Grease**, 1972–80	3,388
10 **Chicago**, 1996–	3,385*

* Still running; total as of Jan. 1, 2005

Source: The League of American Theaters and Producers

All the longest-running musicals date from the past 40 years. Prior to these record-breakers, the longest runner of the 1940s was *Oklahoma!*, which debuted in 1943 and ran for 2,212 performances, and from the 1950s *My Fair Lady*, which opened in 1956 and closed after 2,717 performances.

top 10 OLDEST AMERICAN THEATERS AND OPERA HOUSES

THEATER / LOCATION	BUILT*
1 **The Walnut Street Theatre**, Philadelphia, Pennsylvania	1809
2 **The Woodward Opera House**, Mount Vernon, Ohio	1851
3 **The Fulton Opera House**, Lancaster, Pennsylvania	1852
4 **Loring Hall, Hingham**, Massachusetts	1852
5 **Institute Hall,** Natchez, Mississippi	1853
6 **The Majestic Theatre**, Chillicothe, Ohio	1853
7 **Saco Town Hall**, Saco, Maine	1856
8 **The Academy of Music**, Philadelphia, Pennsylvania	1857
9 **Thespian Hall**, Boonville, Missouri	1857
10 **Thalian Hall**, Wilmington, North Carolina	1858

* Most have been remodeled inside and/or outside since

The Walnut Street Theatre has operated continuously since it opened in 1809. Once owned by Edwin Booth, the brother of Lincoln's assassin John Wilkes Booth, it was the first theater with gas footlights and the first with air-conditioning. Pre-Broadway runs of many plays there have starred some of the world's leading actors, including Jack Lemmon and Audrey Hepburn.

top 10 LONGEST-RUNNING NONMUSICALS ON BROADWAY

SHOW / YEARS RUNNING	PERFORMANCES
1 **Oh! Calcutta!**, 1976–89	5,959
2 **Life with Father**, 1939–47	3,224
3 **Tobacco Road**, 1933–41	3,182
4 **Abie's Irish Rose**, 1922–27	2,327
6 **Gemini**, 1977–81	1,819
5 **Deathtrap**, 1978–82	1,793
7 **Harvey**, 1944–49	1,775
8 **Born Yesterday**, 1946–49	1,642
9 **Mary, Mary**, 1961–64	1,572
10 **The Voice of the Turtle**, 1943–48	1,557

Source: The League of American Theaters and Producers

More than half the longest-running nonmusical shows on Broadway began their runs before World War II; the others all date from the period up to the 1970s, before the long-running musical completely dominated the Broadway stage.

the 10 LATEST NEW YORK DRAMA CRITICS CIRCLE AWARDS FOR BEST NEW PLAY*

YEAR	PLAY	PLAYWRIGHT
2004	**Intimate Apparel**	Lynn Nottage
2003	**Take Me Out**	Richard Greenberg
2002	**The Goat or Who Is Sylvia**	Edward Albee
2001	**The Invention of Love**	Tom Stoppard
2000	**Jitney**	August Wilson
1999	**Wit**	Margaret Edson
1998	**Art**	Yasmina Reza
1997	**How I Learned to Drive**	Paula Vogel
1996	**Seven Guitars**	August Wilson
1995	**Arcardia**	Tom Stoppard

* Award was for "Best Play" prior to 1996

The New York Drama Critics Circle was established in 1935 as a reaction against the decisions of the Pulitzer committee, which similarly presents awards for plays, rather than individual performances or directors. In contrast to the Tony Awards, they also recognize off-Broadway productions. If the winning play is American, a second award is presented for the Best Foreign Play, while if the winner is foreign, another award is presented for Best American Play. Musicals have been acknowledged separately since 1945.

⏱ **See how it runs**
Richard Attenborough, a member of the original cast of *The Mousetrap*, celebrates the 50th anniversary of the world's longest-running play.

the 10 LATEST **TONY AWARDS** FOR A PLAY

YEAR	PLAY	PLAYWRIGHT
2004	I Am My Own Wife	Doug Wright
2003	Take Me Out	Richard Greenberg
2002	The Goat or Who Is Sylvia	Edward Albee
2001	Proof	David Auburn
2000	Copenhagen	Michael Frayn
1999	Side Man	Warren Leight
1998	Art	Yasmina Reza
1997	The Last Night of Ballyhoo	Alfred Uhry
1996	Master Class	Terrence McNally
1995	Love! Valour! Compassion!	Terrence McNally

The Tony Awards, established in 1947 by the American Theater Wing, honor outstanding Broadway plays and musicals, actors and actresses, music, costume, and other contributions. They are named for the actress and director Antoinette Perry (1888– 1946), who headed the American Theater Wing during World War II.

THE **LONGEST-RUNNING** SHOWS OF ALL TIME

SHOW / LOCATION / RUN	PERFORMANCES
1 **The Golden Horseshoe Revue**, Disneyland,California, 1955–86	47,250
2 **The Mousetrap**, London, 1952–	21,708*
3 **The Fantasticks**, New York, 1960–2002	17,162
4 **La Cantatrice Chauve (The Bald Soprano)**, Paris, 1957–	14,863*
5 **Shear Madness**, Boston, 1980–	10,367*
6 **The Drunkard**, Los Angeles, 1933–59	9,477
7 **The Mousetrap**, Toronto, 1977–2004	9,000
8 **Cats**, London, 1981–2002	8,949
9 **Les Misérables**, London, 1985–	7,916*
10 **Cats**, New York, 1982–2000	7,485

* Still running; total as of Jan. 1, 2005

Movie Hits

top 10 HIGHEST-GROSSING MOVIES OF ALL TIME IN THE US (ADJUSTED FOR INFLATION)

MOVIE	YEAR	US BOX OFFICE INCOME ($)	
		(ACTUAL US GROSS)	(ADJUSTED FOR INFLATION*)
1 Gone With the Wind	1939	198,676,459	2,730,013,223
2 Snow White and the Seven Dwarfs#	1937	187,670,866	2,489,247,600
3 Star Wars†	1977	460,998,007	1,452,973,518
4 Bambi#	1942	102,797,000	1,204,554,687
5 Pinocchio#	1940	84,254,167	1,149,471,175
6 Fantasia#	1940	76,408,097	1,042,428,027
7 The Exorcist	1973	232,671,011	1,000,094,155
8 The Sound of Music	1965	163,214,286	989,649,823
9 One Hundred and One Dalmatians#	1961	153,000,000	977,364,000
10 Jaws	1975	260,000,000	923,052,000

* As of Jan.1, 2005

Animated

† Later retitled *Star Wars: Episode IV—A New Hope*

⊙ **Frankly, my dear...**
Clark Gable and Vivien Leigh co-starred in *Gone with the Wind*, the inflation-adjusted top-earning movie of all time.

Unless inflation is factored in, the escalating price of movie tickets—and hence the total income that movies generate—makes the list of all-time blockbusters biased toward recent releases: box office income of $1 million earned 50 years ago (1955), for example, would be worth over $7 million today. However, any inflation-indexing inevitably assumes that the bulk of a movie's income was earned in its release year, which is clearly not the case, since the total gross of any movie is cumulative often over many years from its release (and, with rereleases, may even increase decades later). The ranking indicated by this list must therefore be taken only as a guide and an impressionistic answer to the question, "If the box office income of movie X had been earned today, how much would it be worth?", rather than a precise reflection of the inflation-adjusted earning of every dollar ever earned by each movie.

top 10 MOVIES IN THE US

MOVIE	YEAR	US GROSS ($)
1 Titanic*	1997	600,788,188
2 Star Wars#	1977	460,998,007
3 Shrek 2†	2004	441,226,247
4 E.T. the Extra-Terrestrial	1982	435,110,554
5 Star Wars: Episode I—The Phantom Menace	1999	431,088,297
6 Spider-Man	2002	403,706,375
7 The Lord of the Rings: The Return of the King	2003	377,027,325
8 Spider-Man 2	2004	373,585,825
9 The Passion of the Christ	2004	370,274,604
10 Jurassic Park	1993	357,067,947

* Winner of "Best Picture" Academy Award

Later retitled *Star Wars: Episode IV—A New Hope*

† Animated

⬆ **World-wide web** Globally, *Spider-Man 2* was the highest-earning live-action movie of 2004 and the 9th of all time.

top 10 MOVIES **WORLDWIDE**, 2004

MOVIE	WORLDWIDE GROSS ($)*
1 Shrek 2#	918,506,048
2 Harry Potter and the Prisoner of Azkaban	789,791,069
3 Spider-Man 2	783,964,497
4 The Incredibles#	631,068,449
5 The Passion of the Christ	623,489,009
6 The Day After Tomorrow	542,545,811
7 Meet the Fockers	507,392,324
8 Troy	497,378,256
9 Ocean's Twelve	362,144,280
10 I, Robot	338,780,585

* Including income from ongoing US and overseas releases through 2005

Animated

top 10 **MOVIES** IN THE US, 2004

MOVIE	US GROSS ($)*
1 Shrek 2#	436,471,036
2 Spider-Man 2#	373,377,893
3 The Passion of the Christ	370,270,943
4 The Incredibles#	251,657,004
5 Harry Potter and the Prisoner of Azkaban	249,358,727
6 The Day After Tomorrow	186,739,919
7 The Bourne Supremacy	176,049,130
8 Meet the Fockers	162,461,370
9 Shark Tale#	160,762,022
10 The Polar Express#	155,112,441

* During 2004; some continued to earn through 2005

Animated

top 10 **TRILOGIES**

MOVIES / YEARS	WORLDWIDE TOTAL GROSS ($)*	MOVIES / YEARS	WORLDWIDE TOTAL GROSS ($)*
1 The Lord of the Rings, 2001–03	2,916,544,743	6 Indiana Jones, 1981–89	1,211,716,531
2 Harry Potter, 2001–2004	2,652,297,210	7 Back to the Future, 1985–90	927,715,544
3 Jurassic Park, 1993–2002	1,902,110,926	8 The Silence of the Lambs, 1991–2001	833,916,591
4 The Matrix, 1999–2003	1,623,924,804	9 American Pie, 1999–2003	754,039,152
5 Terminator, 1984–2003	1,212,019,531	10 Die Hard, 1988–95	743,562,298

* Cumulative global earnings of all three parts

Film Genres

top 10 WAR MOVIES

FILM / SETTING	YEAR
1 **Troy**, Trojan Wars	2004
2 **Saving Private Ryan**, World War II	1998
3 **Pearl Harbor**, World War II	2001
4 **The Last Samurai**, Japanese Emperor vs. Samurai	2003
5 **Gone With the Wind**, US Civil War	1939
6 **Schindler's List**, World War II	1993
7 **The English Patient**, World War II	1996
8 **Life Is Beautiful (La Vita è bella)**, World War II	1997
9 **Master and Commander: The Far Side of the World**, Napoleonic Wars	2003
10 **The Patriot**, American Revolution	2000

This list excludes successful movies that are not technically "war" movies but have military themes, such as *Top Gun* (1986), *Rambo: First Blood Part II* (1985), and *A Few Good Men* (1992), which would otherwise appear in the Top 10, all of which have earned more than $200 million each at the world box office.

War chest

Starring Brad Pitt as Achilles, *Troy* earned almost $3.7 billion at the world box office.

top 10 BIOGRAPHICAL MOVIES*

FILM	SUBJECT	YEAR
1 **Catch Me if You Can**	Frank Abagnale Jr.	2002
2 **Pocahontas**#	Pocahontas	1995
3 **Schindler's List**	Oskar Schindler	1993
4 **A Beautiful Mind**	John Nash	2001
5 **Erin Brockovich**	Erin Brockovich	2000
6 **Out of Africa**	Karen Blixen	1985
7 **Braveheart**	William Wallace	1995
8 **The Aviator**	Howard Hughes	2004
9 **Patch Adams**	Hunter "Patch" Adams	1998
10 **Born on the Fourth of July**	Ron Kovic	1989

* Excluding musical biographies

Animated

top 10 DOCUMENTARY FILMS

	FILM	SUBJECT	YEAR
1	Fahrenheit 9/11	War on terrorism	2004
2	The Dream is Alive	Space Shuttle	1985
3	Everest	Exploration	1998
4	Grand Canyon: The Hidden Secrets	Exploration	1984
5	To Fly	History of flying	1976
6	Jackass: The Movie	Comedy stunts	2002
7	Space Station 3-D	International Space Station	2002
8	Blue Planet	Earth from space	1990
9	Mysteries of Egypt	Historical	1998
10 =	Antarctica	Exploration/nature	1991
=	Into the Deep	Underwater exploration	1994

⊙ Hot date
Michael Moore and friend in the all-time documentary hit and Cannes Film Festival "Palme d'Or" winner *Fahrenheit 9/11*.

top 10 ROBOT MOVIES

	FILM	YEAR
1	Star Wars: Episode I— The Phantom Menace	1999
2	Star Wars*	1977
3	Star Wars: Episode VI— Return of the Jedi	1983
4	Star Wars: Episode V— The Empire Strikes Back	1980
5	Terminator 2: Judgment Day	1991
6	Terminator 3: Rise of the Machines	2003
7	I, Robot	2004
8	Lara Croft: Tomb Raider	2001
9	A.I.: Artificial Intelligence	2001
10	Wild Wild West	1999

* Later retitled *Star Wars: Episode IV— A New Hope*

These are the most successful movies in which robots or cyborgs play central or significant roles. All of those in the Top 10 earned upward of $220 million each worldwide.

top 10 HORROR MOVIES

	FILM	YEAR
1	Jurassic Park	1993
2	The Sixth Sense	1999
3	The Lost World: Jurassic Park	1997
4	Jaws	1975
5	The Mummy Returns	2001
6	The Mummy	1999
7	Signs	2002
8	Godzilla	1998
9	Jurassic Park III	2001
10	Hannibal	2001

This list encompasses supernatural and science-fiction horror and monster creatures such as dinosaurs and oversized sharks. It has long been a successful genre: each of the movies listed has earned $350 million or more at the world box office.

top 10 SUPERHERO MOVIES

	FILM	YEAR
1	Spider-Man	2002
2	Spider-Man 2	2004
3	The Incredibles*	2004
4	Batman	1989
5	X2: X-Men United	2003
6	Batman Forever	1995
7	The Mask	1994
8	Superman	1978
9	X-Men	2000
10	Batman Returns	1992

* Animated

Superman makes a single showing in this Top 10, since it is in the unusual situation where the first film made a large amount (over $300 million) at the world box office while each of its three sequels made progressively less.

Oscar-Winning Actors

top 10 **OLDEST** OSCAR-WINNING ACTORS

	ACTOR	MOVIE	YEAR	AGE* (YRS	MTHS	DAYS)
1	George Burns	The Sunshine Boys	1975	80	2	9
2	Melvyn Douglas	Being There	1979	79	0	9
3	John Gielgud	Arthur	1981	77	11	15
4	Don Ameche	Cocoon	1985	77	9	24
5	Henry Fonda	On Golden Pond	1981	76	10	13
6	Edmund Gwenn	Miracle on 34th Street	1947	72	5	24
7	Jack Palance	City Slickers	1991	72	0	1
8	John Houseman	The Paperchase	1973	71	6	0
9	Morgan Freeman	Million Dollar Baby	2004	67	8	27
10	Charles Coburn	The More the Merrier	1943	66	8	13

* Age at time of award ceremony

All of the Academy Awards listed here are for "Best Supporting Actor," apart from Henry Fonda's award for "Best Actor" in *On Golden Pond*. The oldest person to win the "Best Actor" award prior to Henry Fonda was John Wayne, who was 62 when he received his 1969 award for *True Grit*.

the 10 LATEST "**BEST ACTOR**" OSCAR WINNERS

YEAR	ACTOR	MOVIE
2004	Jamie Foxx	Ray
2003	Sean Penn	Mystic River
2002	Adrien Brody	The Pianist
2001	Denzel Washington	Training Day
2000	Russell Crowe	Gladiator*
1999	Kevin Spacey	American Beauty*
1998	Roberto Benigni	Life is Beautiful
1997	Jack Nicholson	As Good As It Gets
1996	Geoffrey Rush	Shine
1995	Nicolas Cage	Leaving Las Vegas

* Won "Best Picture" Academy Award

"And the winner is..."

🔽 **Piano man**
Jamie Foxx played the title role in *Ray*. Like previous Oscar-winner Holly Hunter in *The Pianist*, he played the piano himself in the movie.

top 10 ACTORS WITH THE **MOST NOMINATIONS***

	ACTOR	WINS (SUPPORTING)	(BEST)	NOMINATIONS
1	Jack Nicholson	1	2	12
2	Laurence Olivier	0	1	10
3	=Paul Newman	0	1	9
	=Spencer Tracy	0	2	9
5	=Marlon Brando	0	2	8
	=Jack Lemmon	1	1	8
	=Al Pacino	0	1	8
8	=Richard Burton	0	0	7
	=Dustin Hoffman	0	2	7
	=Peter O'Toole	0	0	7

* In all acting categories

⬅ **Wild about Oscar**
Jack Nicholson's Academy Award nominations span 33 years, from *Easy Rider* (1969) to *About Schmidt* (2002). He won the "Best Actor" award for *One Flew Over the Cuckoo's Nest* (1975) and *As Good as It Gets* (1997), and "Best Supporting Actor" for *Terms of Endearment* (1983).

top 10 **YOUNGEST** OSCAR-WINNING ACTORS

	ACTOR	AWARD / MOVIE	YEAR	(YRS	AGE* MTHS	DAYS)
1	Vincent Winter	Honorary Award: Outstanding Juvenile Performance, *The Little Kidnappers*	1954	7	3	1
2	Jon Whiteley	Honorary Award: Outstanding Juvenile Performance, *The Little Kidnappers*	1954	10	1	11
3	Ivan Jandl	Special Award: Outstanding Juvenile Performance of 1948, *The Search*	1948	12	2	0
4	Claude Jarman Jr.	Special Award: Outstanding Child Actor of 1946, *The Yearling*	1946	12	4	14
5	Bobby Driscoll	Special Award: Outstanding Juvenile Actor of 1949, *The Window*	1949	13	0	20
6	Mickey Rooney	Special Award for juvenile players setting a high standard of ability and achievement[#]	1938	18	5	0
7	Timothy Hutton	Best Supporting Actor, *Ordinary People*	1980	20	7	15
8	George Chakiris	Best Supporting Actor, *West Side Story*	1961	26	7	1
9	Cuba Gooding Jr.	Best Supporting Actor, *Jerry Maguire*	1996	29	3	22
10	Adrien Brody	Best Actor, *The Pianist*	2002	29	11	9

* Age at time of award ceremony

[#] Shared with fellow teen star Deanna Durbin

Oscar-Winning Actresses

the 10 LATEST ACTRESSES TO WIN TWO "BEST ACTRESS" OSCARS

	ACTRESS	FIRST WIN	YEAR	SECOND WIN	YEAR
1	Hilary Swank	Boys Don't Cry	1999	Million Dollar Baby	2004
2	Jodie Foster	The Accused	1988	The Silence of the Lambs	1991
3	Sally Field	Norma Rae	1979	Places in the Heart	1984
4	Jane Fonda	Klute	1971	Coming Home	1978
5	Glenda Jackson	Women in Love	1970	A Touch of Class	1973
6	Katharine Hepburn	The Lion in Winter	1968	On Golden Pond	1981
7	Katharine Hepburn	Morning Glory	1932/33	Guess Who's Coming to Dinner?	1967
8	Elizabeth Taylor	Butterfield 8	1960	Who's Afraid of Virginia Woolf?	1966
9	Ingrid Bergman	Gaslight	1944	Anastasia	1956
10	Vivien Leigh	Gone With the Wind	1939	A Streetcar Named Desire	1951

top 10 OLDEST OSCAR-WINNING ACTRESSES

	ACTRESS	MOVIE	YEAR	AGE* (YRS	MTHS	DAYS)
1	Jessica Tandy	Driving Miss Daisy	1989	80	9	21
2	Peggy Ashcroft	A Passage to India	1984	77	3	3
3	Katharine Hepburn	On Golden Pond	1981	74	4	11
4	Ruth Gordon	Rosemary's Baby	1968	72	5	15
5	Margaret Rutherford	The VIPs	1963	71	11	2
6	Helen Hayes	Airport	1970	70	5	25
7	Ethel Barrymore	None But the Lonely Heart	1944	65	7	0
8	Josephine Hull	Harvey	1950	65	1	26
9	Judi Dench	Shakespeare in Love	1998	64	3	12
10	Beatrice Straight	Network	1976	62	7	26

* Age at time of award ceremony

All of the Academy Awards listed here are for "Best Supporting Actress," apart from Jessica Tandy in *Driving Miss Daisy* and Katharine Hepburn in *On Golden Pond*, who both won "Best Actress" awards. Jessica Tandy holds the record as both the oldest nominee and oldest winner of a "Best Actor" or "Best Actress" Academy Award. Among those female senior citizens who received nominations but did not win Oscars are Gloria Stuart, age 87, for "Best Supporting Actress" in *Titanic* (1997), and May Robson, who was 75 when she was nominated as "Best Actress" in *Lady for a Day* (1933).

⬇ Veteran winner
Two years after becoming the most senior recipient of an Oscar—and almost 60 years after making her first movie—Jessica Tandy was again nominated for "Best Supporting Actress" for her role in *Fried Green Tomatoes* (1991), but lost out to Mercedes Ruehl in *The Fisher King*.

the 10 LATEST "BEST ACTRESS" OSCAR WINNERS

YEAR	ACTRESS	MOVIE
2004	Hilary Swank	Million Dollar Baby*
2003	Charlize Theron	Monster
2002	Nicole Kidman	The Hours
2001	Halle Berry	Monster's Ball
2000	Julia Roberts	Erin Brockovich
1999	Hilary Swank	Boys Don't Cry
1998	Gwyneth Paltrow	Shakespeare in Love*
1997	Helen Hunt	As Good As It Gets
1996	Frances McDormand	Fargo
1995	Susan Sarandon	Dead Man Walking

* Won "Best Picture" Academy Award

Hilary Swank's second win is unique in that both her wins were for roles in films that also won "Best Picture" Oscars. She was the second youngest (after Jodie Foster) to win two Oscars. The youngest "Best Actress" winner was Marlee Matlin, aged 21, for *Children of a Lesser God* (1986), and the youngest nominee Keisha Castle-Hughes, who was 13 when nominated for her role in *Whale Rider* (2002).

Top dollar
Hilary Swank's Oscar for *Million Dollar Baby* was matched by a Golden Globe and other major awards.

Oscar-Winning Movies

the 10 LATEST **"BEST PICTURE"** OSCAR-WINNERS

YEAR	MOVIE	DIRECTOR
2004	**Million Dollar Baby**	Clint Eastwood
2003	**The Lord of the Rings: The Return of the King**	Peter Jackson
2002	**Chicago**	Rob Marshall*
2001	**A Beautiful Mind**	Ron Howard
2000	**Gladiator**	Ridley Scott*
1999	**American Beauty**	Sam Mendes
1998	**Shakespeare in Love**	John Madden*
1997	**Titanic**	James Cameron
1996	**The English Patient**	Anthony Minghella
1995	**Braveheart**	Mel Gibson

* Did not also win "Best Director" Academy Award

top 10 **HIGHEST-EARNING** "BEST PICTURE" OSCAR WINNERS

MOVIE	YEAR*	WORLD BOX OFFICE ($)
1 **Titanic**	1997	1,845,000,000
2 **The Lord of the Rings: The Return of the King**	2003	1,118,900,000
3 **Forrest Gump**	1994	677,400,000
4 **Gladiator**	2000	457,600,000
5 **Dances With Wolves**	1990	424,200,000
6 **Rain Man**	1988	416,000,000
7 **Gone With the Wind**	1939	400,200,000
8 **American Beauty**	1999	356,300,000
9 **Schindler's List**	1993	321,300,000
10 **A Beautiful Mind**	2001	313,500,000

* Of release; Academy Awards are made the following year

For a few million dollars more
With his latest Oscar wins, actor-director Clint Eastwood repeated the "Best Picture" and "Best Director" double victory of *Unforgiven* (1992).

Although since equaled by two recent blockbusters, *Ben-Hur* was the first movie to win more than 10 Oscars. Based on the 1880 book by Lew Wallace, *Ben-Hur* was directed by William Wyler, who had worked as an assistant director on the original 1925 silent version of the film, and had two previous Oscars to his credit. Had it won in the one other category in which it was nominated—"Best Writing, Screenplay Based on Material from Another Medium"—it would have secured a record 12 wins.

➲ Racing ahead
Ben-Hur's amazing haul of 11 Oscars set a record that remained unbeaten for almost 40 years.

top 10 MOVIES TO **WIN THE MOST OSCARS**

MOVIE	YEAR	NOMINATIONS	AWARDS
1 = Ben-Hur	1959	12	11
= Titanic	1997	14	11
= The Lord of the Rings: The Return of the King	2003	11	11
4 West Side Story	1961	11	10
5 = Gigi	1958	9	9
= The Last Emperor	1987	9	9
= The English Patient	1996	12	9
8 = Gone With the Wind	1939	13	8*
= From Here to Eternity	1953	13	8
= On the Waterfront	1954	12	8
= My Fair Lady	1964	12	8
= Cabaret	1972	10	8
= Gandhi	1982	11	8
= Amadeus	1984	11	8

* Plus two special awards

Ten other movies have won seven Oscars each: *Going My Way* (1944), *The Best Years of Our Lives* (1946), *The Bridge on the River Kwai* (1957), *Lawrence of Arabia* (1962), *Patton* (1970), *The Sting* (1973), *Out of Africa* (1985), *Dances With Wolves* (1991), *Schindler's List* (1993), and *Shakespeare in Love* (1998). *Titanic* (1997) matched the previous record of 14 nominations of *All About Eve* (1950), but outshone it by winning 11, compared with the latter's six.

top 10 MOVIES **NOMINATED FOR THE MOST OSCARS**

MOVIE	YEAR	NOMINATIONS	AWARDS
1 = All About Eve	1950	14	6
= Titanic	1997	14	11
3 = Gone With the Wind	1939	13	8*
= From Here to Eternity	1953	13	8
= Shakespeare in Love	1998	13	7
= Mary Poppins#	1964	13	5
= Who's Afraid of Virginia Woolf?#	1966	13	5
= Forrest Gump	1994	13	6
= The Lord of the Rings: The Fellowship of the Ring	2001	13	4
= Chicago	2002	13	6

* Plus two special awards
# Did not win "Best Picture" Academy Award

A total of eight films have received 13 Oscar nominations. They, and the two movies with 14, have received the greatest share of votes from Academy members (currently over 5,500 in total), using a system that creates a shortlist of five nominees in each of 24 categories. Eliminating certain special categories reduces the potential number of awards for which a movie may be nominated, and they may be nominated in one category that excludes another—screenplays, for example, are divided into two awards according to whether they are based on material previously produced or published, or written for the screen.

TOP 10 MOVIES OF ALL TIME

	FILM	YEAR	(US)	GROSS INCOME ($) (OVERSEAS)	(WORLD TOTAL)
1	Titanic*	1997	600,788,188	1,244,246,000	1,845,034,188
2	The Lord of the Rings: The Return of the King	2003	377,027,325	741,861,654	1,118,888,979
3	Harry Potter and the Sorcerer's Stone	2001	317,575,550	668,242,109	985,817,659
4	The Lord of the Rings: The Two Towers	2002	341,784,377	584,500,642	926,287,400
5	Star Wars: Episode I—The Phantom Menace	1999	431,088,297	494,511,703	925,600,000
6	Shrek 2#	2004	441,226,247	470,823,405	918,506,048
7	Jurassic Park	1993	357,067,947	557,623,171	914,691,118
8	Harry Potter and the Chamber of Secrets	2002	261,988,482	614,700,000	876,688,482
9	The Lord of the Rings: The Fellowship of the Ring	2001	314,776,170	556,592,194	871,368,364
10	Finding Nemo#	2003	339,714,978	524,911,000	864,625,978

* Winner of "Best Picture" Academy Award

\# Animated

Prior to the release of *Star Wars* in 1977, no movie had ever made more than $500 million worldwide. Since then, some 35 movies have done so. *Titanic* remains the only movie to have made more than this amount in the US alone, and just 10 movies have exceeded this total outside the US. To date, those in the Top 10, along with *Spider-Man 2* (2004), *Spider-Man* (2002), and *Independence Day* (1996) are the only movies to earn more than $800 million globally.

← **Titanic prowess**
Leonardo DiCaprio and Kate Winslet co-star as ill-fated *Titanic* passengers Jack Dawson and Rose DeWitt Bukater in the US and world's highest-earning film

⬆ Golden Rings

Each of the *Lord of the Rings* movies earned progressively more than its predecessor. Cumulatively, the trilogy has earned almost $3 billion worldwide.

Movie Actors

top 10 TOM CRUISE MOVIES

FILM	YEAR
1 Mission: Impossible II	2000
2 Mission: Impossible	1996
3 The Last Samurai	2003
4 Rain Man	1988
5 Minority Report	2002
6 Top Gun	1986
7 Jerry Maguire	1996
8 The Firm	1993
9 A Few Good Men	1992
10 Interview with the Vampire: The Vampire Chronicles	1994

Tom Cruise (real name Thomas Cruise Mapother IV) built his career on playing a combination of handsome all-American hero, military, and light comedy roles, but has shown himself equally at home with dramatic parts, for which he has been nominated for Oscars on three occasions. Few actors have matched his commercial success: every one of his Top 10 movies has earned more than $220 million worldwide, a total of more than $3.6 billion. Cruise appeared as himself in *Austin Powers in Goldmember*, which, if included in this list, would be ranked 7th.

◑ On the ball
Samuel L. Jackson in the title role of *Coach Carter* (2005). His prolific filmography includes so many high-earning movies that he heads the list of box office total earnings.

top 10 ACTORS BY US BOX OFFICE TOTALS

ACTOR	FILMS	US TOTAL ($)
1 Samuel L. Jackson	60	3,316,546,256
2 Harrison Ford	33	3,255,071,377
3 Tom Hanks	33	3,083,738,308
4 Eddie Murphy	30	2,916,492,624
5 Tom Cruise	28	2,673,139,642
6 Bruce Willis	45	2,475,454,726
7 James Earl Jones	40	2,343,822,050
8 Mel Gibson	35	2,316,662,303
9 Gene Hackman	59	2,253,788,994
10 Jim Cummings	26	2,250,222,445

top 10 JIM CARREY MOVIES

FILM	YEAR
1 Bruce Almighty	2003
2 Dr. Seuss's How the Grinch Stole Christmas	2000
3 Batman Forever	1995
4 The Mask	1994
5 Liar Liar	1997
6 The Truman Show	1998
7 Dumb & Dumber	1994
8 Ace Ventura: When Nature Calls	1995
9 Lemony Snicket's A Series of Unfortunate Events	2004
10 Me, Myself & Irene	2000

Jim Carrey is a member of an elite club of actors, all of whose Top 10 movies have earned more than $100 million worldwide. In fact, such is his international appeal that the average for the movies in this list is over $250 million.

↑ **High-flier** Leonardo DiCaprio as Howard Hughes in *The Aviator*, one of his highest-earning movies.

top 10 **LEONARDO DICAPRIO** MOVIES

	FILM	YEAR
1	Titanic	1997
2	Catch Me If You Can	2002
3	The Aviator	2004
4	Gangs of New York	2002
5	The Man in the Iron Mask	1998
6	Romeo + Juliet	1996
7	The Beach	2000
8	The Quick and the Dead	1995
9	Marvin's Room	1996
10	What's Eating Gilbert Grape	1993

top 10 **JOHNNY DEPP** MOVIES

	FILM	YEAR
1	Pirates of the Caribbean: The Curse of the Black Pearl	2003
2	Sleepy Hollow	1999
3	Platoon	1986
4	Chocolat	2000
5	Donnie Brasco	1997
6	Desperado II: Once Upon a Time in Mexico	2003
7	Secret Window	2004
8	Edward Scissorhands	1990
9	Blow	2001
10	From Hell	2001

top 10 **BRAD PITT** MOVIES

	FILM	YEAR
1	Troy	2004
2	Ocean's Eleven	2001
3	Ocean's Twelve	2004
4	Se7en	1995
5	Interview with the Vampire: The Vampire Chronicles	1994
6	Twelve Monkeys	1995
7	Sleepers	1996
8	Legends of the Fall	1994
9	The Mexican	2001
10	Spy Game	2001

Movie Actresses

top 10 ACTRESSES BY US BOX OFFICE TOTALS

	ACTRESS	MOVIES	US TOTAL ($)
1	Julia Roberts	31	2,100,225,877
2	Carrie Fisher	28	1,862,987,964
3	Cameron Diaz	23	1,829,146,650
4	Whoopi Goldberg	41	1,705,812,987
5	Maggie Smith	26	1,582,143,126
6	Drew Barrymore	30	1,539,958,383
7	Kathy Bates	33	1,496,552,561
8	Kirsten Dunst	25	1,466,237,842
9	Bonnie Hunt	17	1,409,452,306
10	Sally Field	24	1,389,128,778

Julia Roberts' place at the head of this list derives from a career in which it is almost impossible to identify a movie in which she has starred that has not enjoyed success ranging from moderate to spectacular. *Pretty Woman* (1990), her seventh film, is still her highest-earning at some $842 million worldwide.

⊙ **Star earner**
Carrie Fisher (and wookie Chewbacca) at the MTV Movie Awards. Fisher's role as Princess Leia in three of the *Star Wars* movies has contributed to her overall tally.

top 10 RENEE ZELLWEGER MOVIES

	MOVIE	YEAR
1	Chicago	2002
2	Bridget Jones's Diary	2001
3	Jerry Maguire	1996
4	Bridget Jones: The Edge of Reason	2004
5	Cold Mountain	2003
6	Me, Myself & Irene	2000
7	Down with Love	2003
8	Nurse Betty	2000
9	The Bachelor	1999
10	Reality Bites	1994

Aside from some unmemorable early roles in movies such as *The Return of the Texas Chainsaw Massacre* (1994), Renée Zellweger has followed an ever-upward trajectory in her film career, gaining consecutive Best Actress Oscar nominations for *Bridget Jones's Diary* (2001) and *Chicago* (2002), and winning Best Actress in a Supporting Role for *Cold Mountain* (2003). Although discounted here, the animated *Shark Tale*, for which she provided the voice of Angie, has outearned all the movies in which she has appeared.

top 10 KATE WINSLET MOVIES

	MOVIE	YEAR
1	Titanic	1997
2	Sense and Sensibility	1995
3	Finding Neverland	2004
4	Eternal Sunshine of the Spotless Mind	2004
5	The Life of David Gale	2003
6	Quills	2000
7	Iris	2001
8	Enigma	2001
9	A Kid in King Arthur's Court	1995
10	Hamlet	1996

↑ Elf queen
Cate Blanchett as elf queen Galadriel in the *Lord of the Rings* trilogy.

top 10 **CATE BLANCHETT** MOVIES

MOVIE	YEAR
1 The Lord of the Rings: The Return of the King	2003
2 The Lord of the Rings: The Two Towers	2002
3 The Lord of the Rings: The Fellowship of the Ring	2001
4 The Aviator	2004
5 The Talented Mr. Ripley	1999
6 Bandits	2001
7 Elizabeth	1998
8 The Gift	2000
9 The Missing	2003
10 The Life Aquatic with Steve Zissou	2004

top 10 **UMA THURMAN** MOVIES

MOVIE	YEAR
1 Batman & Robin	1997
2 Pulp Fiction	1994
3 Kill Bill: Vol. 1	2003
4 Kill Bill: Vol 2	2004
5 Paycheck	2003
6 The Truth About Cats & Dogs	1996
7 The Avengers	1998
8 Final Analysis	1992
9 Dangerous Liaisons	1988
10 Beautiful Girls	1996

Although featuring in her Top 10 by virtue of its global box office income, *The Avengers* did not earn back its substantial production budget, and may thus be regarded as a flop. Conversely, *Pulp Fiction* had a budget of some $8 million, but went on to make more than $200 million worldwide.

top 10 **NICOLE KIDMAN** MOVIES

MOVIE	YEAR
1 Batman Forever	1995
2 The Others	2001
3 Moulin Rouge!	2001
4 Cold Mountain	2003
5 Days of Thunder	1990
6 Eyes Wide Shut	1999
7 Far and Away	1992
8 The Peacemaker	1997
9 The Hours*	2002
10 The Stepford Wives	2004

* Won Academy Award for "Best Actress"

Honolulu-born Nicole Kidman was raised in Australia, where she acted on TV before her break into film, in which she has pursued a highly successful career: her Top 10 movies have each earned upward of $100 million worldwide.

Film Directors

↑ **Express delivery** Robert Zemeckis–directed *Polar Express* was a pioneering exercise in 3-D motion capture technology.

top 10 **DIRECTORS**

	DIRECTOR	FILMS	HIGHEST-EARNING FILM	TOTAL US GROSS OF ALL FILMS ($)
1	Steven Spielberg	22	ET the Extra-Terrestrial	3,223,585,018
2	Robert Zemeckis	13	Forrest Gump	1,696,212,782
3	Chris Columbus	11	Harry Potter and the Sorcerer's Stone	1,530,121,285
4	Ron Howard	15	Dr. Seuss's How the Grinch Stole Christmas	1,316,036,170
5	George Lucas	5	Star Wars*	1,309,272,429
6	Richard Donner	16	Lethal Weapon 2	1,194,703,637
7	James Cameron	7	Titanic	1,142,636,142
8	Peter Jackson	5	The Lord of the Rings: The Return of the King	1,052,251,914
9	Ivan Reitman	12	Ghostbusters	974,005,978
10	Tim Burton	10	Batman	973,377,367

* Later retitled *Star Wars: Episode IV—A New Hope*

While the cumulative total US box office income of all the movies of these directors provides a comparative view of the overall earning power of the group, the most impressive representative is George Lucas, with relatively few but extremely high-grossing releases, a per-picture average of $264 million.

top 10 MOVIES DIRECTED BY **ROBERT ZEMECKIS**

	FILM	YEAR
1	Forrest Gump*	1994
2	Cast Away	2000
3	Back to the Future	1985
4	Who Framed Roger Rabbit	1988
5	Back to the Future Part II	1989
6	What Lies Beneath	2000
7	The Polar Express	2004
8	Back to the Future Part III	1990
9	Contact	1997
10	Death Becomes Her	1992

* Won Academy Award for "Best Director"; movie won Academy Award for "Best Picture"

top 10 MOVIES DIRECTED BY **PETER WEIR**

FILM	YEAR
1 The Truman Show	1998
2 Dead Poets Society	1989
3 Master and Commander: The Far Side of the World	2003
4 Witness	1985
5 Green Card	1990
6 The Mosquito Coast	1986
7 The Year of Living Dangerously	1982
8 Fearless	1993
9 Gallipoli	1981
10 Picnic at Hanging Rock	1975

top 10 MOVIES DIRECTED BY **MARTIN SCORSESE**

FILM	YEAR
1 The Aviator	2004
2 Gangs of New York	2002
3 Cape Fear	1991
4 Casino	1995
5 The Color of Money	1986
6 Goodfellas	1990
7 The Age of Innocence	1993
8 Taxi Driver	1976
9 Raging Bull	1980
10 Bringing Out the Dead	1999

top 10 MOVIES DIRECTED BY **CLINT EASTWOOD**

FILM	YEAR
1 The Bridges of Madison County	1995
2 Million Dollar Baby*	2004
3 Unforgiven*	1992
4 Mystic River	2003
5 A Perfect World	1993
6 Space Cowboys	2000
7 Absolute Power	1997
8 The Rookie	1990
9 Sudden Impact	1983
10 Firefox	1982

* Won Academy Award for "Best Director"; film won Academy Award for "Best Picture"

⊙ **Commanding presence**
Fellow Australian Russell Crowe as Jack Aubrey in Peter Weir–directed *Master and Commander*.

top 10 MOVIES DIRECTED BY **WOMEN**

FILM	DIRECTOR	YEAR
1 Shrek*	Victoria Jenson#	2001
2 What Women Want	Nancy Meyers	2000
3 Deep Impact	Mimi Leder	1998
4 Look Who's Talking	Amy Heckerling	1989
5 Doctor Dolittle	Betty Thomas	1998
6 Bridget Jones's Diary	Sharon Maguire	2001
7 Something's Gotta Give	Nancy Meyers	2003
8 You've Got M@il	Nora Ephron	1998
9 Sleepless in Seattle	Nora Ephron	1993
10 The Prince of Egypt*	Brenda Chapman†	1998

* Animated

Co-director with Andrew Adamson

† Co-director with Steve Hickner and Simon Wells

Bridget Jones: The Edge of Reason (2004), directed by Beeban Kidron, the highest-earning movie by a British woman director, just fails to find a place in this Top 10. Kelly Asbury directed segments of *Shrek 2* (2004); if included, it would easily top this list.

Film Studios

A small group of studios once controlled the entire movie industry, owning all production facilities and acting as producers, distributors and, before the 1950s, through their ownership of theater chains, exhibitors. Some of the original studios no longer exist, while as a result of mergers and takeovers, most of the leading names are now components of large global media conglomerates operating alongside some newer independent studios, such as Artisan and Dimension, the specialist studio within Miramax. Today the studios are primarily financial and distribution organizations, with the actual production undertaken by independent production companies—often more than one may be involved in a coproduction. The movies listed here represent the Top 10 productions distributed by each of the major studios based on US revenue. In many instances, other companies acted as distributors outside the US.

top 10 STUDIOS 2004

STUDIO	MARKET SHARE (PERCENTAGE)	TOTAL US GROSS 2004 ($)
1 Sony	14.3	1,342,300,000
2 Warner Bros.	13.0	1,223,500,000
3 Buena Vista	12.4	1,165,700,000
4 DreamWorks	9.9	935,300,000
5 20th Century Fox	9.9	929,500,000
6 Universal	9.8	918,700,000
7 Paramount	6.8	635,100,000
8 New Line	4.5	418,800,000
9 Newmarket	4.3	406,700,000
10 Miramax	4.0	373,800,000

top 10 SONY MOVIES*

FILM	YEAR
1 Spider-Man	2002
2 Spider-Man 2	2004
3 Men in Black	1997
4 Ghostbusters	1984
5 Terminator 2: Judgment Day	1991
6 Men in Black II	2002
7 Tootsie	1982
8 Air Force One	1997
9 Big Daddy	1999
10 Jerry Maguire	1997

* Including Columbia and TriStar

top 10 20TH CENTURY FOX MOVIES

FILM	YEAR
1 Star Wars*	1977
2 Star Wars: Episode I—The Phantom Menace	1999
3 Star Wars: Episode II—Attack of the Clones	2002
4 Star Wars: Episode VI—Return of the Jedi	1983
5 Independence Day	1996
6 Star Wars: Episode V—The Empire Strikes Back	1980
7 Home Alone	1990
8 Cast Away	2000
9 Mrs. Doubtfire	1993
10 X2: X-Men United	2003

* Later retitled Star Wars: Episode IV—A New Hope

William Fox, a New York nickelodeon owner, founded a film production company in 1912. At his California studios he created a number of popular movies, pioneering the use of sound, especially through the medium of Fox Movietone newsreels. The company was merged with 20th Century Pictures in 1935, and under the control of Darryl F. Zanuck and Joseph M. Schenck achieved some of its greatest successes in the 1940s, later producing The Sound of Music (1965) and Star Wars (1977).

top 10 BUENA VISTA MOVIES

FILM*	YEAR
1 Pirates of the Caribbean: The Curse of the Black Pearl	2003
2 The Sixth Sense	1999
3 Signs	2002
4 Armageddon	1998
5 Pearl Harbor	2001
6 Pretty Woman	1990
7 Three Men and a Baby	1987
8 The Waterboy	1998
9 Who Framed Roger Rabbit	1988
10 The Santa Clause	1994

* Excluding animated Disney features

Following Walt Disney's death in 1966, a new management team launched the company in novel directions, establishing Touchstone Pictures, a production company concentrating on movies aimed at a more adult audience, with Buena Vista acting as the distributor for these and for Disney's animated films.

top 10 MIRAMAX MOVIES

FILM*	YEAR
1 Chicago	2002
2 Scary Movie	2000
3 Good Will Hunting	1997
4 Spy Kids	2001
5 Pulp Fiction	1994
6 Shakespeare in Love	1998
7 The Others	2001
8 Cold Mountain	2003
9 The Talented Mr. Ripley	1999
10 The English Patient	1996

* Excluding Dimension films

Founded in 1979 by brothers Harvey and Bob Weinstein, Miramax is a production and distribution company that has been part of the Walt Disney Company since 1993. It continues to operate as a major force, achieving both critical acclaim and commercial success for releases that might otherwise have been disregarded as "art films."

Pirate treasure
Pirates of the Caribbean is Buena Vista's most successful movie.

Funny money
DreamWorks' comedy *Meet the Fockers* is among its top earners.

top 10 DREAMWORKS MOVIES

FILM	YEAR
1 Shrek 2*	2004
2 Shrek*	2001
3 Saving Private Ryan	1998
4 Meet the Fockers	2004
5 Gladiator	2000
6 Meet the Parents	2000
7 Catch Me if You Can	2003
8 Shark Tale*	2004
9 What Lies Beneath	2000
10 American Beauty	1999

* Animated

Animation

⬆ **Just incredible** Disney's latest smash hit *The Incredibles* has earned some $628 million around the world.

top 10 ANIMATED FILM **OPENING WEEKENDS** IN THE US

FILM	US RELEASE	OPENING WEEKEND GROSS ($)
1 Shrek 2	May 19, 2004	108,037,878
2 The Incredibles	Nov. 5, 2004	70,467,623
3 Finding Nemo	May 30, 2003	70,251,710
4 Monsters, Inc.	Nov. 2, 2001	62,577,067
5 Toy Story 2*	Nov. 26, 1999	57,388,839
6 Shark Tale	Oct. 1, 2004	47,604,606
7 Ice Age	Mar. 15, 2002	46,312,454
8 Shrek	May 18, 2001	42,347,760
9 The Lion King	June 24, 1994	40,888,194
10 Dinosaur	May 19, 2000	38,854,851

* Second weekend; opening weekend release in limited number of theaters only

top 10 ANIMATED **FILM BUDGETS**

FILM	YEAR	BUDGET ($)
1 The Polar Express	2004	150,000,000
2 Tarzan	1999	145,000,000
3 Treasure Planet	2002	140,000,000
4 Final Fantasy: The Spirits Within	2001	137,000,000
5 Dinosaur	2000	128,000,000
6 Monsters, Inc.	2001	115,000,000
7 Home on the Range	2004	110,000,000
8 The Emperor's New Groove	2000	100,000,000
9 The Road to El Dorado	2000	95,000,000
10 Finding Nemo	2003	94,000,000

Animated film budgets have risen progressively since *Snow White and the Seven Dwarfs* (1937) set a then-record of $1.49 million. Budgets of $50 million or more have been commonplace since the 1990s, while *Tarzan* became the first to break through the $100 million barrier.

top 10 **WALT DISNEY** ANIMATED FEATURE FILMS

	FILM	YEAR
1	Finding Nemo	2003
2	The Lion King	1994
3	The Incredibles	2004
4	Monsters, Inc.	2001
5	Aladdin	1992
6	Toy Story 2	1999
7	Tarzan	1999
8	Beauty and the Beast	1991
9	A Bug's Life	1998
10	Toy Story	1995

Within just a month of its May 30, 2003 release, *Finding Nemo* had earned more than $256 million at the US box office, and has more than tripled that figure since its international release. In addition to these high-earners (all of which have earned over $350 million worldwide), some of the studio's earlier productions, including *Bambi* (1942) and *Snow White and the Seven Dwarfs* (1937), are close runners-up.

the 10 **LATEST OSCAR-WINNING** ANIMATED FILMS*

YEAR	FILM	DIRECTOR / COUNTRY
2004	Ryan	Chris Landreth, US
2003	Harvie Krumpet	Adam Elliot, Australia
2002	The ChubbChubbs!	Eric Armstrong, Canada
2001	For the Birds	Ralph Eggleston, US
2000	Father and Daughter	Michael Dudok de Wit, Netherlands
1999	The Old Man and the Sea	Aleksandr Petrov, US
1998	Bunny	Chris Wedge, US
1997	Geri's Game	Jan Pinkava, US
1996	Quest	Tyron Montgomery, UK
1995	Wallace & Gromit: A Close Shave	Nick Park, UK

* In the category "Short Films (Animated)"

Latest winner 14-minute short *Ryan* is the story of Canadian film animator Ryan Larkin, who won an Oscar in the same category for his *En Marchant* (1969).

⊙ **On the line**
Computer-animated DreamWorks movie *Shark Tale* has earned over $337 million.

top 10 **NON-DISNEY** ANIMATED FEATURE FILMS

	FILM	PRODUCTION COMPANY	YEAR
1	Shrek 2	DreamWorks	2004
2	Shrek	DreamWorks	2001
3	Ice Age	Fox Animation	2002
4	Shark Tale	DreamWorks	2004
5	Casper*	Amblin Entertainment	1995
6	The Polar Express	Castle Rock	2004
7	Spirited Away (Sento Chihiro no Kamikakushi)	Studio Ghibli	2001
8	Space Jam*	Warner Bros.	1996
9	Chicken Run	DreamWorks	2000
10	The Prince of Egypt	DreamWorks	1998

* Part animated, part live-action

Movie Mosts

top 10 COUNTRIES WITH MOST MOVIE THEATER ADMISSIONS PER CAPITA

COUNTRY	ADMISSIONS PER CAPITA, 2003
1 US	5.53
2 Iceland	5.40
3 Singapore	4.75
4 Ireland	4.56
5 New Zealand	4.49
6 Australia	4.45
7 Canada	3.83
8 Spain	3.43
9 India	3.15
10 Luxembourg	2.98
World average	*1.14*

top 10 MOVIE-GOING COUNTRIES (TOTAL)

COUNTRY	TOTAL ATTENDANCE, 2003
1 India	3,420,000,000
2 US	1,570,000,000
3 France	174,100,000
4 UK	167,200,000
5 Japan	162,300,000
6 Germany	149,000,000
7 Mexico	139,000,000
8 Spain	137,420,000
9 Canada	124,600,000
10 China	117,000,000
World	*7,261,070,000*

Source: Screen Digest

top 10 COUNTRIES WITH MOST MOVIE SCREENS

COUNTRY	SCREENS PER MILLION, 2003
1 Iceland	154.8
2 Sweden	130.8
3 US	126.1
4 Spain	106.1
5 Australia	94.6
6 France	89.2
7 Norway	88.5
8 Canada	86.6
9 Ireland	86.0
10 Malta	84.4
World average	*24.4*

Source: Screen Digest

top 10 MOVIE-PRODUCING COUNTRIES

	COUNTRY	FILMS PRODUCED, 2003
1	India	1,100
2	US	593
3	Japan	287
4	France	212
5	UK	175
6	China	140
7	Italy	117
8	Spain	110
9	Germany	107
10	Bangladesh	96

Source: *Screen Digest*

Based on the number of full-length feature films produced, Hollywood's "golden age" was the 1920s and 1930s, with a peak of 854 films made in 1921, and its nadir reached in 1978 with just 354.

⬅ **Hurray for Bollywood!**
The Indian film industry's output overtook that of Hollywood as early as 1954, and—50 years on—Bollywood produces almost twice as many feature films.

top 10 FILM BUDGETS

	FILM	YEAR	BUDGET ($)
1	The Chronicles of Narnia: The Lion, the Witch, and the Wardrobe	2005	216,000,000*
2	= Battle Angel	2007#	200,000,000
	= Spider-Man 2	2004	200,000,000
	= Titanic	1997	200,000,000
5	Troy	2004	185,000,000
6	Waterworld	1995	175,000,000
7	= Terminator 3: Rise of the Machines	2003	170,000,000
	= Wild, Wild West	1999	170,000,000
9	Van Helsing	2004	160,000,000
10	Pearl Harbor	2001	152,700,000

* Budget reputedly NZ$292 million

Scheduled release

Battle Angel is *Titanic* director James Cameron's latest blockbuster, a science-fiction epic based on a graphic novel and containing an unprecedented array of state-of-the art CGI effects.

TV & Radio Listings

top 10 PRIME-TIME PROGRAMS ON NETWORK TELEVISION, 2004

	PROGRAM TITLE*	DATE	%	AVERAGE VIEWERS TOTAL
1	Friends	May 6	42	52,462,000
2	CSI	Nov. 18	26	31,463,000
3	American Idol	Feb. 3	24	30,093,000
4	Apprentice	Apr. 15	25	28,047,000
5	Desperate Housewives	Nov. 28	21	27,240,000
6	ER	May 13	23	23,882,000
7	Survivor: All-Stars	Mar. 4	21	23,304,000
8	CSI: Miami	Sept. 20	21	22,455,000
9	Without a Trace	Nov. 4	21	21,774,000
10	Will & Grace	Apr. 29	21	20,527,000

* Excluding sports; highest-ranked screening only listed

Source: Nielsen Media Research

Final episodes of long-running comedy series commonly attract record audiences, and after its 10-year run, *Friends* was no exception, being out-viewed only by *M*A*S*H* (1983, 109 million viewers in 50.15 million homes), *Cheers* (1993, 80.4 million viewers), and *Seinfeld* (1998, 76.3 million viewers).

top 10 TV AUDIENCES IN THE US

	PROGRAM / DATE	AUDIENCE (HOUSEHOLDS)	(%)
1	M*A*S*H Special, Feb. 28, 1983	50,150,000	60.2
2	Dallas, Nov. 21, 1980	41,470,000	53.3
3	Roots Part 8, Jan. 30, 1977	36,380,000	51.1
4	Super Bowl XVI, Jan. 24, 1982	40,020,000	49.1
5	Super Bowl XVII, Jan. 30, 1983	40,480,000	48.6
6	XVII Winter Olympics, Feb. 23, 1994	45,690,000	48.5
7	Super Bowl XX, Jan. 26, 1986	41,490,000	48.3
8	Gone With the Wind Pt.1, Nov. 7, 1976	33,960,000	47.7
9	Gone With the Wind Pt.2, Nov. 8, 1976	33,750,000	47.4
10	Super Bowl XII, Jan. 15, 1978	34,410,000	47.2

Source: Nielsen Media Research

Historically, as more households acquired television sets (there are currently 108.4 million "TV households" in the US), audiences generally increased. However, the rise in channel choice and the use of VCRs has somewhat checked this trend. Listing the Top 10 according to percentage of households viewing provides a clearer picture of who watches what.

top 10 RADIO FORMATS IN THE US

	FORMAT	NO. OF STATIONS	AUDIENCE SHARE (%)
1	News/talk/information	2,179	15.9
2	Country	2,066	13.2
3	Adult contemporary	1,556	12.8
4	Contemporary hit radio	569	10.3
5	Rock	869	9.0
6	Urban	352	7.6
7	Oldies	1,060	7.1
8	Spanish	750	6.4
9	Religious	2,014	5.5
10	Alternative	454	4.0

Source: Arbitron, *Radio Today 2005*

top 10 RADIO-OWNING COUNTRIES

	COUNTRY	RADIOS PER 1,000 POPULATION, 2001
1	Norway	3,324
2	Sweden	2,811
3	USA	2,117
4	Australia	1,999
5	Finland	1,624
6	UK	1,446
7	Denmark	1,400
8	Estonia	1,136
9	Canada	1,047
10	South Korea	1,034
	World average	*419*

Source: World Bank, *World Development Indicators 2003*

top 10 **SATELLITE** TELEVISION COUNTRIES

COUNTRY	HOME SATELLITE ANTENNAE 2002 (% OF TV-OWNING HOMES)
1 **Algeria**	92.2
2 **Palestine**	86.1
3 **Burkina Faso**	83.3
4 **Bahrain**	65.3
5 **Saudi Arabia**	64.3
6 **Austria**	48.0
7 **Lebanon**	45.0
8 **Syria**	44.8
9 **Slovenia**	43.5
10 **Jordan**	40.1
US	*16.8*
World	*14.6*

Source: International Telecommunication Union, *World Telecommunication Development Report 2003*

➔ Satellite country

Algeria has adopted satellite TV with unrivaled enthusiasm, as the proliferation of receivers on this typical Algiers apartment building testifies.

top 10 **TV-OWNING** COUNTRIES

COUNTRY	TVS PER 1,000 POPULATION, 2000
1 **Qatar**	869
2 **USA**	854
3 **Denmark**	807
4 **Latvia**	789
5 **Australia**	738
6 **Japan**	725
7 **Canada**	715
8 **Finland**	692
9 **Norway**	669
10 **UK**	653
World average	*270*

Source: International Telecommunication Union, *World Telecommunication Development Report 2002*

DVD & Video

⊕ **Monster hit** The DVD release of *Shrek 2* mirrored the popularity of the movie release, and earned almost twice as much as *Shrek*.

top 10 VHS RENTALS IN THE US, 2004

TITLE	VHS RENTAL, REVENUE 2004 ($)
1 Open Range	18,150,000
2 Out of Time	17,860,000
3 Radio	17,090,000
4 Cheaper by the Dozen	16,940,000
5 Something's Gotta Give	16,210,000
6 Mystic River	16,160,000
7 American Wedding	15,850,000
8 Secondhand Lions	15,450,000
9 School of Rock	15,110,000
10 The Day After Tomorrow	15,080,000

Source: Rentrak Home Video Essentials/ *Video Business*

VHS rentals have experienced a marked decline in the face of competition from DVD, as reflected in the relatively lower level of earnings generated by them.

TOP 10 BESTSELLING DVDS IN THE US, 2004

TITLE	DVD SALES, 2004 ($)
1 Shrek 2	316,000,000
2 Lord of the Rings: Return of the King (all editions)	257,000,000
3 Star Wars Trilogy	215,000,000
4 The Passion of the Christ	189,000,000
5 Harry Potter and the Prisoner of Azkaban	171,000,000
6 Spider-Man 2	162,000,000
7 Matrix Revolutions	116,000,000
8 Elf	114,000,000
9 Lion King 1 ½	113,000,000
10 Brother Bear	112,000,000

Source: *Video Business*

top 10 DVD RENTALS IN THE US, 2004

TITLE	DVD RENTAL, REVENUE 2004 ($)
1 The Day After Tomorrow	52,280,000
2 Man on Fire	52,010,000
3 Mystic River	50,780,000
4 50 First Dates	50,670,000
5 The Butterfly Effect	47,420,000
6 Along Came Polly	44,370,000
7 The Last Samurai	44,150,000
8 Secret Window	43,470,000
9 Cold Mountain	41,840,000
10 Radio	41,010,000

Source: Rentrak Home Video Essentials/ *Video Business*

The DVD rental income of *The Day After Tomorrow* was equivalent to 28 percent of the movie's US box office income.

top 10 VIDEO GAMES IN THE US, 2004*

GAME / PLATFORM

 Grand Theft Auto: San Andreas
Playstation 2

 Halo 2
Xbox

 Madden NFL 2005
Playstation 2

 ESPN NFL 2K5
Playstation 2

 Need for Speed: Underground 2
Playstation 2

 Pokémon Fire Red
(with free wireless adaptor), Nintendo

 NBA Live 2005
Playstation 2

 Spiderman: The Movie 2
Playstation 2

Halo
Xbox

ESPN NFL 2K5
Xbox

* Ranked by units sold

Source: The NPD Group/NPD Funworld®/Point-of-sale

⬆ Game winners
The global success of video game *Grand Theft Auto: San Andreas* owes much to its movie-based style, featuring the images and voices of real stars, including Ice-T and Samuel L. Jackson.

top 10 BESTSELLING DVDS IN THE US

TITLE	YEAR*	REVENUE ($)#
1 **Finding Nemo**	2003	320,400,000
2 **Shrek 2**	2004	316,000,000
3 **The Lord of the Rings: The Two Towers**	2003	280,500,000
4 **The Lord of the Rings: The Fellowship of the Ring**	2002	257,300,000
5 **The Lord of the Rings: The Return of the King**	2004	257,000,000
6 **Pirates of the Caribbean: The Curse of the Black Pearl**	2003	235,300,000
7 **Spider-Man**	2002	215,300,000
8 **Star Wars trilogy**	2004	215,000,000
9 **Monsters, Inc.**	2002	202,000,000
10 **The Passion of the Christ**	2004	189,000,000

* Of DVD release   # In release year

Chapter

789101

the 10 countries
consuming the most
energy: page 182

123456

Commercial World

top 10 richest countries: page 169

BANQUE

Workers

top 10 **COMPANIES** WITH THE MOST WORKERS

COMPANY / BASE	INDUSTRY	EMPLOYEES*
1 **Wal-Mart Stores**, US	Retail	1,400,000
2 **PetroChina**, China	Oil and gas	422,554
3 **China Petroleum and Chemical**, China	Oil and gas	418,871
4 **Siemens**, Germany	Conglomerates	417,000
5 **McDonald's**, US	Fast food restaurants	413,000
6 **Carrefour**, France	Food markets	396,662
7 **DaimlerChrysler**, Germany	Automotive	370,677
8 **United Parcel Service**, US	Transportation	360,000
9 **Ford Motor**, US	Automotive	350,321
10 **General Motors**, US	Automotive	350,000

* As of Feb. 13, 2004

Source: *Forbes 2000*

This list excludes public-sector organizations and hence discounts the 1.6 million employed by the Indian railroad network, the 1.3 million who work for the British National Health Service, and the almost 800,000 employees of the US Postal Service.

top 10 **COUNTRIES** WITH THE MOST WORKERS

COUNTRY	WORKERS*, 2004 EST.
1 **China**	778,100,000
2 **India**	472,000,000
3 **US**	146,500,000
4 **Indonesia**	105,700,000
5 **Brazil**	82,590,000
6 **Russia**	71,680,000
7 **Japan**	66,660,000
8 **Bangladesh**	64,020,000
9 **Nigeria**	54,360,000
10 **Vietnam**	45,740,000

* Based on people aged 15–64 who are currently employed; unpaid groups are not included

Source: Central Intelligence Agency

The International Labor Organization defines the "labor force" as people between the ages of 15 and 64 who are currently employed (excluding unpaid groups) or unemployed but seeking employment. In practice, it is difficult to count the unemployed accurately, especially in developing countries, so it may be just as difficult to know who is fully employed.

↓ Labor intensive
China is able to call on the world's largest labor force as it progressively modernizes its outdated factories and production lines.

Work force

Almost half the total world population—some 3 billion people in total—are identified as economically productive workers. .

top 10 COUNTRIES WITH LOWEST PROPORTION OF ELDERLY PEOPLE AT WORK

	COUNTRY	EST. PERCENTAGE OF OVER-74-YEAR-OLDS ECONOMICALLY ACTIVE*
1	Spain	0.2
2	Slovakia	0.4
3	France	0.5
4	Belgium	0.6
5	Germany	0.9
6	= Lithuania	1.1
	= Netherlands	1.1
8	Greece	1.2
9	Italy	1.4
10	Latvia	1.5
	US	5.8

* Excludes unpaid work; 2003 or latest for which data are available (some countries excluded because data are not collected for this age group)

Source: International Labor Organization

the 10 COUNTRIES WITH HIGHEST PROPORTION OF ELDERLY PEOPLE AT WORK

	COUNTRY	EST. PERCENTAGE OF OVER-74-YEAR-OLDS ECONOMICALLY ACTIVE*
1	Malawi	84.2
2	Ghana	52.9
3	Madagascar	52.1
4	Philippines	42.4
5	Papua New Guinea	40.5
6	Sudan	39.6
7	Rwanda	38.6
8	Dominican Republic	35.9
9	Bolivia	35.1
10	Georgia	31.7

* Excludes unpaid work; 2003 or latest for which data are available (some countries excluded because data are not collected for this age group)

Source: International Labor Organization

Cross-country comparisons of workers in terms of their ages are difficult because methods of collecting data vary from country to country.

top 10 COUNTRIES WITH THE HIGHEST PROPORTION OF CHILD WORKERS

	COUNTRY	PERCENTAGE OF 10–14-YEAR-OLDS AT WORK*, 2000
1	Mali	51.14
2	Bhutan	51.10
3	Burundi	48.50
4	Uganda	43.79
5	Niger	43.62
6	Burkina Faso	43.45
7	Ethiopia	42.45
8	Nepal	42.05
9	Rwanda	41.35
10	Kenya	39.15
	World average	11.24

* Excludes unpaid work

Source: International Labor Organization (ILO)

The ILO's International Program on the Elimination of Child Labor (IPEC) estimates that some 29 percent of children in Africa and 19 percent in Asia are working.

The Global Economy

top 10 **AID** DONORS

COUNTRY	NET ODA*, 2004 (% OF GNI#)	NET ODA*, 2004 (TOTAL, $)
1 US	0.16	18,999,000,000
2 Japan	0.19	8,859,000,000
3 France	0.42	8,475,000,000
4 UK	0.36	7,836,000,000
5 Germany	0.28	7,497,000,000
6 Netherlands	0.74	4,235,000,000
7 Sweden	0.77	2,704,000,000
8 Spain	0.26	2,547,000,000
9 Canada	0.26	2,537,000,000
10 Italy	0.15	2,484,000,000

* ODA = Official Development Assistance

GNI = Gross National Income

Source: Organization for Economic Co-operation and Development (OECD)

The amounts the 30 full members of the OECD give in aid ranges in terms both of overall totals and as a percentage of each country's Gross National Income: Italy's and the US's contributions are the lowest and Norway (which provided $2.2 billion in 2004) the highest at 0.87 percent.

the 10 COUNTRIES **MOST IN DEBT**

COUNTRY	EXTERNAL DEBT, 2002 (TOTAL, $)	EXTERNAL DEBT, 2002 (% OF GNI*)
1 Congo	5,152,000,000	228
2 Dem. Rep. of Congo	8,726,000,000	171
3 Zambia	5,969,000,000	127
4 Angola	10,134,000,000	120
5 Syria	21,504,000,000	117
6 Burundi	1,204,000,000	110
7 Sierra Leone	1,448,000,000	103
8 = Lebanon	17,077,000,000	102
= Serbia and Montenegro	12,688,000,000	102
10 Ecuador	16,452,000,000	95

* GNI = Gross National Income

Source: World Bank, *World Development Indicators 2005*

Expressed as a percentage of their gross national income, these countries stand out, but in terms of total external debt (the amount owed to foreign agencies, rather than their domestic banking sector), certain countries have even higher levels, among them Brazil at $228 billion; China, $168 billion; Russia, $147 billion; and Mexico, $141 billion.

⊕ US aid

Workers unload food aid destined for Afghanistan. The country was ranked 9th among US aid recipients at $427 million in 2003, compared with No. 1 recipient Egypt's $831 million in assistance.

top 10 FASTEST-GROWING ECONOMIES

	COUNTRY	GDP* PER CAPITA, 2002 ($)	ANNUAL GROWTH RATE, 1990–2002 (%)
1	Equatorial Guinea	4,394	20.8
2	Bosnia and Herzegovina	1,362	18.0
3	China	989	8.6
4	Ireland	30,982	6.8
5	Albania	1,535	6.0
6	Vietnam	436	5.9
7 =	Maldives	2,182	4.7
=	South Korea	10,006	4.7
9	Mozambique	195	4.5
10	Chile	4,115	4.4
	US	*36,006*	
	World average	*5,174*	*1.2*

* GDP = Gross Domestic Product

Source: United Nations, *Human Development Indicators 2004*

top 10 AREAS OF US FEDERAL GOVERNMENT EXPENDITURE

	AREA OF EXPENDITURE	ESTIMATED EXPENDITURE 2004 ($)
1	Social security	496,200,000,000
2	National defense	453,700,000,000
3	Income security	339,500,000,000
4	Medicare	270,500,000,000
5	Health	243,500,000,000
6	Net interest	156,300,000,000
7	Education, training, employment, and social services	87,200,000,000
8	Transportation	68,100,000,000
9	Veterans' benefits and services	60,500,000,000
10	Administration of justice	41,600,000,000

Source: US Office of Management and Budget

the 10 POOREST COUNTRIES

	COUNTRY	GDP* PER CAPITA, 2002 ($)
1	Sierra Leone	520
2 =	Tanzania	580
=	Malawi	580
4	Burundi	630
5	Dem. Rep. of Congo	650
6	Guinea-Bissau	710
7	Madagascar	740
8	Ethiopia	780
9	Niger	800
10	Zambia	840

* GDP = Gross Domestic Product

Source: United Nations, *Human Development Indicators 2004*

First Fact The first credit card was issued in 1950 in the US by Diners Club, the brainchild of Frank X. McNamara. Initially, just 200 cards were issued, allowing holders to use them to pay for meals in 14 New York restaurants. Within a year, the numbers had expanded to 20,000 customers and 1,000 restaurants.

top 10 RICHEST COUNTRIES

	COUNTRY	GDP* PER CAPITA, 2002 ($)
1	Luxembourg	47,354
2	Norway	41,974
3	Switzerland	36,687
4	US	36,006
5	Denmark	32,179
6	Japan	31,407
7	Ireland	30,982
8	Iceland	29,749
9	Qatar	28,634
10	Sweden	26,929
	World average	*5,174*

* GDP = Gross Domestic Product

Source: United Nations, *Human Development Indicators 2004*

➔ De Luxe
Despite being one of the world's smallest countries, Luxembourg enjoys enviable economic prosperity.

Personal Wealth

top 10 RICHEST AMERICANS

	NAME	SOURCE	NET WORTH ($)
1	Bill Gates	Microsoft	46,500,000,000
2	Warren Buffett	Berkshire Hathaway	44,000,000,000
3	Paul Allen	Microsoft	21,000,000,000
4	Larry Ellison	Oracle	18,400,000,000
5	S. Robson Walton	Wal-Mart	18,300,000,000
6 =	Jim C. Walton	Wal-Mart	18,200,000,000
=	John T. Walton	Wal-Mart	18,200,000,000
8 =	Alice L. Walton	Wal-Mart	18,000,000,000
=	Helen R. Walton	Wal-Mart	18,000,000,000
10	Michael Dell	Dell	16,000,000,000

Source: *Forbes Billionaires List 2005*

The estimated net worth of the world's richest man, William Henry (Bill) Gates III, the cofounder of Microsoft, has increased by a factor of 18.6 since he entered the Top 10 in 1990 with assets of "only" $2.5 billion. The Bill & Melinda Gates Foundation, which Gates set up in 2000 with his wife, provides over $1 billion a year to healthcare and other causes, especially in the developing world.

top 10 HIGHEST-EARNING DEAD CELEBRITIES

	CELEBRITY	PROFESSION	EARNINGS* ($)
1	Elvis Presley	Musician	40,000,000
2	Charles M. Schultz	"Peanuts" cartoonist	35,000,000
3	J. R. R. Tolkien	Author	23,000,000
4	John Lennon	Musician	21,000,000
5	Theodor "Dr. Seuss" Geisel	Author	18,000,000
6	Marilyn Monroe	Actress	8,000,000
7 =	Irving Berlin	Songwriter	7,000,000
=	George Harrison	Musician	7,000,000
=	Bob Marley	Musician	7,000,000
10	Richard Rodgers	Songwriter	6,500,000

* 2003–04 financial year

Source: *Forbes, Top-Earning Dead Celebrities,* 2004

Through the sales of their work or image and licensing in a range of media and merchandise, the continuing earning power of an élite group of deceased celebrities means that some are arguably worth more dead than alive.

top 10 HIGHEST-EARNING CELEBRITIES

	CELEBRITY	PROFESSION	EARNINGS* ($)
1 =	Mel Gibson	Film producer/director	210,000,000
=	Oprah Winfrey	Talk show host/producer	210,000,000
3	J. K. Rowling	Author	147,000,000
4 =	Michael Schumacher	Racing driver	80,000,000
=	Tiger Woods	Golfer	80,000,000
6	Steven Spielberg	Film producer/director	75,000,000
7	Jim Carrey	Actor	66,000,000
8	Bruce Springsteen	Musician	64,000,000
9	Nora Roberts (J. D. Robb)	Author	60,000,000
10	David Copperfield	Magician	57,000,000

* June 2003–June 2004

Source: *Forbes, The Celebrity 100,* 2004

◉ Mel's wealth
Mel Gibson has long figured prominently in the celebrity earnings league table, but the huge success of *The Passion of The Christ* (2004), which he directed, propelled him to the top alongside Oprah Winfrey, who has headed the list for many years.

top 10 RICHEST **NON-AMERICANS**

NAME / COUNTRY	SOURCE	NET WORTH ($)
1 **Lakshmi Mittal**, India	Steel	25,000,000,000
2 **Carlos Slim Helu**, Mexico	Telecom	23,800,000,000
3 **Prince Alwaleed Bin Talal Alsaud**, Saudi Arabia	Investments	23,700,000,000
4 **Ingvar Kamprad**, Sweden	Ikea	23,000,000,000
5 **Karl Albrecht**, Germany	Retail	18,500,000,000
6 **Kenneth Thomson and family**, Canada	Publishing	17,900,000,000
7 **Liliane Bettencourt**, France	L'Oréal	17,200,000,000
8 **Bernard Arnault**, France	LVMH	17,000,000,000
9 **Theo Albrecht**, Germany	Retail	15,500,000,000
10 **Roman Abramovich**, Russia	Oil	13,300,000,000

Source: *Forbes Billionaires List 2005*

First Fact John D. Rockefeller (1839–1937) was the first-ever billionaire. From modest beginnings, he founded Standard Oil (Esso) and became the world's richest man. Despite giving away over $500 million during his lifetime, at his death Rockefeller was thought to be worth $1.4 billion, the equivalent to 1/65th of the entire Gross National Income of the US. In modern money, such a proportion of the US's GNI would be worth some $200 billion, dwarfing the fortunes of today's mega-rich.

top 10 RICHEST **RUSSIANS**

NAME	SOURCE	NET WORTH ($)
1 **Roman Abramovich**	Oil	13,300,000,000
2 = **Mikhail Fridman**	Oil, banking	7,000,000,000
= **Vladimir Lisin**	Steel	7,000,000,000
4 **Oleg Deripaska**	Manufacturing	5,500,000,000
5 **Viktor Vekselberg**	Oil, metals	5,000,000,000
6 **Alexei Mordashov**	Steel	4,800,000,000
7 = **Vladimir Potanin**	Metals	4,400,000,000
= **Mikhail Prokhorov**	Metals	4,400,000,000
9 **Vagit Alekperov**	Oil	4,300,000,000
10 **Victor Rashnikov**	Iron, steel	3,600,000,000

Source: *Forbes Billionaires List 2005*

Since the collapse of the Soviet Union and the privatization of its industries, a new breed of Russian oligarchs has emerged. Several of these multibillionaires, including Abramovich, Deripaska, and Mordahshov, are under age 40.

● Roman emperor
The oil and other business interests of Roman Abramovich have made him the richest Russian and the 21st richest person in the world.

Diamonds & Gold

top 10 GOLD-PRODUCING COUNTRIES

COUNTRY	2003 PRODUCTION (TROY OUNCES)	(TONS)
1 South Africa	13,316,820	414.2
2 USA	10,108,180	314.4
3 Australia	10,050,308	312.6
4 China	7,552,199	234.9
5 Russia	6,462,290	201.0
6 Peru	6,082,912	189.2
7 Indonesia	5,764,620	179.3
8 Canada	2,835,691	88.2
10 Ghana	2,491,679	77.5
World	*91,828,829*	*2,856.2*

Source: Gold Fields Mineral Services Ltd., Gold Survey 2004

As reported by Gold Fields Mineral Services Ltd., output by world-dominating gold producer South Africa experienced a decline for the tenth consecutive year since its 1993 all-time high of 682.9 tons. Australia's output increased again in 2003 for the first time since 1999: the country's record annual production had stood at 131.2 tons since 1903, but in 1988 rocketed to 167.6 tons, peaking at 345.2 tons in 1997.

top 10 COUNTRIES WITH THE MOST GOLD

COUNTRY	GOLD RESERVES* (TROY OUNCES)	(TONS)
1 USA	261,584,525	8,968.6
2 Germany	110,389,783	3,784.5
3 France	95,738,354	3,282.5
4 Italy	78,827,086	2,702.6
5 Switzerland	42,827,947	1,468.4
6 Netherlands	24,675,662	846.0
7 Japan	24,601,715	843.5
8 China	19,290,420	661.4
9 Spain	16,824,461	576.8
10 Portugal	14,863,268	509.6

* As at March 2005

Source: World Gold Council

Gold reserves are the government holdings of gold in each country – which are often far greater than the gold owned by private individuals. In the days of the "Gold Standard", this provided a tangible measure of a country's wealth, guaranteeing the convertibility of its currency, and determined such factors as exchange rates. Though less significant today, gold reserves remain a component in calculating a country's international reserves, alongside its holdings of foreign exchange and SDRs (Special Drawing Rights).

top 10 DIAMOND PRODUCERS BY VOLUME

COUNTRY	VALUE, 2003 ($)	VOLUME, 2003 (CARATS)
1 Australia	417,000,000	30,994,000
2 Botswana	2,489,000,000	30,412,000
3 Dem. Rep. of Congo	686,000,000	29,000,000
4 Russia	1,600,000,000	19,000,000
5 South Africa	1,100,000,000	12,400,000
6 Canada	1,240,000,000	11,200,000
7 Angola	1,100,000,000	6,300,000
8 Namibia	474,000,000	1,550,000
9 Ghana	23,000,000	900,000
10 Brazil	83,000,000	700,000

Source: De Beers

top 10 **MOST EXPENSIVE** SINGLE DIAMONDS*

DIAMOND / DETAILS	SALE	PRICE
1 **Star of the Season**, pear-shaped 100.10 carat D[#] IF[†] diamond	Sotheby's, Geneva, May 17, 1995	$16,548,750 (SF19,858,500)
2 **The Mouawad Splendor**, pear-shaped 101.84 carat D[#] IF[†] diamond	Sotheby's, Geneva, Nov. 14, 1990	$12,760,000 (SF15,950,000)
3 **Star of Happiness**, cut-cornered rectangular-cut 36 carat D[#] IF[†]	Sotheby's, Geneva, Nov. 17, 1993	$11,882,333 (SF17,883,500)
4 **Fancy blue emerald-cut** 20.17 carat diamond VS2[†]	Sotheby's, New York, Oct. 18, 1994	$9,902,500
5 **Eternal Light**, pear-shaped 85.91 carat D[#] IF[†] diamond	Sotheby's, New York, Apr. 19, 1988	$9,130,000
6 **Rectangular-cut fancy deep-blue** 13.49 carat diamond IF[†]	Christie's, New York, Apr. 13, 1995	$7,482,500
7 **Rectangular-cut** 52.59 carat D[#] IF[†] diamond	Christie's, New York, Apr. 20, 1985	$7,480,000
8 **Fancy pink rectangular-cut** 19.66 carat diamond VVS2[†]	Christie's, Geneva, Nov. 17, 1994	$7,421,318 (SF9,573,500)
9 **The Jeddah Bride**, rectangular-cut 80.02 carat D[#] IF[†] diamond	Sotheby's, New York, Oct. 24, 1991	$7,150,000
10 **The Agra Diamond**, fancy light pink cushion-shaped 32.24 carat diamond VS1[†]	Christie's, London, June 20, 1990	$6,959,700 (£4,070,000)

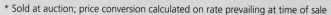

* Sold at auction; price conversion calculated on rate prevailing at time of sale

[#] A color grade given to a diamond for its whiteness, D being the highest grade

[†] A clarity grade, which gives the relative position of a diamond on a flawless-to-imperfect scale: IF = internally flawless, VS = very slightly flawed, VVS = very, very slightly flawed; the numbers indicate the degree of the flaw

Saudi jeweler Sheikh Ahmed Hassan Fitaihi, also the owner of the Jeddah Bride (named after his home town) at No. 8, fought off competing buyers to establish a new world record with his acquisition of the flawless Star of the Season, and has since declined even higher private offers for the unique gem. The 100.10-carat diamond weighs only 8 carats less than the famed Koh-I-Noor of the British Crown Jewels, and is one of few diamonds of over 100 carats ever to be auctioned.

Fast Fact

The Cullinan diamond—the largest ever discovered—was found by Frederick Wells in 1905 at the Premier Mine, South Africa and named after Sir Thomas Cullinan, the president of diamond company De Beers. About 5 inches (12.7 cm) across and weighing 3,106 carats, it was presented to King Edward VII on his 66th birthday in 1907 and the following year was cut by Dutch expert Joseph Asscher, producing 105 separate gems. The most important of these are now among the British Crown Jewels and include the 530.2-carat Great Star of Africa—the largest cut diamond in the world—which is mounted in the royal scepter, and the 317.40-carat Second Star of Africa, set in the Imperial State Crown beneath the Black Prince's Ruby.

top 10 COUNTRIES THAT
SPEND THE MOST
ON ADVERTISING

COUNTRY / EST. EXPENDITURE, 2004*

($)

1 **US** $155,000,000,000   **2** *Japan* $37,000,000,000

3 **China** $23,000,000,000

4 **GERMANY** $19,000,000,000   **5** **UK** $14,000,000,000

6 *France* $11,000,000,000   **7** **Italy** $8,000,000,000

8 = **Canada** $6,000,000,000   = **Spain** $6,000,000,000

10 = **AUSTRALIA** $5,000,000,000

= *Brazil* $5,000,000,000

* BY FORECAST ADVERTISING EXPENDITURE
SOURCE: *INITIATIVE GLOBAL ADEX 2004*

top 10 COUNTRIES IN WHICH COCA-COLA IS THE TOP COLA BRAND

COUNTRY	PERCENTAGE OF TOTAL STANDARD COLA MARKET
1 Morocco	86.5
2 Indonesia	86.3
3 Bulgaria	81.3
4 Greece	77.4
5 Chile	76.2
6 Brazil	75.2
7 Mexico	73.7
8 Singapore	72.2
9 Japan	69.5
10 France	65.2
US	*27.7*
World average	*46.2*

Source: Euromonitor

top 10 WORLD RETAIL SECTORS

SECTOR	NO. OF COMPANIES*
1 Specialty	108
2 Supermarket	96
3 Department	56
4 Convenience	50
5 Discount	48
6 Superstore	40
7 Hypermarket	37
8 Cash and carry	25
9 Drug	23
10 Home improvement	22

* Of those listed in *Stores' Top 250 Global Retailers*; stores can operate in more than one area

Source: *Stores* magazine

➲ Great Wal-Mart of China
In 1996, American retail giant Wal-Mart opened its first store in China, in Shenzen. By 2004, its sales in China were $917.75 million, and by March 2005 it had opened 44 outlets.

TOP 10 **MOST VALUABLE** GLOBAL BRANDS

BRAND NAME / COUNTRY OF OWNERSHIP*	INDUSTRY	BRAND VALUE 2004 ($)
1 **Coca-Cola**	Beverages	67,394,000,000
2 **Microsoft**	Technology	61,372,000,000
3 **IBM**	Technology	53,791,000,000
4 **General Electric**	Diversified	44,111,000,000
5 **Intel**	Technology	33,499,000,000
6 **Disney**	Leisure	27,113,000,000
7 **McDonald's**	Food retail	25,001,000,000
8 **Nokia**, Finland	Technology	24,041,000,000
9 **Toyota**, Japan	Automobiles	22,673,000,000
10 **Marlboro**	Tobacco	22,128,000,000

* All US-owned unless otherwise stated

Source: Interbrand/*BusinessWeek*

Brand consultants Interbrand use a method of estimating

Food

top 10 EGG CONSUMERS

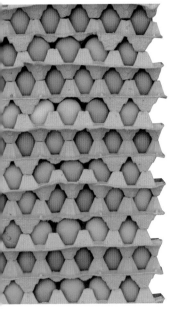

COUNTRY	AVERAGE CONSUMPTION PER CAPITA, 2002 (LB / OZ)		(KG)
1 Japan	42	1	19.1
2 China	38	5	17.4
3 Hungary	37	7	17.0
4 Denmark	36	2	16.4
5 Brunei	35	14	16.3
6 Mexico	35	4	16.0
7 Netherlands	34	6	15.6
8 France	33	11	15.3
9 US	32	2	14.6
10 Spain	31	8	14.3
World average	*18*	*8*	*8.4*

Source: Food and Agriculture Organization of the United Nations

top 10 VEGETABLE CONSUMERS

COUNTRY	AVERAGE CONSUMPTION PER CAPITA, 2002 (LB / OZ)		(KG)
1 Cuba	587	12	266.6
2 China	560	3	254.1
3 Greece	541	3	245.5
4 Israel	502	3	227.8
5 Turkey	494	7	224.3
6 Lebanon	494	0	224.1
7 Libya	491	6	222.9
8 United Arab Emirates	479	15	217.7
9 Macedonia	474	10	215.3
10 South Korea	461	3	209.2
US	*281*	*8*	*127.7*
World average	*251*	*8*	*114.1*

Source: Food and Agriculture Organization of the United Nations

top 10 MEAT CONSUMERS

COUNTRY	AVERAGE CONSUMPTION PER CAPITA, 2002 (LB / OZ)		(KG)
1 US	273	9	124.1
2 Spain	261	3	118.5
3 Denmark	251	8	114.1
4 Austria	245	2	111.2
5 = Australia	239	13	108.8
= Mongolia	239	13	108.8
7 New Zealand	235	3	106.7
8 Cyprus	229	8	104.1
9 France	225	8	102.3
10 Canada	221	9	100.5
World average	*86*	*10*	*39.3*

Source: Food and Agriculture Organization of the United Nations

top 10 FISH CONSUMERS

COUNTRY	AVERAGE CONSUMPTION PER CAPITA*, 2002 (LB / OZ)		(KG)
1 Maldives	409	13	185.9
2 Samoa	201	15	91.6
3 Iceland	200	9	91.0
4 Kiribati	165	12	75.2
5 Japan	146	2	66.3
6 Seychelles	136	10	62.0
7 Lithuania	131	13	59.8
8 Portugal	130	11	59.3
9 South Korea	129	6	58.7
10 Malaysia	125	10	57.0
US	*46*	*15*	*21.3*
World average	*35*	*14*	*16.3*

* Marine only

Source: Food and Agriculture Organization of the United Nations

The majority of the fish consumed comes from the sea. The average annual consumption of freshwater fish is 10 lb 5 oz (4.7 kg), with the largest consumers being Norway, whose population consume 57 lb 5 oz (26 kg) of freshwater fish per person per year.

top 10 FOODS CONSUMED IN THE US*

ITEM / AVERAGE CONSUMPTION
PER CAPITA, 2003 (LB / OZ / KG)

1

Milk and cream
205 lb 4 oz / 93.1 kg

2

Meat 199 lb 6 oz / 90.4 kg
(red meat 111 lb 14 oz / 50.7 kg)

3

= Fresh vegetables (excl. potatoes)
148 lb 3 oz / 67.2 kg

= Processed fruit 148 lb 3 oz / 67.2 kg

Sweeteners 141 lb 11 oz / 64.2 kg
(sugar 61 lb 1 oz / 27.7 kg#)

Potatoes (fresh and processed)
138 lb 8 oz / 62.8 kg

Wheat flour and flour products
137 lb 14 oz / 62.5 kg

Processed vegetables (excl. potatoes)
129 lb 1 oz / 58.5 kg

Fresh fruit 126 lb 11 oz / 57.4 kg

Fats 87 lb 14 oz / 39.8 kg

* By weight

Excludes sugar imported in blends and mixtures

Source: US Department of Agriculture,
Economic Research Service

top 10 BREAKFAST CEREAL CONSUMERS

COUNTRY	AVERAGE CONSUMPTION PER CAPITA, 2004		
	(LB / OZ)		(KG)
1 UK	17	10	8.0
2 Sweden	16	15	7.7
3 Australia	16	8	7.5
4 Finland	14	12	6.7
5 Canada	13	7	6.1
6 Ireland	12	5	5.6
7 US	11	14	5.4
8 New Zealand	11	0	5.0
9 Denmark	8	6	3.8
10 Norway	8	2	3.7

Source: Euromonitor

top 10 RICE CONSUMERS

COUNTRY	AVERAGE CONSUMPTION PER CAPITA*, 2002		
	(LB / OZ)		(KG)
1 Myanmar	676	9	306.9
2 Vietnam	558	6	253.3
3 Laos	554	7	251.5
4 Bangladesh	541	0	245.4
5 Cambodia	492	1	223.2
6 Indonesia	490	11	222.6
7 Philippines	345	10	156.8
8 Thailand	339	1	153.8
9 Nepal	336	13	152.8
10 Madagascar	315	7	143.1
US	*31*	*1*	*14.1*
World average	*189*	*6*	*85.9*

* Paddy equivalent

Source: Food and Agriculture Organization of the United Nations

Rice is the staple diet of more than half the world's population.
Perhaps surprisingly, given that it has been cultivated since
ancient times and the place of rice in its cuisine, China does
not figure in the Top 10—its annual consumption is estimated
at 273 lb 9 oz (124.1 kg) per capita—while that of Japan is only
fractionally greater than the world average.

◐ **National diet**
Touted as a healthy and wholesome drink,
milk features prominently in the shopping
basket of the average US consumer.

Drinks

top 10 COFFEE DRINKERS
COUNTRY / CONSUMPTION PER CAPITA, 2003 (LB/OZ / KG / CUPS*)

1 Finland 24 lb 11 oz / 11.21 kg / 1,681 cups

2 Belgium and Luxembourg 21 lb 2 oz / 9.60 kg / 1,440 cups

3 Norway 19 lb 11 oz / 8.95 kg / 1,342 cups

4 Denmark 17 lb 13 oz / 8.10 kg / 1,215 cups

5 Sweden 17 lb 6 oz / 7.88 kg / 1,182 cups

6 Switzerland 15 lb 3 oz / 6.90 kg / 1,035 cups

7 Netherlands 14 lb 14 oz / 6.76 kg / 1,014 cups

8 Germany 14 lb 10 oz / 6.64 kg / 996 cups

9 Greece 13 lb 4 oz / 6.01 kg / 901 cups

10 Italy 12 lb 10 oz / 5.73 kg / 859 cups

US 9 lb 5 oz / 4.24 kg / 636 cups

* Based on 150 cups per kilogram (2 lb 3 oz)
Source: International Coffee Organization

top 10 TEA DRINKERS
COUNTRY / ANNUAL CONSUMPTION PER CAPITA* (LB/OZ / KG / CUPS#)

1 Ireland 6 lb 8 oz / 2.96 kg / 1,302 cups

2 Libya 6 lb 7 oz / 2.92 kg / 1,284 cups

3 Qatar 6 lb 6 oz / 2.89 kg / 1,271 cups

4 Iraq 5 lb 5 oz / 2.42 kg / 1,064 cups

5 Kuwait 5 lb 0 oz / 2.29 kg / 1,007 cups

6 UK 4 lb 15 oz / 2.24 kg / 985 cups

7 Turkey 4 lb 5 oz / 1.98 kg / 871 cups

8 Afghanistan 4 lb 0 oz / 1.84 kg / 809 cups

9 Syria 3 lb 9 oz / 1.62 kg / 712 cups

10 Morocco 3 lb 2 oz / 1.42 kg / 624 cups

US 0 lb 11 oz / 0.33 kg / 145 cups

* 2001–2003
# Based on 440 cups per kilogram (2 lb 3 oz)
Source: International Tea Committee Ltd., London

top 10 WINE DRINKERS

	COUNTRY	CONSUMPTION PER CAPITA, 2003 (GALLONS)	(LITERS)
1	Luxembourg	17.5	66.1*
2	France	12.8	48.5
3	Italy	12.5	47.5
4	Portugal	11.1	42.0*
5	Switzerland	10.8	40.9
6	Hungary	9.9	37.4*
7	Argentina	9.1	34.6
8	Greece	8.9	33.8*
9	Uruguay	8.8	33.3*
10	Denmark	8.6	32.6*
	US	2.5	9.5

* Estimated from wine production data due to lack of consumption data

Source: Commission for Distilled Spirits

The US still does not make it into the Top 10 or even the Top 30 wine-drinking countries, but consumption of wine has become increasingly popular over the last 33 years. Between 1970 and 2003, wine consumption in the US increased by over 90 percent.

top 10 BEER DRINKERS

	COUNTRY	CONSUMPTION PER CAPITA, 2003 (GALLONS)	(LITERS)
1	Czech Republic	41.5	157.0*
2	Ireland	37.3	141.2
3	Germany	31.0	117.5
4	Austria	29.1	110.6
5	Luxembourg	26.8	101.6
6	UK	26.8	101.5
7	= Belgium	25.4	96.2
	= Denmark	25.4	96.2
9	Australia	24.2	91.5*
10	Slovak Republic	23.4	88.4*
	US	21.5	81.6*

* Estimated from beer production data due to lack of consumption data

Source: Commission for Distilled Spirits

Despite its position as the world's leading producer of beer, the US is ranked 12th in consumption. In African countries, many people drink a lot of beer, but since bottled beer is often prohibitively expensive, they tend to consume homemade beers sold in local markets and hence excluded from national statistics.

top 10 SOFT DRINK CONSUMERS

	COUNTRY	CONSUMPTION PER CAPITA, 2003* (GALLONS)	(LITERS)
1	US	87.2	330.0
2	Mexico	77.5	293.3
3	Spain	74.6	282.1
4	Belgium	72.7	275.2
5	Germany	69.1	261.6
6	Italy	66.1	250.3
7	Switzerland	66.0	249.9
8	Austria	65.4	247.5
9	France	59.1	223.6
10	Canada	56.5	213.7
	World	17.0	64.4

* In those countries for which data available

Source: Euromonitor

➲ **Wine growth**
The identities of the world's leading wine consumers have shifted, with three of those outside the Top 10, Japan, Finland, and the UK, experiencing the greatest increases in the past three decades.

top 10 BOTTLED WATER DRINKERS

	COUNTRY	CONSUMPTION PER CAPITA, 2003 (GALLONS)	(LITERS)
1	Italy	46.8	177.1
2	Spain	41.4	156.7
3	France	40.3	152.5
4	Mexico	40.2	152.1
5	Belgium	34.4	130.1
6	Germany	31.3	118.6
7	Switzerland	29.6	112.0
8	Austria	25.9	98.0
9	Portugal	25.6	96.8
10	Argentina	21.5	81.4
	US	18.9	71.6
	World average	6.0	22.9

Source: Euromonitor

Worldwide consumption of bottled mineral water has more than doubled in the past decade, hitting a 2003 total of 38.2 billion gallons (144.5 billion liters). Although its total consumption of 4.8 billion gallons (18.3 billion liters) makes it the world's leading overall consumer, on a per capita basis the US remains unusually absent from the Top 10.

Energy & Environment

the 10 COUNTRIES CONSUMING THE MOST ENERGY

COUNTRY	(OIL)	(GAS)	ENERGY CONSUMPTION, 2003* (COAL)	(NUCLEAR)	(HEP)[#]	(TOTAL)
1 US	914.3	566.8	573.9	181.9	60.9	2,297.8
2 China	275.2	29.5	799.7	9.8	64.0	1,178.2
3 Russia	124.7	365.2	111.3	34.0	35.6	670.8
4 Japan	248.7	68.9	112.2	52.2	22.8	504.8
5 India	113.3	27.1	185.3	4.1	15.6	345.4
6 Germany	125.1	77.0	87.1	37.3	5.7	332.2
7 Canada	96.4	78.7	31.0	16.8	68.6	291.5
8 France	94.2	39.4	12.4	99.8	14.8	260.6
9 UK	76.8	85.7	39.1	20.1	1.3	223.0
10 South Korea	105.7	24.4	51.1	27.0	1.6	209.8
World total	3,636.6	2,591.0	2,578.4	598.8	595.4	10,000.2

* Millions of metric tons of oil equivalent

\# HEP = Hydroelectric power

Source: *BP Statistical Review of World Energy 2004*

the 10 COUNTRIES CONSUMING THE MOST OIL

COUNTRY / CONSUMPTION, 2003 (TONNES)

 1 US 914,300,000

 2 China 275,200,000

 3 Japan 248,700,000

 4 Germany 125,100,000

 5 Russia 124,700,000

 6 India 113,300,000

 7 South Korea 105,700,000

 8 Canada 96,400,000

 9 France 94,200,000

10 Italy 92,100,000

World total 3,636,600,000

Source: *BP Statistical Review of World Energy 2004*

⊖ **Environmentally unfriendly**
Pollution and its effects on the environment and human health are among the biggest challenges facing the world.

the 10 COUNTRIES EMITTING THE MOST CARBON DIOXIDE

COUNTRY	CO₂ EMISSIONS PER CAPITA, 2002 (METRIC TONS OF CO₂)
1 Qatar	46.08
2 United Arab Emirates	43.53
3 Bahrain	33.07
4 Singapore	27.22
5 Kuwait	25.49
6 Trinidad and Tobago	23.71
7 Luxembourg	22.96
8 Australia	21.00
9 US	19.97
10 Canada	18.92
World average	3.93

Source: Energy Information Administration

CO_2 emissions derive from three principal sources—fossil fuel burning, cement manufacturing, and gas flaring. Since World War II, increasing industrialization in many countries has resulted in huge increases in carbon output, a trend that most countries are now actively trying to reverse, with some degree of success among the former leaders in this Top 10, although the US remains the worst offender in total, with over 5,749,410,000 metric tons released in 2002. Around the world there are a number of island territories with small populations but a high CO_2 output resulting from such industries as the production of liquid fuels. Among them, Gibraltar (144.11 metric tons per head) and the US Virgin Islands (114.55 metric tons per head) have greater per-capita emissions than those countries in the Top 10.

First Fact The first person to suggest the notion of the greenhouse effect was French mathematician Baron Jean-Baptiste-Joseph Fournier, in 1827. In 1908, Swedish chemist and Nobel Prize winner Svante Arrhenius was the first to warn of the danger of global warming as a result of the release of carbon dioxide from the use of fossil fuels.

top 10 LEAST ENVIRONMENTALLY FRIENDLY COUNTRIES

COUNTRY / ESI RANKING*

1 **North Korea** 29.2

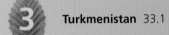
2 **Taiwan** 32.7

3 **Turkmenistan** 33.1

4 **Iraq** 33.6

5 **Uzbekistan** 34.4

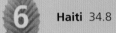
6 **Haiti** 34.8

7 **Sudan** 35.9

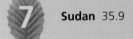
8 **Trinidad and Tobago** 36.3

9 **Kuwait** 36.6

10 **Yemen** 37.3

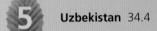

* Based on calculations of 20 key indicators in five categories: environmental systems, environmental stresses, human vulnerability to environmental risks, a society's institutional capacity to respond to environmental threats, and a nation's stewardship of the shared resources of the global commons

Source: World Economic Forum, *2005 Environmental Sustainability Index*

top 10 ENVIRONMENTALLY FRIENDLY COUNTRIES

COUNTRY / ESI RANKING*

1 **Finland** 75.1

2 **Norway** 73.4

3 **Uruguay** 71.8

4 **Sweden** 71.7

5 **Iceland** 70.8

6 **Canada** 64.4

7 **Switzerland** 63.7

8 **Guyana** 62.9

9 = **Argentina** 62.7
= **Austria** 62.7

* Based on calculations of 20 key indicators in five categories: environmental systems, environmental stresses, human vulnerability to environmental risks, a society's institutional capacity to respond to environmental threats, and a nation's stewardship of the shared resources of the global commons

Source: World Economic Forum, *2005 Environmental Sustainability Index*

Chapter

89 **10** **12**

the 10 latest holders of the water speed record: page 187

234567

ransportation & Tourism

Speed Records

the 10 LATEST HOLDERS OF THE **AIR SPEED** RECORD **BY JETS***

	PILOT(S) / COUNTRY	LOCATION	AIRCRAFT	SPEED (MPH)	(KM/H)	DATE
1	**Eldon W. Joersz**, US **George T. Morgan Jr.**, US	Beale AFB, US	Lockheed SR-71A	2,193.167	3,529.560	July 28, 1976
2	**Robert L. Stephens**, US **Daniel Andre**, US	Edwards AFB, US	Lockheed YF-12A	2,070.102	3,331.507	May 1, 1965
3	**Georgi Mossolov**, USSR	Podmoskownoe, USSR	Mikoyan E-166	1,665.896	2,681.000	July 7, 1962
4	**Robert B. Robinson**, US	Edwards AFB, US	McDonnell F4H-1F Phantom II	1,606.509	2,585.425	Nov. 22, 1961
5	**Joseph W. Rogers**, US	Edwards AFB, US	Convair F-106A Delta Dart	1,525.924	2,455.736	Dec. 15 1959
6	**Georgi Mossolov**	Jukowski-Petrowskol, USSR	Mikoyan E-66	1,483.834	2,388.000	Oct. 31, 1959
7	**Walter W. Irwin**, US	Edwards AFB, US	Lockheed YF-104A Starfighter	1,404.012	2,259.538	May 16, 1958
8	**Adrian E. Drew**, US	Edwards AFB, US	McDonnell F-101A Voodoo	1,207.635	1,943.500	Dec. 12, 1957
9	**Peter Twiss**, US	Chichester, UK	Fairey Delta Two	1,132.138	1,822.000	Mar. 10, 1956
10	**Horace A. Hanes**, US	Palmdale, US	North American F-100C Super Sabre	822.268	1,323.312	Aug. 20, 1955

* Ground-launched only, hence excludes X-15 records

The flight of Horace A. Hanes was the first official supersonic record-holder. The next holder, that of Peter Twiss, was the greatest-ever incremental increase—309.870 mph (498.688 km/h). It should be noted that although air records are traditionally expressed to three decimal places, few flights have ever been recorded to such a level of accuracy.

top 10 **FASTEST** RAIL JOURNEYS

	JOURNEY*/ COUNTRY	TRAIN	DISTANCE (MILES)	(KM)	SPEED (MPH)	(KM/H)
1	**Hiroshima to Kokura**, Japan	15 Nozomi	119.3	192.0	162.7	261.8
2	**Valence TGV to Avignon TGV**, France	TGV 5102	80.6	129.7	161.2	259.4
3	**Brussels Midi to Valence TGV**, International	ThalysSoleil	516.5	831.3	150.4	242.1
4	**Frankfurt Flughafen to Siegburg/Bonn**, Germany	19 ICE trains	89.0	143.3	144.4	232.4
5	**Madrid Atocha to Sevilla (Seville)**, Spain	2 AVE trains	292.4	470.5	129.9	209.1
6	**Alvesta to Hassleholm**, Sweden	X2000 541	61.0	98.0	111.0	178.2
7	**Darlington to York**, UK	6 Voyager trains	44.1	71.0	110.3	177.5
8	**Roma (Rome) Termini to Firenze (Florence) SMN**, Italy	Eurostar 9458	162.2	261.0	103.5	166.6
9	**Wilmington, DE, to Baltimore**, MD	Acela Express	68.4	110.1	102.6	165.1
10	**Salo to Karjaa**, Finland	2 Pendolinos	33.0	53.1	94.3	151.7

* Fastest journey for each country; all those countries in the Top 10 have other equally or similarly fast services

Source: *Railway Gazette International*

the 10 LATEST HOLDERS OF THE **WATER SPEED** RECORD

DRIVER / BOAT / LOCATION	SPEED (MPH)	(KM/H)	DATE
1 **Dave Villwock**, Miss Budweiser, Lake Oroville, California	220.493	354.849	Mar. 13, 2004
2 **Russ Wicks**, Miss Freei, Lake Washington, Washington	205.494	330.711	June 15, 2000
3 **Roy Duby**, Miss US1, Lake Guntersville, Alabama	200.419	322.543	Apr. 17, 1962
4 **Bill Muncey**, Miss Thriftaway, Lake Washington, Washington	192.001	308.996	Feb. 16, 1960
5 **Jack Regas**, Hawaii Kai III, Lake Washington, Washington	187.627	301.956	Nov. 30, 1957
6 **Art Asbury**, Miss Supertest II, Lake Ontario, Canada	184.540	296.988	Nov. 1, 1957
7 **Stanley Sayres**, Slo-Mo-Shun IV, Lake Washington, Washington	178.497	287.263	July 7, 1952
8 **Stanley Sayres**, Slo-Mo-Shun IV, Lake Washington, Washington	160.323	258.015	June 26, 1950
9 **Malcolm Campbell**, Bluebird K4, Coniston Water, UK	141.740	228.108	Aug. 19, 1939
10 **Malcolm Campbell**, Bluebird K3, Hallwiler See, Switzerland	130.910	210.679	Aug. 17, 1938

All these record-holders were propeller-driven craft, taking the average of two runs over a measured kilometer or mile course. Since the 1950s, jet-powered boats, which skim over the surface of the water, have achieved consistently faster speeds, with Ken Warby's *Spirit of Australia* setting the jet record of 317.58 mph (511.11 km/h) on *Blowering Dam*, New South Wales, Australia, on October 8, 1978.

⊕ Miss Budweiser
Powered by a 2,650-hp Chinook helicopter engine, hydroplane *Miss Budweiser* set a new world water speed record in 2004.

the 10 LATEST HOLDERS OF THE **LAND SPEED** RECORD

DRIVER / COUNTRY / CAR / SPEED / DATE

1 **Andy Green**, UK, Thrust SSC*, 763.04 mph (1,227.99 km/h), Oct. 15, 1997

2 **Richard Noble**, UK, Thrust 2*, 633.47 mph (1,013.47 km/h), Oct. 4, 1983

3 **Gary Gabelich**, US, The Blue Flame, 622.41 mph (995.85 km/h), Oct. 23, 1970

4 **Craig Breedlove**, US, Spirit of America—Sonic 1, 600.60 mph (960.96 km/h), Nov. 15, 1965

5 **Art Arfons**, US, Green Monster, 576.55 mph (922.48 km/h), Nov. 7, 1965

6 **Craig Breedlove**, Spirit of America—Sonic 1, 555.48 mph (888.76 km/h), Nov. 2, 1965

7 **Art Arfons**, Green Monster, 536.71 mph (858.73 km/h), Oct. 27, 1964

8 **Craig Breedlove**, Spirit of America, 526.28 mph (842.04 km/h), Oct. 15, 1964

9 **Craig Breedlove**, Spirit of America, 468.72 mph (749.95 km/h), Oct. 13, 1964

10 **Art Arfons**, Green Monster, 434.02 mph (694.43 km/h), Oct. 5, 1964

* Location Black Rock Desert, NV; all other speeds were achieved at Bonneville Salt Flats, UT

On the Road

top 10 CARS IN THE US

	CAR	SALES, 2004
1	Ford F-Series	939,511
2	Chevrolet Silverado	680,768
3	Toyota Camry	426,990
4	Dodge Ram	426,289
5	Honda Accord	386,770
6	Ford Explorer	339,333
7	Honda Civic	309,196
8	Chevrolet Impala	290,259
9	Chevrolet Trailblazer	283,484
10	Ford Taurus	248,148

Source: Automotive News Data Center

top 10 CAR PRODUCERS

	COUNTRY	CAR PRODUCTION, 2004*
1	Japan	8,720,385
2	Germany	5,192,101
3	US	4,229,625
4	France	3,220,329
5	South Korea	3,122,600
6	Spain	2,402,103
7	China	2,316,262
8	UK	1,646,881
9	Brazil	1,756,166
10	Canada	1,335,464

* Provisional figures

Source: OICA Correspondents Survey

top 10 COUNTRIES WITH THE LONGEST ROAD NETWORKS

	COUNTRY	LENGTH (MILES)	LENGTH (KM)
1	US	3,980,687 miles	6,406,296 km
2	India	2,062,731 miles	3,319,644 km
3	Brazil	1,071,821 miles	1,724,929 km
4	Canada	875,388 miles	1,408,800 km
5	China	871,596 miles	1,402,698 km
6	Japan	721,967 miles	1,161,894 km
7	France	555,506 miles	894,000 km
8	Australia	504,307 miles	811,603 km
9	Spain	412,463 miles	663,795 km
10	Russia	330,814 miles	532,393 km

Source: Central Intelligence Agency

The CIA's assessment of road lengths includes both paved (mostly asphalt-surfaced) and unpaved (gravel and dirt-surfaced) highways. In many developing countries the proportion of unpaved is greater than paved.

top 10 MOTOR VEHICLE **MANUFACTURERS**

MANUFACTURER	MOTOR VEHICLE PRODUCTION*, 2003
1 General Motors	8,185,997
2 Ford	6,566,089
3 Toyota	6,240,526
4 Volkswagen Group	5,024,032
5 DaimlerChrysler	4,231,603
6 PSA Peugeot Citroën	3,310,368
7 Nissan	2,942,306
8 Honda	2,922,526
9 Hyundai-Kia	2,697,435
10 Renault-Dacia-Samsung	2,386,098

* Includes cars, light trucks, lorries, buses, and coaches

Source: OICA Correspondents Survey

top 10 MOTOR VEHICLE **PRODUCERS**

COUNTRY	MOTOR VEHICLE PRODUCTION, 2004*
1 US	11,989,387
2 Japan	10,511,518
3 Germany	5,569,954
4 China	5,070,527
5 France	3,665,990
6 South Korea	3,469,464
7 Spain	3,011,010
8 Canada	2,710,683
9 Brazil	2,210,062
10 UK	1,856,049

* Provisional figures; includes cars, light trucks, lorries, buses, and coaches

Source: OICA Correspondents Survey

⊕ Traffic jam

In the past 50 years, annual motor vehicle production has risen from 13.6 million to over 60 million globally, with more than 500 million cars alone on the world's roads.

Track Records

TOP 10 LONGEST UNDERGROUND RAILROAD NETWORKS

London UK
1
1863
267
244 miles
392 km

New York US
2
1904
468
231 miles
371 km

Moscow Russia
3
1935
160
163 miles
262 km

Tokyo Japan*
4
1927
241
159 miles
256 km

Paris France#
5
1900
297
126 miles
202 km

CITY   OPENED   STATIONS   TOTAL TRACK LENGTH (MILES)   (KM)

the 10 FIRST COUNTRIES WITH RAILROADS

COUNTRY	FIRST RAILROAD ESTABLISHED
1 UK	Sept. 27, 1825
2 France	Nov. 7, 1829
3 US	May 24, 1830
4 Ireland	Dec. 17, 1834
5 Belgium	May 5, 1835
6 Germany	Dec. 7, 1835
7 Canada	July 21, 1836
8 Russia	Oct. 30, 1837
9 Austria	Jan. 6, 1838
10 Netherlands	Sept. 24, 1839

Inaugurated with the UK's Stockton & Darlington Railway, the first steam (rather than horse-drawn) services rapidly launched a "golden age" of railway building across the world.

top 10 LONGEST RAIL NETWORKS

	TOTAL RAIL LENGTH	
LOCATION	(MILES)	(KM)
1 US	141,961	228,464
2 Russia	54,157	87,157
3 China	43,532	70,058
4 India	39,233	63,140
5 Canada	30,391	48,909
6 Germany	28,607	46,039
7 Australia	27,350	44,015
8 Argentina	21,183	34,091
9 France	19,993	32,175
10 Brazil	18,276	29,412
World	*692,956*	*1,115,205*

Source: Central Intelligence Agency

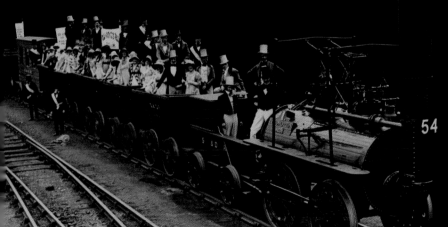

54

← Early train
Pioneer passengers in open cars savor the revolutionary experience of traveling by rail.

Mexico City Mexico	**San Francisco** US	**Chicago** US	**Madrid** Spain	**Washington, DC** US
6	**7**	**8**	**9**	**10**
1969	1972	1943	1919	1976
175	42	140	201	83
125 miles	124 miles	107 miles	106 miles	103 miles
201 km	200 km	173 km	171 km	166 km

* Includes Toei, Eidan lines   # Metro and RER   Source: Tony Pattison, Center for Environmental Initiatives Researcher

top 10 **BUSIEST** RAIL NETWORKS

LOCATION	PASSENGER-MILES PER ANNUM	PASSENGER-KMS PER ANNUM
1 Japan	354,137,000,000	568,036,000,000
2 China	243,900,000,000	390,484,000,000
3 India	222,994,000,000	357,013,000,000
4 Russia	106,371,000,000	170,300,000,000
5 France	38,620,000,000	61,830,000,000
6 Egypt	37,539,000,000	60,100,000,000
7 Germany	37,071,000,000	59,350,000,000
8 Ukraine	36,902,000,000	59,080,000,000
9 Italy	31,936,000,000	51,129,000,000
10 UK	19,771,000,000	31,653,000,000
US	*13,619,000,000*	*21,918,000,000*

* Number of passengers multiplied by distance carried; totals include national and local services where applicable

Source: *Railway Gazette International*

Though coming to rail transportation later than many other countries, Japan (first railroad 1872), China (1880), and India (1853) today have the world's busiest systems.

 Rush hour
Morning on the Yamanote Line, Tokyo's busiest commuter route: as many as half of all employees in Japan commute to work by train.

Water Ways

top 10 LARGEST YACHTS

	YACHT	OWNER / COUNTRY	BUILT / REFITTED	LENGTH (FT	IN)	(M)
1	Octopus	Paul Allen, US	2003	414	0	126.1
2	Savarona	Kahraman Sadikoglu, Turkey (charter)	1931/1992	408	0	124.3
3	Alexander	Latsis family, Greece	1976/1986	400	2	122.0
4	Atlantis II	Niarchos family, Greece	1981	379	7	115.6
5	Pelorus	Roman Abramovich, Russia	2003	377	3	114.9
6	Le Grand Bleu	Roman Abramovich	2000	370	0	112.7
7	Lady Moura	Nasser al-Rashid, Saudi Arabia	1990	344	0	104.8
8	Christina O	John Paul Papanicolaou, Greece	1943/2001	325	3	99.1
9	Carinthia VII	Heidi Horten, Germany	2002	321	5	97.9
10	Limitless	Leslie Wexner, US	1997	315	7	96.1

Source: *Power & Motoryacht*, August 2004

Owned by Microsoft cofounder Paul Gardner Allen, German-built *Octopus*—the world's largest privately-owned yacht—boasts such equipment as a 60-ft (18-m) landing craft and a submarine.

top 10 BUSIEST PORTS

	PORT / COUNTRY	CONTAINER TRAFFIC, 2003 (TEUS*)
1	**Hong Kong**, China	20,499,000
2	**Singapore**, Singapore	18,411,000
3	**Shanghai**, China	11,280,000
4	**Shenzhen**, China	10,615,000
5	**Busan**, South Korea	10,408,000
6	**Kaohsiung**, Taiwan	8,843,000
7	**Los Angeles**, US	7,149,000
8	**Rotterdam**, Netherlands	7,107,000
9	**Hamburg**, Germany	6,138,000
10	**Antwerp**, Belgium	5,445,000

* TEUS = Twenty-foot Equivalent Units

Source: American Association of Port Authorities

A "Twenty-foot Equivalent Unit" is a measurement used in quantifying container traffic, in which Hong Kong is the world leader, although Singapore is the largest in terms of total weight handled, with over 347 million tonnes in 2003, compared with Hong Kong's 207 million.

top 10 LARGEST OIL TANKERS*

TANKER / YEAR BUILT / OPERATOR'S COUNTRY / DEADWEIGHT TONNAGE#

5 Marine Pacific

1	=TI Africa	2002	UK	441,893
	=TI Asia	2002	UK	441,893
	=TI Europe	2002	UK	441,893

4	TI Oceania	2003	UK	441,585

* As of April 2004

Total weight of the vessel, including its cargo, crew, passengers, and supplies

Source: Lloyd's Register-Fairplay Ltd. www.lrfairplay.com

top 10 LONGEST SHIP CANALS

	CANAL / COUNTRY	OPENED	LENGTH (MILES)	(KM)
1	**Grand Canal**, China	283*	1,114	1,795
2	**Erie Canal**, US	1825	363	584
3	**Göta Canal**, Sweden	1832	240	386
4	**St. Lawrence Seaway**, Canada/US	1959	180	290
5	**Canal du Midi**, France	1692	149	240
6	**Main-Danube**, Germany	1992	106	171
7	**Suez**, Egypt	1869	101	162
8	=**Albert**, Belgium	1939	80	129
	=**Moscow-Volga**, Russia	1937	80	129
10	**Volga-Don**, Russia	1952	63	101

* Extended from 605–10 and rebuilt during 1958–72

Connecting Hang Zhou in the south to Beijing in the north, China's Grand Canal was largely built by manual labor, long before the invention of the mechanized digging used in the construction of the other major artificial waterways. The Panama Canal, opened in 1914 (51 miles/82 km), just fails to find a place in the Top 10.

⬆ **Slow boats in China**
China's Grand, or Jinghang, Canal combines sections of navigable rivers, lakes, and human-made canals to form a major water highway from Beijing to Zhejiang.

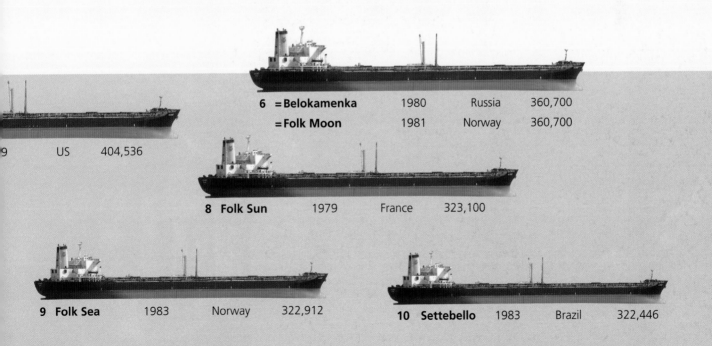

6	=**Belokamenka**	1980	Russia	360,700
	=**Folk Moon**	1981	Norway	360,700

9 · US · 404,536

| 8 | **Folk Sun** | 1979 | France | 323,100 |

| 9 | **Folk Sea** | 1983 | Norway | 322,912 |

| 10 | **Settebello** | 1983 | Brazil | 322,446 |

Airlines

top 10 **BUSIEST** AIRPORTS

Source: Airports Council International

	Airport	Location	Country	Passengers, 2003
1	ATLANTA HARTSFIELD INTERNATIONAL	ATLANTA	US	79,086,792
2	CHICAGO O'HARE	CHICAGO	US	69,508,672
3	LONDON HEATHROW	LONDON	UK	63,487,136
4	TOKYO INTERNATIONAL	TOKYO	JAPAN	62,876,269
5	LOS ANGELES INTERNATIONAL	LOS ANGELES	US	54,982,838
6	DFW INTERNATIONAL	DALLAS/FORT WORTH	US	53,253,607
7	FRANKFURT	FRANKFURT	GERMANY	48,351,664
8	CHARLES DE GAULLE	PARIS	FRANCE	48,220,436
9	SCHIPHOL	AMSTERDAM	NETHERLANDS	39,960,400
10	DENVER INTERNATIONAL	DENVER	US	37,505,138

top 10 AIRLINES WITH THE **MOST AIRCRAFT**

AIRLINE / COUNTRY*	MAIN FLEET SIZE, 2004[#]
1 American Airlines	840
2 Delta Air Lines	587
3 United Airlines	523
4 Northwest Airlines	452
5 Southwest Airlines	417
6 Lufthansa German Airlines, Germany	368
7 Air France, France	363
8 Continental Airlines	358
9 US Airways	279
10 British Airways, UK	220

* All from the US unless otherwise stated

[#] 2003 data where 2004 not yet available

American Airlines has not only the largest fleet but also the greatest passenger traffic and employs the largest number of staff. It serves 172 cities, averages 2,600 departures a day, and handles some 80 million passengers a year.

top 10 COUNTRIES WITH THE **MOST AIRPORTS**

COUNTRY	AIRPORTS, 2003 EST.
1 US	14,807
2 Brazil	3,803
3 Russia	2,609
4 Mexico	1,827
5 Canada	1,357
6 Argentina	1,335
7 Bolivia	1,067
8 Colombia	980
9 Paraguay	880
10 South Africa	728

Source: Central Intelligence Agency

➔ Runway success
Handling more international traffic than any other airport, London Heathrow is also Europe's busiest for passenger traffic. Its 5th terminal, scheduled for 2008–2015, will enable it to handle 90 million passengers a year.

↑ Lost luggage
Some 18 percent of all complaints to airlines concern mishandled baggage, a greater proportion than for any other issue.

top 10 AIRLINES WITH THE MOST PASSENGER TRAFFIC

AIRLINE / COUNTRY	PASSENGER-MILES FLOWN, 2003*
1 **American Airlines**, US	119,987,000,000
2 **United Airlines**, US	101,532,000,000
3 **Delta Airlines**, US	89,105,000,000
4 **Northwest Airlines**, US	68,475,000,000
5 **British Airways**, UK	63,131,000,000
6 **Air France**, France	60,646,000,000
7 **Lufthansa German Airlines**, Germany	60,024,000,000
8 **Continental Airlines**, US	56,855,000,000
9 **Japan Airlines**, Japan	45,298,000,000
10 **Qantas Airways**, Australia	42,812,000,000

* Total distance traveled on scheduled flights by aircraft of these airlines multiplied by the number of passengers carried

Source: International Civil Aviation Organization (ICAO)

British Airways, the largest non-US airline, was created in 1973 by the merging of the British Overseas Airways Corporation and British European Airways. In the 1990s it proclaimed itself "The World's Favorite Airline," and until 2003 it was, along with Air France, one of the operators of the supersonic Concorde.

top 10 COMPLAINTS AGAINST US AIRLINES

TYPE OF COMPLAINT	2003*	2004*
1 **Flight problems**	971	1,391
2 **Baggage**	885	1,015
3 **Reservations/ticketing/boarding problems**	696	747
4 **Customer service**	550	695
5 **Refund problems**	573	455
6 **Disability**	266	415
7 **Oversales**	228	286
8 **Frequent flyer problems**	157	191
9 **Fares**	258	164
10 **Discrimination**	70	93
Total (including those not in the Top 10)	4,736	5,558

* Jan.–Sept.

Source: Office of Aviation Enforcement and Proceedings

These are claims filed by consumers to the US Department of Transportation. "Flight problems" includes cancellations (469 complaints), delays (344), and missed connections (244). They exclude the much greater numbers of complaints—led by those relating to the mishandling of baggage and bumping from flights—that are made directly to the airlines.

Transport Disasters

the 10 WORST **AIR** DISASTERS (EXCLUDING TERRORISM)

LOCATION / DATE / INCIDENT   NO. KILLED

1 Tenerife, Canary Islands, Mar. 27, 1977   583
Two Boeing 747s (Pan Am and KLM, carrying 380 passengers and 16 crew and 234 passengers and 14 crew, respectively) collided and caught fire on the runway of Los Rodeos airport after the pilots received incorrect control tower instructions. A total of 61 people escaped.

2 Mt. Ogura, Japan, Aug. 12, 1985   520
A JAL Boeing 747 on an internal flight from Tokyo to Osaka crashed, killing all but four of the 509 passengers and all 15 crew on board.

3 Charkhi Dadri, India, Nov. 12, 1996   349
Soon after taking off from New Delhi's Indira Gandhi International Airport, a Saudi Airways Boeing 747 collided with a Kazakh Airlines Ilyushin IL-76 cargo aircraft on its descent and exploded, killing all 312 people (289 passengers and 23 crew) on the Boeing and all 37 people (27 passengers and 10 crew) on the Ilyushin in the world's worst midair crash.

4 Paris, France, Mar. 3, 1974   346
Immediately after takeoff for London, a Turkish Airlines DC-10 crashed at Ermenonville, north of Paris, killing all 335 passengers, including many English rugby fans, and its crew of 11.

5 Riyadh, Saudi Arabia, Aug. 19, 1980   301
A Saudia (Saudi Arabian) Airlines Lockheed TriStar caught fire during an emergency landing, killing all 287 passengers and 14 crew.

6 Off the Iranian coast, July 3, 1988   290
An Iran Air A300 airbus was shot down in error by a missile fired by the USS *Vincennes*, with 274 passengers and 16 crew killed.

7 Chicago, IL, May 25, 1979   273
The worst air disaster in the US occurred when an engine fell off an American Airlines DC-10 as it took off from Chicago O'Hare airport and the plane plunged out of control, killing all 258 passengers and 13 crew on board and two on the ground.

8 Sakhalin Island, off the Siberian coast, Sept. 1, 1983   269
A Korean Air Lines Boeing 747 that had strayed into Soviet airspace was shot down by a Soviet fighter.

9 Belle Harbor, NY, Nov. 12, 2001   265
An American Airlines Airbus A.300B4-605R broke up in midair and crashed in a residential area, killing all 260 on board and five on the ground.

10 Nagoya airport, Japan, Apr. 26, 1994   264
A China Airlines Airbus A300, on a flight from Taipei, Taiwan, stalled at 980 ft (300 m) and crashed while landing, killing all 15 crew and 249 out of the 256 passengers on board.

the 10 WORST **AIR** DISASTERS CAUSED BY TERRORISM

LOCATION / DATE / INCIDENT   NO. KILLED

1 New York, NY, Sept. 11, 2001   c. 1,622
Following a hijacking by terrorists, an American Airlines Boeing 767 was deliberately flown into the North Tower of the World Trade Center, killing all 81 passengers and 11 crew on board and an estimated 1,530 on the ground, both as a direct result of the crash, and the subsequent fire and collapse of the building.

2 New York, NY, Sept. 11, 2001   c. 677
As part of the coordinated attack, hijackers commandeered a second Boeing 747 and crashed it into the South Tower of the World Trade Center, killing all 56 passengers and 9 crew on board and approximately 612 on the ground.

3 Off the Irish coast, June 23, 1985   329
An Air India Boeing 747 on a flight from Vancouver to Delhi exploded in midair, probably as a result of a terrorist bomb, killing all 307 passengers and 22 crew in the worst-ever air disaster over water.

4 Lockerbie, Scotland, Dec. 21, 1988   270
Pan Am Flight 103—a Boeing 747—en route from London Heathrow to New York exploded in midair as a result of a terrorist bomb, killing 243 passengers, 16 crew, and 11 on the ground in the UK's worst-ever air disaster.

5 Pentagon, Washington, DC, Sept. 11, 2001   189
As part of the 9/11 hijackings, a Boeing 757 was deliberately crashed into the Pentagon, killing 64 on board and 125 on the ground.

6 Tenere Desert, Niger, Sept. 19, 1989   171
A Union de Transports Ariens DC-10 flying out of Ndjamena, Chad, exploded over Niger. French investigators implicated Libyan and Syrian terrorists.

7 Baiyun Airport, China, Oct. 2, 1990   128
A Xiamen Airlines Boeing 737 was hijacked in flight and, during a forced landing, crashed into a taxiing Boeing 757.

8 Comoros Islands, Indian Ocean, Nov. 23, 1996   125
An Ethiopian Airlines Boeing 767 was hijacked and ditched in the sea when it ran out of fuel.

9 Andaman Sea, off Myanmar, Nov. 29, 1987   115
A Korean Air Boeing 707 exploded in midair. Two North Korean terrorists were captured; one of them committed suicide, while the other was sentenced to death but later pardoned.

10 Near Abu Dhabi, United Arab Emirates, Sept. 23, 1983   113
A Gulf Air Boeing 737 exploded as it prepared to land. Evidence indicated that the explosion had been caused by a bomb in the cargo hold.

the 10 WORST MARINE DISASTERS

LOCATION / DATE / INCIDENT	APPROXIMATE NO. KILLED
1 Off Gdansk, Poland, Jan. 30, 1945 The German liner *Wilhelm Gustloff*, laden with refugees, was torpedoed by a Soviet submarine, *S-13*. The precise death toll remains uncertain, but is in the range of 5,348 to 7,800.	up to 7,800
2 Off Cape Rixhöft (Rozeewie), Poland, Apr. 16, 1945 A German ship, *Goya*, carrying evacuees from Gdansk, was torpedoed in the Baltic.	6,800
3 Off Yingkow, China, Dec. 3, 1948 The boilers of an unidentified Chinese troopship carrying Nationalist soldiers from Manchuria exploded, detonating ammunition.	over 6,000
4 Lübeck, Germany, May 3, 1945 The German ship *Cap Arcona*, carrying concentration-camp survivors, was bombed and sunk by British Typhoon fighter-bombers.	5,000
5 Off British coast, Aug. to Oct. 1588 Military conflict and storms combined to destroy the Spanish Armada.	c. 4,000
6 Off Stolpmünde (Ustka), Poland, Feb. 10, 1945 German war-wounded and refugees were lost when the *General Steuben* was torpedoed by the same Russian submarine that had sunk the *Wilhelm Gustloff* 10 days earlier.	3,500
7 Off St. Nazaire, France, June 17, 1940 The British troop ship *Lancastria* sank.	3,050
8 Tabias Strait, Philippines, Dec. 20, 1987 The ferry *Dona Paz* was struck by oil tanker *MV Victor*.	up to 3,000
9 Woosung, China, Dec. 3, 1948 The overloaded steamship *Kiangya*, carrying refugees, struck a Japanese mine.	over 2,750
10 Lübeck, Germany, May 3, 1945 The refugee ship *Thielbeck* sank along with the *Cap Arcona* during the British bombardment of Lübeck harbor in the closing weeks of World War II.	2,750

Recent reassessments of the death tolls in some of the World War II marine disasters means that the most famous marine disaster of all, the *Titanic*, the British liner that struck an iceberg in the North Atlantic and sank on April 15, 1912, with the loss of 1,517 lives, no longer ranks in the Top 10. However, the *Titanic* tragedy remains one of the worst-ever peacetime disasters, along with such notable incidents as that involving the *General Slocum*, an excursion liner that caught fire in the port of New York on June 15, 1904 with the loss of 1,021 lives.

the 10 WORST LAND TRANSPORT DISASTERS

LOCATION / DATE / INCIDENT	NO. KILLED
1 Afghanistan, Nov. 3, 1982 Following a collision with a Soviet army truck, a gasoline tanker exploded in the 1.7-mile (2.7-km) Salang Tunnel. Some authorities have put the death toll from the explosion, fire, and fumes as high as 3,000.	over 2,000
2 Colombia, Aug. 7, 1956 Seven army ammunition trucks exploded at night in the center of Cali, destroying eight city blocks, including a barracks where 500 soldiers were sleeping.	1,200
3 Bagmati River, India, June 6, 1981 The cars of a train traveling from Samastipur to Banmukhi in Bihar plunged off a bridge over the Bagmati River near Mansi when the driver braked, apparently to avoid hitting a sacred cow. Although the official death toll was said to have been 268, many authorities have claimed that the train was so massively overcrowded that the actual figure was in excess of 800, making it probably the worst rail disaster of all time.	c. 800
4 Chelyabinsk, Russia, June 3, 1989 Two passenger trains, laden with vacationers heading to and from Black Sea resorts, were destroyed when liquid gas from a nearby pipeline exploded.	up to 800
5 Guadalajara, Mexico, Jan. 18, 1915 A train derailed on a steep incline, but political strife in the country meant that full details of the disaster were suppressed.	over 600
6 Modane, France, Dec. 12, 1917 A troop-carrying train ran out of control and was derailed. It has been claimed that it was overloaded and that as many as 1,000 may have died.	573
7 Balvano, Italy, Mar. 2, 1944 A heavily laden train stalled in the Armi Tunnel, and many passengers were asphyxiated. Like the disaster at Torre (No. 8), wartime secrecy prevented the full details from being published.	521
8 Torre, Spain, Jan. 3, 1944 A double collision and fire in a tunnel resulted in many deaths—some have put the total as high as 800.	over 500
9 Awash, Ethiopia, Jan. 13, 1985 A derailment hurled a train laden with some 1,000 passengers into a ravine.	428
10 Cireau, Romania, Jan. 7, 1917 An overcrowded passenger train crashed into a military train and was derailed.	374

World Tourism

top 10 TOURIST **DESTINATIONS**

	COUNTRY	INTERNATIONAL VISITORS, 2003
1	*France*	75,048,000
2	*Spain*	52,477,000
3	*US*	40,356,000
4	*Italy*	39,604,000
5	*China*	32,970,000
6	*UK*	24,785,000
7	*Austria*	19,078,000
8	*Mexico*	18,665,000
9	*Germany*	18,399,000
10	*Canada*	17,468,000

Source: World Tourism Organization

Greetings

⬆ Italian treasures
Italy's picturesque towns and villages and the cultural attractions of its cities have been a magnet for tourists since the days of the 18th-century Grand Tour.

⬆ Spanish pleasures
The resorts of Spain and its islands, with their beaches and leisure facilities, attract increasing numbers of tourists.

top 10 WORLDWIDE AMUSEMENT AND **THEME PARKS**

PARK / LOCATION	ESTIMATED ATTENDANCE, 2004
1 **The Magic Kingdom at Walt Disney World**, Lake Buena Vista, Florida	15,170,000
2 **Disneyland**, Anaheim, California	13,360,000
3 **Tokyo Disneyland**, Tokyo, Japan	13,200,000
4 **Disneysea**, Tokyo, Japan	12,200,000
5 **Disneyland Paris**, Marne-La-Vallée, France	10,200,000
6 **Universal Studios Japan**, Osaka, Japan	9,900,000
7 **Epcot at Walt Disney World**, Lake Buena Vista, Florida	9,400,000
8 **Disney-MGM Studios at Walt Disney World**, Lake Buena Vista, Florida	8,260,000
9 **Lotte World**, Seoul, South Korea	8,000,000
10 **Disney's Animal Kingdom at Walt Disney World**, Lake Buena Vista, Florida	7,820,000

Source: *Amusement Business*

After experiencing flat or declining entrance numbers in recent years, most amusement parks recorded increases in 2004. New parks in Japan, such as Tokyo's Disneysea and Universal Studios and Osaka's Universal Studios, which all opened in 2001, and the enormous Dubai Land scheduled to open in 2006, are shifting the global balance from the US to the East and Middle East.

↑ Disneyland's domination
Including Epcot, eight of the world's Top 10 amusement parks are members of The Walt Disney Company. Its pioneering Disneyland, in second place, opened in 1955.

top 10 **COUNTRIES OF ORIGIN** OF OVERSEAS VISITORS TO THE US

COUNTRY	OVERSEAS VISITORS TO THE US, 2003
1 **UK**	3,936,112
2 **Japan**	3,169,682
3 **Germany**	1,180,212
4 **France**	688,887
5 **South Korea**	617,573
6 **Italy**	408,633
7 **Australia**	405,698
8 **Netherlands**	373,690
9 **Brazil**	348,945
10 **Venezuela**	284,423

Source: US Department of Commerce, International Trade Administration, Office of Travel and Tourism Industries

Fears of global terrorism and economic and other factors have adversely affected US tourist visitor numbers. The total declined from 41,891,707 in 2002 to 40,356,213 in 2003, and is more than 10 million lower than the peak year of 2000.

top 10 **COUNTRIES EARNING THE MOST** FROM TOURISM

COUNTRY	INTERNATIONAL TOURISM RECEIPTS, 2003 ($)
1 **US**	65,100,000,000
2 **Spain**	41,700,000,000
3 **France**	36,600,000,000
4 **Italy**	31,300,000,000
5 **Germany**	23,000,000,000
6 **UK**	19,400,000,000
7 **China**	17,400,000,000
8 **Austria**	13,600,000,000
9 **Turkey**	13,200,000,000
10 **Greece**	10,700,000,000

Source: World Tourism Organization

top 10 *FASTEST* ROLLER COASTERS

ROLLER COASTER / LOCATION	YEAR OPENED	SPEED (MPH)	(KMH)
1 **Kingda Ka**, Six Flags Great Adventure, Jackson, New Jersey	2005*	128	206
2 **Top Thrill Dragster**, Cedar Point, Sandusky, Ohio	2003	120	193
3 **Dodonpa**, Fuji-Q Highlands, ShinNishihara, FujiYoshida-shi, Yamanashi, Japan	2001	106.9	172
4 = **Superman The Escape**, Six Flags Magic Mountain, Valencia, California	1997	100	161
= **Tower of Terror**, Dreamworld, Coomera, Queensland, Australia	1997	100	161
6 **Steel Dragon 2000**, Nagashima Spa Land, Nagashima, Mie, Japan	2000#	95	153
7 **Millennium Force**, Cedar Point, Sandusky, Ohio	2000	93	149
8 = **Goliath**, Six Flags Magic Mountain, Valencia, California	2000	85	137
= **Titan**, Six Flags Over Texas, Arlington, Texas	2001	85	137
10 = **Phantom's Revenge**, Kennywood Park, West Mifflin, Pennsylvania	2001	82	132
= **Xcelerator**, Knott's Berry Farm, Buena Park, California	2002	82	132

* Scheduled opening date Spring 2005

\# Still standing but not operating since Aug. 23, 2003

➔ **Millennium Force**
When it was built, Cedar Point's 14th roller coaster set new records as the world's fastest and, at 310 ft (94.5 m), the tallest.

Chapter

9 10 1 2 3

top 10 longest-standing outdoor field athletics world records: page 214

top 10 transfers in international soccer: page 232

Sports

Summer Olympics

TOP 10 SUMMER OLYMPICS **GOLD MEDAL** WINNERS

	ATHLETE / COUNTRY	SPORT	YEARS	GOLD MEDALS
1	Ray Ewry, US	Track & Field	1900–08	10
2 =	Paavo Nurmi, Finland	Track & Field	1920–28	9
=	Larissa Latynina, USSR	Gymnastics	1956–64	9
=	Mark Spitz, US	Swimming	1968–72	9
=	Carl Lewis, US	Track & Field	1984–96	9
6 =	Sawao Kato, Japan	Gymnastics	1968–76	8
=	Matt Biondi, US	Swimming	1984–92	8
=	Jenny Thompson, US	Swimming	1992–2000	8
9 =	Aladár Gerevich, Hungary	Fencing	1932–60	7
=	Viktor Chukarin, USSR	Gymnastics	1952–56	7
=	Boris Shakhlin, USSR	Gymnastics	1956–64	7
=	Vera Cáslavská, Czechoslovakia	Gymnastics	1964–68	7
=	Nikolay Andrianov, USSR	Gymnastics	1972–80	7

All Ewry's golds were in the standing jumps—long jump, high jump, and triple jump—that once formed part of the track and field competition. Born in 1873, Ewry contracted polio as a boy and seemed destined to be confined to a wheelchair for life, but through a determined effort to overcome his handicap, he exercised and developed his legs to such a remarkable degree that he went on to become one of the world's greatest athletes. Spitz's seven gold medals in 1972 is a record for medals won at a single celebration. Latynina is the all-time top Olympic medalist, with 18 medals to her credit (9 gold, 5 silver, 4 bronze).

the 10 FIRST ATHLETES TO WIN MEDALS AT **FIVE** SUMMER OLYMPICS

	ATHLETE / COUNTRY	SPORT	YEARS
1	Heikki Ilmari Savolainen, Finland	Gymnastics	1928–52
2	Aladár Gerevich*, Hungary	Fencing	1932–56
3	Edoardo Mangiarotti, Italy	Fencing	1936–60
4	Gustav Fischer, Switzerland	Dressage	1952–68
5	Hans Günther Winkler#, West Germany	Show jumping	1956–72
6	Ildikó Ságiné–Rejtö (née Uljaki–Rejtö), Hungary	Fencing	1960–76
7	John Michael Plumb, US	Three Day Event	1964–84
8	Reiner Klimke, West Germany	Dressage	1964–88
9 =	Teresa Edwards, US	Basketball	1984–2000
=	Birgit Fischer-Schmidt, East Germany	Canoeing	1980–2000
=	Stephen Redgrave, UK	Rowing	1984–2000

* Also won medal at the 1960 Games

Also won medal at the 1976 Games

top 10 SUMMER OLYMPICS MEDAL-WINNERS (MEN)

	ATHLETE / COUNTRY	SPORT	YEARS	MEDALS* (GOLD)	(SILVER)	(BRONZE)	(TOTAL)
1	**Nikolai Andrianov**, USSR	Gymnastics	1972–80	7	5	3	15
2 =	**Edoardo Mangiarotti**, Italy	Fencing	1936–60	6	5	2	13
=	**Takashi Ono**, Japan	Gymnastics	1952–64	5	4	4	13
=	**Boris Shakhlin**, USSR	Gymnastics	1956–64	7	4	2	13
5 =	**Paavo Nurmi**, Finland	Track & Field	1920–28	9	3	0	12
=	**Sawao Kato**, Japan	Gymnastics	1968–76	8	3	1	12
=	**Alexei Nemov**, Russia	Gymnastics	1996–2000	4	2	6	12
8 =	**Carl Osburn**, US	Shooting	1912–24	5	4	2	11
=	**Viktor Chukarin**, USSR	Gymnastics	1952–56	7	3	1	11
=	**Mark Spitz**, US	Swimming	1968–72	9	1	1	11
=	**Matt Biondi**, US	Swimming	1984–92	8	2	1	11

* 1896–2004 inclusive

Nikolai Andrianov is married to Olympic gymnast Lyubov Burda, who herself won two Olympic gold medals. Fencer Edoardo Mangiarotti won his first gold at the age of 17, making him the youngest male medalist at the 1936 Berlin Games. Although his overall total relegates him to the bottom of this list, Mark Spitz has the distinction of winning the most gold medals at a single Olympics, with seven in 1972.

top 10 SUMMER OLYMPICS MEDAL-WINNERS (WOMEN)

	ATHLETE / COUNTRY	SPORT	YEARS	MEDALS* (GOLD)	(SILVER)	(BRONZE)	(TOTAL)
1	**Larissa Latynina**, USSR	Gymnastics	1956–64	9	5	4	18
2	**Birgit Fischer-Schmidt**, East Germany	Canoeing	1980–2004	8	4	0	12
3	**Vera Cáslavská**, Czechoslovakia	Gymnastics	1960–68	7	4	0	11
4 =	**Agnes Keleti**, Hungary	Gymnastics	1952–56	5	3	2	10
=	**Polina Astakhova**, USSR	Gymnastics	1956–64	5	2	3	10
=	**Jenny Thompson**, US	Swimming	1992–2000	8	1	1	10
7 =	**Lyudmila Turishcheva**, USSR	Gymnastics	1968–76	4	3	2	9
=	**Nadia Comaneci**, Romania	Gymnastics	1976–80	5	3	1	9
9 =	**Sofia Muratova**, USSR	Gymnastics	1956–60	2	2	4	8
=	**Dawn Fraser**, Australia	Swimming	1956–64	4	4	0	8
=	**Shirley Babashoff**, US	Swimming	1972–76	2	6	0	8
=	**Kornelia Ender**, East Germany	Swimming	1972–76	4	4	0	8
=	**Dara Torres**, US	Swimming	1984–2000	4	0	4	8

* 1896–2004 inclusive

Larissa Latynina holds the record for total medals won by any athlete in any sport in Olympic history. Vera Cáslavská (1968), and Daniela Silivas of Romania (1988), are the only gymnasts to obtain medals in all six events at one Olympics. Gymnastics and swimming dominate the medal table, with canoeist Birgit Fischer-Schmidt outstanding not only among women competitors but as the holder of the most Olympic canoeing medals of all time.

Winter Olympics

top 10 WINTER OLYMPICS MEDAL-WINNING COUNTRIES

| COUNTRY | (GOLD) | MEDALS* | | (TOTAL) |
		(SILVER)	(BRONZE)	
1 USSR/Unified Team/Russia	113	82	78	273
2 Norway	94	93	73	260
3 US	70	70	51	191
4 Germany/West Germany	68	67	52	187
5 Austria	41	57	65	163
6 Finland	41	51	49	141
7 East Germany	39	37	35	111
8 Sweden	36	28	38	102
9 Switzerland	32	33	36	101
10 Canada	30	28	37	95

* Up to and including the 2002 Salt Lake City Games; includes medals won for figure skating and ice hockey in the Summer Games prior to the launch of the Winter Olympics in 1924

First Fact American athlete Edward "Eddie" Eagan (1897–1967) is the first and—to date—the only person to win gold medals in both Summer and Winter Olympic Games. In 1920 he beat Sverre Sörsdal of Norway in the light-heavyweight boxing final at the Antwerp Olympics. He failed to win a medal at the 1924 Olympics and did not take part in the 1928 Games, but at the 1932 Lake Placid Winter Olympics, he was a member of the winning US four-man bobsled team.

➲ Calgary commemoration
The cross-country skier was one of a series of ten silver $20 coins issued by Canada to commemorate the 1988 Winter Olympics.

top 10 WINTER OLYMPICS GOLD MEDALISTS

	MEDALLIST / COUNTRY	SPORT	GOLD MEDALS*
1	**Bjørn Dählie**, Norway	Cross-country skiing	8
2	= **Lyubov Egorova**, UT#/Russia	Cross-country skiing	6
	= **Lydia Skoblikova**, USSR	Speed skating	6
4	= **Bonnie Blair**, US	Speed skating	5
	= **Eric Heiden**, US	Speed skating	5
	= **Larissa Lazutina**, UT#/Russia	Cross-country skiing	5
	= **Clas Thunberg**, Norway	Speed skating	5
	= **Ole Einar Bjuøerndalen**, Norway	Biathlon	5
9	= **Ivar Ballangrud**, Norway	Speed skating	4
	= **Lee-Kyung Chun**, South Korea	Short-track speed skating	4
	= **Yevgeny Grishin**, USSR	Speed skating	4
	= **Sixten Jernberg**, Sweden	Cross-country skiing	4
	= **Johann Olav Koss**, Norway	Speed skating	4
	= **Galina Kulakova**, USSR	Cross-country skiing	4
	= **Matti Nykänen**, Finland	Ski jumping	4
	= **Claudia Pechstein**, Germany	Speed skating	4
	= **Raisa Smetanina**, UT#/Russia	Cross-country skiing	4
	= **Gunde Svan**, Sweden	Cross-country skiing	4
	= **Alexander Tikhonov**, USSR	Biathlon	4
	= **Thomas Wassberg**, Sweden	Cross-country skiing	4
	= **Nikolai Zimyatov**, USSR	Cross-country skiing	4

* All events up to and including the 2002 Salt Lake City Games
# UT = Unified Team, Commonwealth of Independent States, 1992

top 10 WINTER OLYMPICS **MEDAL WINNERS**

	MEDALLIST / COUNTRY	SPORT	YEARS	(GOLD)	MEDALS* (SILVER)	(BRONZE)	(TOTAL)
1	**Bjørn Dählie**, Norway	Cross-country skiing	1992–98	8	4	0	12
2	**Raisa Smetanina**, USSR	Cross-country skiing	1976–92	4	5	1	10
3 =	**Sixten Jernberg**, Sweden	Cross-country skiing	1956–64	4	3	2	9
=	**Lyubov Egorova**, UT#/Russia	Cross-country skiing	1992–94	6	3	0	9
=	**Stefania Belmondo**, Italy	Cross-country skiing	1992–2002	2	3	4	9
=	**Larisa Lazutina**, UT#/Russia	Cross-country skiing	1992–2002	5	3	1	9
7 =	**Galina Kulakova**, USSR	Cross-country skiing	1968–80	4	2	2	8
=	**Karin Kania (née Enke)**, East Germany	Speed skating	1980–88	3	4	1	8
=	**Gunda Neimann-Stirnemann**, East Germany/Germany	Speed skating	1992–98	3	4	1	8
10 =	**Clas Thunberg**, Norway	Speed skating	1924–28	5	1	1	7
=	**Ivar Ballangrud**, Norway	Speed skating	1928–36	4	2	1	7
=	**Veikko Hakulinen**, Finland	Cross-country skiing	1952–60	3	3	1	7
=	**Eero Mäntyranta**, Finland	Cross-country skiing	1960–68	3	2	2	7
=	**Andrea Ehrig (née Mitscherlich; formerly Schöne)**, East Germany	Speed skating	1976–88	1	5	1	7
=	**Marja-Liisa Kirvesniemi (née Hämäläinen)**, Finland	Cross-country skiing	1980–98	3	0	4	7
=	**Bogdan Musiol**, East Germany/Germany	Bobsledding	1986–92	1	5	1	7
=	**Elena Välbe**, UT#/Russia	Cross-country skiing	1992–98	3	0	4	7
=	**Kjetil Andre Aamoldt**, Norway	Alpine skiing	1992–2002	3	2	2	7
=	**Rico Gross**, Germany	Biathlon	1992–2002	3	2	2	7
=	**Claudia Pechstein**, Germany	Speed skating	1992–2002	4	1	2	7

* All events up to and including the 2002 Salt Lake City Games

UT = Unified Team, Commonwealth of Independent States, 1992

Prior to Bjørn Dählie's Olympic achievements, Russia's Raisa Smetanina was the all-time Winter Olympics medalist. Born on February 29, 1952, she appeared in five Olympics for the Soviet Union and the Unified Team in 1992. Her first medal was silver in the 5-km Cross-Country at Innsbruck in 1976. She came away from those Games with two golds and a silver, won silver and gold in 1980, two silvers in 1984, a bronze and silver in 1988, and her 10th and last medal, a gold, in the 4-x-5-km Relay in 1992. Considered the greatest cross-country skier of all time, Bjørn Dählie (born 1967) gained more golds and more medals than any other Winter Games competitor in three Olympics and might have gone on to further wins in Salt Lake City in 2002 had his career not been cut short by injury.

⊘ **Small wonder**
Despite her diminutive 5-ft (1.55-m) height, Italian skier Stefania Belmondo won Olympic medals in four Games.

top 10 SUMMER OLYMPICS MEDAL-WINNING COUNTRIES

	COUNTRY	(GOLD)	MEDALS* (SILVER) (BRONZE)		(TOTAL)
1	United States	907	697	615	2,219
2	USSR/Unified Team/Russia	525	436	409	1,370
3	Germany/West Germany	229	258	298	785
4	Great Britain	189	242	237	668
5	France	199	202	230	631
6	Italy	189	154	168	511
7	Sweden	140	157	179	476
8	Hungary	158	141	161	460
9	East Germany	159	150	136	445
10	Australia	119	126	154	399

* 1896–2004, inclusive

There have been 25 Summer Olympics since the 1896 Games in Athens (including the 1906 Intercalated Games, also held in Athens). The USSR first entered the Olympic Games in 1952, but boycotted the 1984 Games. The US boycotted the 1980 Games. James Connolly of the US became the first Olympic champion in 1896 when he took the hop, step, and jump (now triple jump) first prize, which in those days was a silver medal. Runners-up used to receive bronze medals and third-place athletes were not rewarded for their efforts. However, all Olympic records consider the first, second, and third-place athletes in 1896 to have received gold, silver, and bronze medals.

➔ **Olympic victors**
The US and USSR/Russia have dominated the Summer Olympics: US athlete Jesse Owens (above) won four gold medals at the 1936 Berlin Olympics; Russian rower Nikolai Spinev (top right) and US athlete Shawn Crawford (bottom right) were both gold medal winners at the 2004 Athens Games; 17-year-old Soviet gymnast Olga Korbut (bottom left) was a triple gold and silver medal-winner at the 1972 Munich Olympics.

⬅ **Munich medals**
US swimmer Mark Spitz won an unprecedented seven of his country's total of 33 gold medals at the 1972 Munich Olympics.

Football

top 10 CAREER **TOUCHDOWNS**

PLAYER	YEARS	TOUCHDOWNS*
1 Jerry Rice	1985–2004	207
2 Emmitt Smith	1990–2004	175
3 Marcus Allen	1982–97	144
4 Marshall Faulk	1994–2004	135
5 Cris Carter	1987–2002	130
6 Jim Brown	1957–65	126
7 Walter Payton	1975–87	125
8 John Riggins	1971–85	116
9 Lenny Moore	1956–67	111
10 Barry Sanders	1989–98	109

* As of end of 2004 season

Source: National Football League

A wide receiver, Jerry Rice also holds Super Bowl records in touchdowns, receptions, and yards receiving, winning three Super Bowls with the San Francisco 49ers (1989, 1990, 1995). He only once topped the NFL scoring list, in 1987, with 130 points.

top 10 NFL **POINT-SCORERS**

PLAYER	YEARS	POINTS*
1 Gary Anderson	1982–2004	2,448
2 Morten Andersen	1982–2004	2,358
3 George Blanda	1949–75	2,002
4 Norm Johnson	1982–99	1,736
5 Nick Lowery	1980–96	1,711
6 Jan Stenerud	1980–85	1,699
7 Eddie Murray	1980–2000	1,594
8 Al Del Greco	1984–2000	1,584
9 John Carney	1988–2004	1,537
10 Matt Stover	1991–2004	1,481

* As of end of 2004 season

Source: National Football League

Born in 1959, Gary Anderson started his career with the Pittsburgh Steelers in 1982 before playing two seasons with the Philadelphia Eagles in 1995–96. He had a year with the San Francisco 49ers in 1997, moved on to the Minnesota Vikings 1998, and then to the Tennessee Titans in 2003. He broke George Blanda's points record in 2000. Anderson came out of retirement in 2003 and again in 2004 to help out the Titans.

First Fact

At the end of the 1932 season, the Chicago Bears were tied with the Portsmouth (Ohio) Spartans, and a playoff was arranged to decide the league champions. On December 18, heavy snow made it impossible to play on Chicago's Wrigley Field, so the game was moved indoors to Chicago Stadium, an indoor arena just vacated by a circus. Since the field for this first-ever indoor NFL game was 80 yards shorter than a normal playing area, with walls at each end, the goal posts had to be repositioned and new rules invented. A crowd of 11,198 saw the Bears win 9-0.

◀ Marshall law
St. Louis Rams running back Marshall Faulk (born 1973) set the NFL record for yards from scrimmage with 1,381 rushing and 1,048 receiving.

top 10 BIGGEST **WINNING MARGINS** IN THE SUPER BOWL

	WINNERS	RUNNERS-UP	YEAR	SCORE	MARGIN
1	San Francisco 49ers	Denver Broncos	1990	55–10	45
2	Chicago Bears	New England Patriots	1986	46–10	36
3	Dallas Cowboys	Buffalo Bills	1993	52–17	35
4	Washington Redskins	Denver Broncos	1988	42–10	32
5	Los Angeles Raiders	Washington Redskins	1984	38–9	29
6	= Baltimore Ravens	New York Giants	2001	34–7	27
	= Tampa Bay Buccaneers	Oakland Raiders	2003	48–21	27
8	Green Bay Packers	Kansas City Chiefs	1967	35–10	25
9	San Francisco 49ers	San Diego Chargers	1995	49–26	23
10	San Francisco 49ers	Miami Dolphins	1985	38–16	22

Source: National Football League

The closest Super Bowl was in 1991, when the New York Giants beat the Buffalo Bills 20–19. Scott Norwood missed a 47-yard field goal eight seconds from the end of time to deprive the Bills of their first-ever Super Bowl win.

top 10 **NFL COACHES** WITH THE MOST WINS

	COACH	GAMES WON*
1	Don Shula	347
2	George Halas	324
3	Tom Landry	270
4	Curly Lambeau	229
5	Chuck Noll	209
6	Dan Reeves	201
7	Chuck Knox	193
8	Marty Schottenheimer	182
9	Paul Brown[#]	170
10	Bud Grant	168

* Regular and post season games

[#] A further 52 wins that came in the AAFC are not recognized by the NFL

Source: National Football League

top 10 **MOST SUCCESSFUL** SUPER BOWL TEAMS

	TEAM	SUPER BOWL GAMES (WINS)	(RUNNERS-UP)	(POINTS*)
1	Dallas Cowboys	5	3	13
2	= Pittsburgh Steelers	4	1	10
	= San Francisco 49ers	5	0	10
4	= Denver Broncos	2	4	8
	= New England Patriots	3	2	8
	= Oakland / Los Angeles Raiders	3	2	8
	= Washington Redskins	3	2	8
8	= Green Bay Packers	3	1	7
	= Miami Dolphins	2	3	7
10	New York Giants	2	1	5

* Based on two points for a Super Bowl win, and one for runner-up; up to and including 2005 Super Bowl

Source: National Football League

top 10 **OLDEST** NFL TEAMS*

	PRESENT NAME / NAME DURING FIRST SEASON	FIRST SEASON
1	= Arizona Cardinals / Chicago Cardinals	1920
	= Chicago Bears / Decatur Staleys	1920
3	Green Bay Packers / Green Bay Packers	1921
4	New York Giants / New York Giants	1925
5	Detroit Lions / Portsmouth [OH] Spartans	1930
6	Washington Redskins / Boston Braves	1932
7	= Philadelphia Eagles / Philadelphia Eagles	1933
	= Pittsburgh Steelers / Pittsburgh Pirates	1933
9	St. Louis Rams / Cleveland Rams	1937
10	= Cleveland Browns / Cleveland Browns	1946
	= San Francisco 49ers / San Francisco 49ers	1946

* Current teams only; based on first season in the League

➲ Ahead of the game
Among the first NFL teams, the NY Giants have gained two and the Washington Redskins three Super Bowl victories.

Track Athletics

top 10 COUNTRIES WITH THE **MOST TRACK MEDALS** AT THE 2004 ATHENS OLYMPIC GAMES

	COUNTRY	(GOLD)	MEDALS (SILVER)	(BRONZE)	(TOTAL)
1	US	6	7	5	18
2	Russia	1	6	2	9
3	=Ethiopia	2	2	3	7
	=Kenya	1	4	2	7
5	Jamaica	2	1	2	5
6	Australia	–	1	3	4
7	=Great Britain	3	–	–	3
	=Morocco	2	1	–	3
9	=Bahrain	1	–	1	2
	=China	2	–	–	2
	=France	–	–	2	2
	=Greece	2	–	–	2
	=Italy	2	–	–	2
	=Nigeria	–	–	2	2
	=Portugal	–	1	1	2
	=Romania	–	1	1	2
	=Ukraine	–	1	1	2

top 10 **FASTEST MILERS** EVER*

	ATHLETE / COUNTRY	YEAR	TIME (MIN:SEC)
1	**Hicham El Guerrouj**, Morocco	1999	3:43.13
2	**Noah Ngeny**, Kenya	1999	3:43.40
3	**Noureddine Morceli**, Algeria	1993	3:44.39
4	**Steve Cram**, GB	1985	3:46.32
5	**Daniel Komen**, Kenya	1997	3:46.38
6	**Vénuste Niyongabo**, Burundi	1997	3:46.70
7	**Saïd Aouita**, Morocco	1987	3:46.76
8	**Bernard Lagat**, Kenya	2001	3:47.28
9	**Sebastian Coe**, GB	1981	3:47.33
10	**Laban Rotich**, Kenya	1997	3:47.65

* Outdoor records as of Jan. 1, 2005; fastest time by each athlete only included

top 10 **FASTEST WOMEN** EVER*

	ATHLETE / COUNTRY	YEAR	TIME (SEC)
1	**Florence Griffith Joyner**, US	1988	10.49
2	**Marion Jones**, US	1998	10.65
3	**Christine Arron**, France	1998	10.73
4	**Merlene Ottey**, Jamaica	1996	10.74
5	**Evelyn Ashford**, US	1984	10.76
6	=**Irina Privalova**, Russia	1994	10.77
	=**Ivet Lalova**, Bulgaria	2004	10.77
8	**Dawn Sowell**, US	1989	10.78
9	=**Xuemei Li**, China	1997	10.79
	=**Inger Miller**, US	1999	10.79

* Based on fastest time for the 100 meters as of Jan. 1, 2005; fastest time by each athlete only included

At the quarter-finals of the US Olympic trials on July 16, 1988, Florence Griffith Joyner (1959–98), nicknamed "Flo Jo," set a women's record that has never been beaten. Her mysterious death at the age of 38 fueled rumors that her achievement had been assisted by performance-enhancing drugs.

⊖ Hayes makes it
Joanna Hayes (b. 1976) wins the 100 meter hurdles at the 2004 Olympics to set a new Olympic record of 12.37 seconds and add to the US track tally of six golds.

the 10 **LATEST TRACK** WORLD RECORDS*

ATHLETE / COUNTRY / EVENT	WINNING TIME (HR:MIN:SEC)	DATE
1 **Saif Saaeed Shaheen**, Qatar Men's 3,000 m steeplechase	7:53:63	Sept. 3, 2004
2 **Denis Nizhegorodov**, Russia Men's 50 km walk	3:35:29	June 13, 2004
3 **Elvan Abeylegesse**, Turkey Women's 5,000 m	14:24.68	June 11, 2004
4 **Kenenisa Bekele**, Ethiopia Men's 10,000 m	26:20.31	June 8, 2004
5 **Kenenisa Bekele**, Ethiopia Men's 5,000 m	12:37.35	May 31, 2004
6 **Paul Tergat**, Kenya Men's marathon	2:04:55	Sept. 28, 2003
7 **Jefferson Pérez**, Ecuador Men's 20 km walk	1:17:21	Aug. 23, 2003
8 **Yuliya Pechonkina**, Russia Women's 400 m hurdles	52.34	Aug. 8, 2003
9 **Paula Radcliffe**, GB Women's marathon	2:15:25	Apr. 13, 2003
10 **Tim Montgomery**, US Men's 100 m	9.78	Sept. 14, 2002

* As of Jan. 1, 2005

⬆ **Long-distance runners**
Kenenisa Bekele leads fellow Ethiopian Sileshi Sihine to set a new 10,000 meter record at the 2004 Olympics.

top 10 **FASTEST MEN** EVER*

ATHLETE / COUNTRY	YEAR	TIME (SEC)
1 **Tim Montgomery**, US	2002	9.78
2 **Maurice Greene**, US	1999	9.79
3 =**Donovan Bailey**, Canada	1996	9.84
=**Bruny Surin**, Canada	1999	9.84
5 =**Leroy Burrell**, US	1994	9.85
=**Justin Gatlin**, US	2004	9.85
7 =**Carl Lewis**, US	1991	9.86
=**Frank Fredericks**, Namibia	1996	9.86
=**Ato Boldon**, Trinidad	1998	9.86
=**Francis Obikwelu**, Portugal	2004	9.86

* Based on fastest time for the 100 meters as of Jan. 1, 2005; fastest time by each athlete only included

Some would argue that Michael Johnson (US) should be in this category with his remarkable 200 meter record of 19.32 seconds in 1996 (equivalent to a 100 meter time of 9.66 seconds), but his best 100 meter time is only 10.09 seconds.

Field Athletics

top 10 LONGEST-STANDING OUTDOOR FIELD ATHLETICS WORLD RECORDS (FEMALE)

ATHLETE / COUNTRY	EVENT	DATE SET	DATE BROKEN	DURATION (YRS	MTHS	DAYS)
1 **Natalya Lisovskaya**, USSR	Shot put	June 7, 1987	*	17	6	24
2 **Stefka Kostadinova**, Bulgaria	High jump	Aug. 30, 1987	*	17	4	1
3 **Galina Chistyakova**, Russia	Long jump	June 11, 1988	*	16	6	21
4 **Gabriele Reinsch**, Germany	Discus	July 9, 1988	*	16	5	23
5 **Jackie Joyner-Kersee**, US	Heptathlon	Sept. 24, 1988	*	16	3	8
6 **Gisela Mauermayer**, Germany	Shot put	July 15, 1934	Aug. 4, 1948	14	0	20
7 **Gisela Mauermayer**	Discus	July 11, 1936	Aug. 8, 1948	12	0	28
8 **Kinue Hitomi**, Japan	Long jump	May 20, 1928	July 30, 1939	11	2	10
9 **Francina Blankers-Koen**, Netherlands	Long jump	Sept. 19, 1943	Feb. 20, 1954	11	5	1
10 **Iolanda Balas**, Romania	High jump	July 16 1961	Sept. 4, 1971	10	1	19

* As of Jan. 1, 2005

top 10 LONGEST-STANDING OUTDOOR FIELD ATHLETICS WORLD RECORDS (MALE)

ATHLETE / COUNTRY	EVENT	DATE SET	DATE BROKEN	DURATION (YRS	MTHS	DAYS)
1 **Jesse Owens**, US	Long jump	May 25, 1935	Aug. 12, 1960	25	2	18
2 **Patrick Ryan**, US	Hammer	Aug. 17, 1913	Aug. 27, 1938	25	0	10
3 **Bob Beamon**, US	Long jump	Oct. 18, 1968	Aug. 30, 1991	22	10	12
4 **Daniel Ahearn**, US	Triple jump	May 30, 1911	Oct. 27, 1931	20	4	28
5 **Peter O'Connor**, GB	Long jump	Aug. 5, 1901	July 23, 1921	19	11	13
6 **Ralph Rose**, US	Shot put	Aug. 21, 1909	May 6, 1928	18	8	15
7 **Jürgen Schult**, Germany	Discus	June 6, 1986	*	18	6	25
8 **Yuriy Syedikh**, Russia	Hammer	Aug. 30, 1986	*	18	4	2
9 **Naoto Tajima**, Japan	Triple jump	Aug. 6, 1936	Sept. 30, 1951	15	1	24
10 **Cornelius Warmerdam**, US	Pole vault	May 23, 1942	Apr. 27, 1957	14	11	4

* As of Jan. 1, 2005

top 10 LONGEST-STANDING CURRENT OLYMPIC FIELD ATHLETICS RECORDS

	ATHLETE / COUNTRY	EVENT	WINNING DISTANCE OR SCORE	DATE
1	Bob Beamon, US	Men's long jump	8.90 m	Oct. 18, 1968
2	Ilona Slupianek, East Germany	Women's shot	22.41 m	July 24, 1980
3	Ulf Timmermann, East Germany	Men's shot	22.47 m	Sept. 23, 1988
4	Jackie Joyner-Kersee, US	Women's heptathlon	7,291 points	Sept. 24, 1988
5	Sergey Litvinov, USSR	Men's hammer	84.80 m	Sept. 26, 1988
6 =	Martina Hellmann, East Germany	Women's discus	72.30 m	Sept. 29, 1988
=	Jackie Joyner-Kersee	Women's long jump	7.40 m	Sept. 29, 1988
8	Inessa Kravets, Ukraine	Women's triple jump	15.33 m	Aug. 4, 1996
9	Kenny Harrison, US	Men's triple jump	18.09 m	July 27, 1996
10	Charles Austin, US	Men's high jump	2.39 m	July 28, 1996

Bob Beamon's record-breaking jump in 1968 is regarded as one of the greatest achievements in athletics. He was aided by Mexico City's rarefied atmosphere, but to add a staggering 22½ in (55 cm) to the old world record, and win the competition by 28 in (71 cm), was no mean feat. Beamon's jump of 29 ft 2½ in (8.90 m) was the first beyond both 28 and 29 ft (8.53 and 8.84 m). The next jump to exceed 28 ft (8.53 m) in the Olympics was not until 1980, 12 years after Beamon's leap.

top 10 COUNTRIES WITH THE MOST FIELD ATHLETICS MEDALS AT THE 2004 ATHENS OLYMPIC GAMES

	COUNTRY	MEDALS (G)	(S)	(B)	(TOTAL)
1	Russia	5	3	5	13
2	US	2	5	–	7
3	Cuba	2	1	1	4
4 =	Greece	–	2	1	3
=	Sweden	3	–	–	3
6 =	Bulgaria	–	1	1	2
=	Czech Republic	1	–	1	2
=	Germany	–	2	–	2
=	Lithuania	1	1	–	2
=	Ukraine	1	–	1	2

the 10 MOST RECENT FIELD ATHLETICS WORLD RECORDS*

	ATHLETE / COUNTRY	EVENT	WINNING DISTANCE OR SCORE	DATE
1	Yelena Isinbayeva, Russia	Women's pole vault	4.92 m	Sept. 3, 2004
2	Osleidys Menéndez, Cuba	Women's javelin throw	71.54 m	July 1, 2001
3	Roman Sebrle, Czech Republic	Men's decathlon	9,026 points	May 27, 2001
4	Mihaela Melinte, Romania	Women's hammer throw	76.07 m	Aug. 29, 1999
5	Jan Zelezny, Czech Republic	Men's javelin throw	98.48 m	May 25, 1996
6	Inessa Kravets, Ukraine	Women's triple jump	15.50 m	Aug. 10, 1995
7	Jonathan Edwards, GB	Men's triple jump	18.29 m	Aug. 7, 1995
8	Sergey Bubka, Ukraine	Men's pole vault	6.14 m	July 31, 1994
9	Javier Sotomayor, Cuba	Men's high jump	2.45 m	July 27, 1993
10	Mike Powell, US	Men's long jump	8.95 m	Aug. 30, 1991

* As of Jan. 1, 2005

◉ Russian and pole

In 2004 in Brussels, Belgium, Yelena Isinbayeva (b. 1982) beat her own gold-medal-winning Olympic height of 4.91 m to set a new world women's pole vault record.

Baseball Teams

top 10 TEAMS WITH THE MOST WORLD SERIES WINS

	TEAM*	WINS
1	New York Yankees	26
2 =	Philadelphia/Kansas City/Oakland Athletics	9
=	St. Louis Cardinals	9
4 =	Boston Red Sox	6
=	Brooklyn/Los Angeles Dodgers	6
6 =	Cincinnati Reds	5
=	New York/San Francisco Giants	5
=	Pittsburgh Pirates	5
9	Detroit Tigers	4
10 =	Boston/Milwaukee/Atlanta Braves	3
=	St. Louis/Baltimore Orioles	3
=	Washington Senators/Minnesota Twins	3

* Teams separated by "/" indicate changes of franchise and are regarded as the same team for Major League record purposes

top 10 TEAMS WITH THE MOST APPEARANCES IN THE WORLD SERIES

	TEAM	WINS	LOSSES	APPS.
1	New York Yankees	26	13	39
2	Brooklyn/Los Angeles Dodgers	6	12	18
3	New York/San Francisco Giants	5	11	16
4	St. Louis Cardinals	9	6	15
5	Philadelphia/Kansas City/Oakland Athletics	9	5	14
6	Chicago Cubs	2	8	10
7 =	Boston/Milwaukee/Atlanta Braves	3	6	9
=	Boston Red Sox	5	4	9
=	Cincinnati Reds	5	4	9
=	Detroit Tigers	4	5	9

The Toronto Blue Jays and the Florida Marlins are the only teams to have appeared in two World Series and not lost, while the San Diego Padres are the only team to have appeared in two Series and not won. The Yankees appeared in 15 of the 18 World Series held between 1947 and 1964, winning 10 and losing five.

the 10 LATEST WINNERS OF THE WORLD SERIES

YEAR	WINNER / LEAGUE*	LOSER / LEAGUE*	SCORE
2004	Boston Red Sox (A)	St. Louis Cardinals (N)	4–0
2003	Florida Marlins (N)	New York Yankees (A)	4–2
2002	Anaheim Angels (A)	San Francisco Giants (N)	4–3
2001	Arizona Diamondbacks (N)	New York Yankees (A)	4–3
2000	New York Yankees (A)	New York Mets (N)	4–1
1999	New York Yankees (A)	Atlanta Braves (N)	4–0
1998	New York Yankees (A)	San Diego Padres (N)	4–0
1997	Florida Marlins (N)	Cleveland Indians (A)	4–3
1996	New York Yankees (A)	Atlanta Braves (N)	4–2
1995	Atlanta Braves (N)	Cleveland Indians (A)	4–2

* A = American League; N = National League

The Boston Red Sox won the first modern World Series in 1903, beating the Pittsburgh Pirates 5–3 in the best-of-seven series. The Pirates led 3–1 after the first four games. The turning point was the Red Sox 7–3 victory in game 7 when they eventually beat Pirates' starting pitcher Deacon Phillippe. The Pirates' right-fielder Jimmy Sebring hit a homer in game one, the first home run in the World Series.

First Fact

Following a meeting of the National Association in February 1876, baseball's first National League was formed and the first match was played on April 22, with Boston beating Philadelphia 6–5 and Jim O'Rourke the first player to get a hit. Chicago's Ross Barnes was the first player to hit a homer, and St. Louis' George Bradley pitched the first no-hitter. Chicago won the first championship pennant after winning 52 of their 66 matches with a 0.788 average. St. Louis was runner-up, while Cincinnati finished last of the eight teams.

top 10 TEAMS WINNING THE MOST AMERICAN LEAGUE SEASON AND DIVISION TITLES

	TEAM	FIRST TITLE	LAST TITLE	TOTAL
1	New York Yankees	1921	2004	40
2	Oakland Athletics	1902	1990	15
3	Boston Red Sox	1903	2004	11
4	Detroit Tigers	1907	1984	9
5	Baltimore Orioles	1944	1983	7
6	Minnesota Twins	1924	1991	6
7	Cleveland Indians	1920	1997	5
8	Chicago White Sox	1906	1959	4
9	= Kansas City Royals	1980	1985	2
	= Toronto Blue Jays	1992	1993	2

The Seattle Mariners, the Tampa Bay Devil Rays, and the Texas Rangers are the only three American League teams never to have won a title. The Anaheim Angels (2002) and the Boston Red Sox (2004) are the only wild-card teams to have won the American League title. Both went on to win the World Series.

top 10 TEAMS WINNING THE MOST NATIONAL LEAGUE SEASON AND DIVISION TITLES

	TEAM	FIRST TITLE	LAST TITLE	TOTAL
1	Los Angeles Dodgers	1890	1988	21
2	San Francisco Giants	1888	1989	20
3	St. Louis Cardinals	1926	2004	17
4	Chicago Cubs	1876	1945	10
5	= Atlanta Braves	1877	1999	9
	= Cincinnati Reds	1919	1990	9
	= Pittsburgh Pirates	1901	1979	9
8	Philadelphia Phillies	1915	1993	5
9	New York Mets	1969	2000	4
10	= Florida Marlins	1997	2003	2
	= San Diego Padres	1984	1998	2

The Colorado Rockies and the Montreal Expos are the only National League teams never to have won a title. The 2002 World Series between Anaheim (American League) and San Francisco (National League) was the first to feature two wild-card teams.

top 10 TEAMS WITH THE MOST WINS IN MAJOR LEAGUE BASEBALL*

	TEAM	GAMES WON
1	New York Yankees	9,097
2	San Francisco Giants	8,688
3	Los Angeles Dodgers	8,421
4	St. Louis Cardinals	8,336
5	Pittsburgh Pirates	8,276
6	Boston Red Sox	8,263
7	Cleveland Indians	8,209
8	Detroit Tigers	8,150
9	Chicago Cubs	8,135
10	Cincinnati Reds	8,107

* Regular season games up to and including 2004

The Yankees made their American League debut as the Baltimore Orioles in 1901, and the following season they finished at the bottom of the League. It was then that they moved to New York and became the Highlanders. They changed their name to the Yankees in 1913.

top 10 TEAMS WITH THE MOST COLLEGE WORLD SERIES TITLES

	TEAM	WINS
1	USC	12
2	= Arizona State	5
	= LSU	5
	= Texas	5
5	= CS–Fullerton	4
	= Miami–FL	4
7	= Arizona	3
	= Minnesota	3
9	= California	2
	= Michigan	2
	= Oklahoma	2
	= Stanford	2

The NCAA Division One College World Series was first held in Kalamazoo, Michigan in 1948. Since 1950 it has been played in Omaha, Nebraska. The biggest winning margin was in 1956, when Minnesota beat Arizona 12–1.

Basketball

top 10 OLYMPIC BASKETBALL COUNTRIES*

	COUNTRY	MEDALS (G)	(S)	(B)	(TOTAL)
1	US	17	2	3	22
2	USSR/Unified Team/Russia	5	4	5	14
3	Yugoslavia	1	5	2	8
4	Brazil	0	1	4	5
5	= Australia	0	2	1	3
	= Lithuania	0	0	3	3
7	= Bulgaria	0	1	1	2
	= China	0	1	1	2
	= France	0	2	0	2
	= Italy	0	2	0	2
	= Uruguay	0	0	2	2

* Based on total of gold, silver, and bronze medals won in the men's and women's competitions

A demonstration sport at the 1904 Olympics, basketball made its official debut at Berlin in 1936, when it was played outdoors. Dr. James Naismith, the Canadian inventor of the game, presented the medals to the winning US team. The US went on to dominate the medals table, with Teresa Edwards (US) the only person to have won five Olympic medals for basketball. She won gold in 1984, 1992, 1996, and 2000, and bronze in 1988.

top 10 TEAMS WITH THE MOST NBA TITLES

	TEAM*	YEARS	TITLES
1	Boston Celtics	1957–86	16
2	Minneapolis Lakers / Los Angeles Lakers	1949–2002	14
3	Chicago Bulls	1991–98	6
4	= Detroit Pistons	1989–2004	3
	= Philadelphia Warriors / Golden State Warriors	1947–75	3
	= Syracuse Nationals / Philadelphia 76ers	1955–83	3
7	= Baltimore Bullets / Washington Bullets	1948–78	2
	= Houston Rockets	1994–95	2
	= New York Knicks	1970–72	2
	= San Antonio Spurs	1999–2003	2

* Teams separated by / indicate change of franchise and mean they have won the championship under both names

Source: National Basketball Association

Basketball is one of the few sports that can trace its exact origins. It was invented by Dr. James Naismith in Springfield, Massachusetts, in 1891. Professional basketball in the US dates back to 1898, but the National Basketball Association (NBA) was not formed until 1949, when the National Basketball League and Basketball Association of America merged. The NBA consists of 27 teams split into Eastern and Western Conferences. At the end of an 82-game regular season, the top eight teams in each Conference play off and the two Conference champions meet in a best-of-seven final for the NBA Championship.

top 10 BIGGEST NBA ARENAS

	ARENA / LOCATION	TEAM	CAPACITY
1	Palace of Auburn Hills, Auburn Hills	Detroit Pistons	22,076
2	United Center, Chicago	Chicago Bulls	21,711
3	MCI Center, Washington, D.C.	Washington Wizards	20,674
4	Gund Arena, Cleveland	Cleveland Cavaliers	20,562
5	First Union Center, Philadelphia	Philadelphia 76ers	20,444
6	Continental Airlines Arena, East Rutherford	New Jersey Nets	20,049
7	Rose Garden, Portland	Portland Trail Blazers	19,980
8	Delta Center, Salt Lake City	Utah Jazz	19,911
9	Air Canada Centre, Toronto	Toronto Raptors	19,800
10	Madison Square Garden, New York	New York Knicks	19,763

Source: National Basketball Association

The Palace of Auburn Hills in a Detroit, Michigan, suburb is the new home of the Detroit Pistons, who previously played at the Pontiac Silverdome. On November 19, 2004 it became notorious for a serious brawl that led to the suspension of a number of NBA players.

top 10 CURRENT NBA PLAYERS WITH THE **HIGHEST POINTS AVERAGE**

PLAYER	GAMES PLAYED	POINTS SCORED	POINTS AVERAGE*
1 Allen Iverson	610	16,738	30.7
2 Shaquille O'Neal	882	23,583	26.7
3 LeBron James	159	3,829	24.1
4 Vince Carter	526	10,989	23.9
5 Paul Pierce	521	12,086	23.0
6 Tim Duncan	586	13,204	22.5
7 Kobe Bryant	627	14,034	22.4
9 Tracy McGrady	565	12,423	22.0
8 Chris Webber	686	14,945	21.8
10 Dirk Nowitzki	522	11,106	21.3

* Regular season games only; as of end of 2004–05 season

Source: National Basketball Association

top 10 NBA **POINT-SCORERS**

PLAYER	YEARS	TOTAL POINTS*
1 Kareem Abdul-Jabbar	1969–89	38,387
2 Karl Malone	1985–2004	36,928
3 Michael Jordan	1984–2003	32,292
4 Wilt Chamberlain	1959–73	31,419
5 Moses Malone	1976–95	27,409
6 Elvin Hayes	1968–84	27,313
7 Hakeem Olajuwon	1984–2002	26,946
8 Oscar Robertson	1960–74	26,710
9 Dominique Wilkins	1982–99	26,668
10 John Havlicek	1962–78	26,395

* Regular season games only; as of end of 2004–05 season

Source: National Basketball Association

If points from the ABA were also considered, then Kareem Abdul-Jabbar would still be No.1, with the same total. The greatest point-scorer in NBA history, he was born as Lew Alcindor but adopted a new name on converting to the Islamic faith in 1969. The next year he turned professional, playing for Milwaukee. His career spanned 20 seasons before he retired at the end of the 1989 season.

Sixers star

As well as securing top place in the points average table, Philadelphia 76ers all-star guard Allen Iverson (b. 1975) was the first player ever to achieve 10 steals in a single NBA playoff game, against the Orlando Magic on May 13, 1999.

First Fact Wilt Chamberlain was the first player to lead the NBA for scoring in seven consecutive years (1960–66), the first to score more than 3,000 points in a single season (3,033 in 1960–61), the first to gain over 4,000 (4,029 in 1961–62), and the first to score 100 in a single game (March 2, 1962).

⬆ **Triple triumph** In 2003 Roy Jones Jr. won his third world title—and appeared in *The Matrix Reloaded*.

The 10 LATEST BOXERS TO WIN **THREE OR MORE WORLD TITLES**

	BOXER / COUNTRY	TITLES WON	DATES
1	**"Sugar" Shane Mosley**, US	Junior Middleweight, WBC Welterweight, IBF Lightweight	Aug. 1997–Sept. 2003
2	**James Toney**, US	IBF Cruiserweight, IBF Super Middleweight, IBF Middleweight	May 1991–Apr. 2003
3	**Roy Jones Jr.**, US	WBA Heavyweight, IBF/WBA/WBC Light Heavyweight, IBF Middleweight	May 1993–Mar. 2003
4	**Johnny Tapia**, US	IBF Featherweight, WBA Bantamweight, IBF Junior Bantamweight	July 1997–Apr. 2002
5	**Oscar De La Hoya**, US	WBA/WBC Junior Middleweight, WBC Welterweight, WBC Junior Welterweight, IBF Lightweight	May 1995–June 2001
6	**Felix Trinidad**, US (Puerto Rico)	IBF/WBA Middleweight, IBF/WBA Junior Middleweight, IBF/WBC Welterweight	May 1993–May 2001
7	**Leo Gamez**, Venezuela	WBA Junior Bantamweight, WBA Flyweight, WBA Junior Flyweight	Aug. 1993–Oct. 2000
8	**Julio Cesar Chavez**, Mexico	IBF/WBC Junior Welterweight, WBC/WBA Lightweight, WBC Junior Lightweight	Sept. 1984–May 1994
9	**Thomas Hearns**, US	WBA/WBC Light Heavyweight, Middleweight, Junior Middleweight, WBA Welterweight	Aug. 1980–May 1991
10	**Roberto Duran**, Panama	WBC Middleweight, Welterweight, WBA Junior Middleweight, Lightweight	May 1972–Feb. 1989

top 10 LONGEST-REIGNING WORLD HEAVYWEIGHT CHAMPIONS

BOXER / COUNTRY	RECOGNITION	DATES	DURATION (YRS)	DURATION (MTHS)
1 Joe Louis, US	World	1937–49*	11	8
2 Larry Holmes, US	WBC, IBF	1978–85#	8	3
3 William Harrison "Jack" Dempsey, US	World	1919–26	7	2
4 John Arthur "Jack" Johnson, US	World	1908–15	6	3
5 James Jackson Jeffries, US	World	1899–1905	5	10
6 James John Corbett, US	World	1892–1897	4	6
7 Lennox Lewis, UK	WBC, WBA, IBF	1997–2001†	4	2
8 Jess Willard, US	World	1915–19	4	1
9 Brian Nielsen, Denmark	IBO	1996–99*	3	8
10 Rocky Marciano, US	World	1952–56*	3	7

* Retired / relinquished title

Relinquished WBC title on Dec. 11, 1983 to assume title of the newly established IBF

† WBC from Feb. 7, 1997; IBF, IBO, WBA, and WBC Nov. 13, 1999–Apr. 29, 2000, when WBA title relinquished; IBF, IBO, and WBC Apr. 29, 2000–Apr. 22, 2001

The first boxing board to be established was the World Boxing Association (WBA) in 1921, originally founded as the National Boxing Association (NBA). In 1963, the World Boxing Council (WBC) was established, followed in 1983 by the International Boxing Federation (IBF), and in 1988 by the World Boxing Organization (WBO). Finally, in 1991, the International Boxing Organization (IBO) was founded.

top 10 OLDEST BOXING WORLD HEAVYWEIGHT CHAMPIONS*

BOXER / COUNTRY	RECOGNITION	DATE OF WIN	AGE (YRS)	AGE (MTHS)	AGE (DAYS)
1 George Foreman#, US	IBF, WBA	Nov. 5, 1994	46	9	14
2 Evander Holyfield#, US	WBA	Aug. 12, 2000	37	9	13
3 Corrie Sanders, South Africa	WBO	Mar. 8, 2003	37	7	1
4 Jersey Joe Walcott, US	Universal	July 18, 1951	37	6	5
5 Muhammad Ali#, US	WBA	Sept. 15, 1978	36	7	29
6 Lennox Lewis#, UK	IBF, IBO, WBC	Nov. 17, 2001	36	2	15
7 Roy Jones Jr., US	WBA	Mar. 1, 2003	34	1	13
8 Bob Fitzsimmons, US	Universal	Mar. 17, 1897	33	9	24
9 Frank Bruno, US	WBC	Sept. 2, 1995	33	9	16
10 Trevor Berbick, Jamaica	WBC	Mar. 22, 1986	33	7	21

* Based on age at date when world title won or regained; only latest titles listed

Age at date of regaining title

⊙ Veteran victory
Corrie Sanders (born 1967) achieved a decisive second-round knockout to become heavyweight champion, despite his advanced (for a boxer) age of 37.

top 10 LATEST UNDISPUTED WORLD HEAVYWEIGHT BOXING CHAMPIONS

BOXER / COUNTRY	YEAR
1 Lennox Lewis, UK	1999
2 Riddick Bowe, US	1992
3 Evander Holyfield, US	1990
4 James "Buster" Douglas, US	1990
5 Mike Tyson, US	1987
6 Leon Spinks, US	1978
7 Muhammad Ali, US	1974
8 George Foreman, US	1973
9 Joe Frazier, US	1970
10 Muhammad Ali, US	1967

"Undisputed" champions are those who are recognized by the main governing bodies at the time of winning their world title. The current main governing bodies are: the World Boxing Council (WBC), World Boxing Association (WBA), International Boxing Federation (IBF), and World Boxing Organization (WBO). Champions not recognized by all the major bodies of the day may coexist with these, so at any one time there may be more than one "world champion" in each weight division.

Cycling

	RACE	FIRST HELD
1	Liège–Bastogne–Liège	1892
2	Paris–Brussels	1893
3 =	Paris–Roubaix	1896
=	ParisParis–Tours*	1896
5	Tour de France	1903
6	Tour of Lombardy	1905
7	Giro d'Italia (Tour of Italy)	1906
8	Milan–San Remo	1907
9	Tour of Flanders	1913
10	Grand Prix des Nations	1932

* Known as the Blois–Chaville 1974–1987

The oldest-ever classic was the Bordeaux to Paris race, inaugurated in 1891. The longest continuous race in the world, it covered around 373 miles (600 km) nonstop, lasting around 16 hours. The riders were paced for part of the journey. Pacing ceased in 1986 and the race was discontinued two years later.

◐ Steady Eddy

Belgian champion Eddy Merckx (born 1945) is considered one of the greatest cyclists of all time. His attempt to win a record sixth Tour de France was thwarted when he was attacked and injured by a spectator.

top 10 CYCLISTS WITH THE MOST WINS IN THE **THREE MAJOR TOURS**

	CYCLIST / COUNTRY	YEARS	TOUR	GIRO	VUELTA	TOTAL
1	**Eddy Merckx**, Belgium	1968–74	5	5	1	11
2	**Bernard Hinault**, France	1978–85	5	3	2	10
3	**Jacques Anquetil**, France	1957–64	5	2	1	8
4 =	**Fausto Coppi**, Italy	1940–53	2	5	0	7
=	**Miguel Induráin**, Spain	1991–95	5	2	0	7
6	**Lance Armstrong**, US	1999–2004	6	0	0	6
7 =	**Gino Bartali**, Italy	1938–48	2	3	0	5
=	**Alfredo Binda**, Italy	1925–33	0	5	0	5
=	**Felice Gimondi**, Italy	1965–76	1	3	1	5
10	**Tony Rominger**, Switzerland	1992–95	0	1	3	4

The three major tours are: the Tour de France, launched in 1903 and won by Maurice Garin, France; the Tour of Italy (Giro d'Italia) first contested in 1909 and won by Luigi Ganna, Italy; and the Tour of Spain (Vuelta de España), first held in 1935 and won by Gustave Deloor, Belgium. Eddy Merckx won a record 33 stages of the Tour de France in 1969–75.

top 10 **FASTEST AVERAGE WINNING SPEEDS** IN THE TOUR DE FRANCE

CYCLIST / COUNTRY	YEAR	AVERAGE SPEED (MPH)	(KM/H)
1 Lance Armstrong, US	2003	25.448	40.956
2 Lance Armstrong	2004	25.198	40.553
3 Lance Armstrong	1999	25.026	40.276
4 Lance Armstrong	2001	24.898	40.070
5 Marco Pantani, Italy	1998	24.844	39.983
6 Lance Armstrong	2002	24.804	39.919
7 Lance Armstrong	2000	24.587	39.570
8 Miguel Indurain, Spain	1992	24.546	39.504
9 Jan Ullrich, Germany	1997	24.380	39.237
10 Bjarne Rijs, Denmark	1996	24.374	39.227

The Tour de France consists of some 20 stages and covers a distance of up to 2,485 miles (4,000 km), over a three-week period, so achieving these *average* speeds represents an extraordinary feat of skill and endurance.

First Fact

The first Tour de France took place in 1903. Originally a publicity event for *L'Auto* newspaper, it took in six stages and covered a total distance of 1,508 miles (2,428 km) with 60 competitors taking part. It was won by Maurice Garin (France) at an average speed of 15.956 mph (25.679 km/h).

top 10 **OLYMPIC CYCLING** COUNTRIES

COUNTRY	MEDALS (GOLD)	(SILVER)	(BRONZE)	(TOTAL)
1 France	37	22	24	83
2 Italy	35	15	7	57
3 Germany/West Germany	16	19	20	55
4 Great Britain	12	23	19	54
5 US	13	15	19	47
6 Australia	13	15	13	41
7 Netherlands	14	16	8	38
8 USSR/Unified Team/Russia	15	8	12	35
9 Belgium	6	8	10	24
10 Denmark	6	7	8	21

France has maintained its dominance of Olympic cycling events since the first modern Games in 1896, when the first-ever gold medal winner was Léon Flameng. He cycled around a 333.3-m track 300 times to win the 100-km race. Flameng also won silver in the 10,000-m race and bronze in the 2,000-m race.

● Tour de Lance

After winning the Tour de France on a record six occasions, American cyclist Lance Armstrong (born 1971) moved to new sponsors Discovery Channel and confirmed his intention to aim for a seventh victory in 2005.

Skateboarding

top 10 SKATEBOARDERS WITH THE MOST MEDALS IN THE X GAMES

SKATER / COUNTRY	YEARS	(GOLD)	MEDALS* (SILVER)	(BRONZE)	(TOTAL)
1 = Tony Hawk, US	1995–2003	9	3	3	15
= Andy Macdonald, US	1996–2003	8	5	2	15
3 = Rodil de Araujo Jr., Brazil	1996–2003	6	4	–	10
= Bucky Lasek, US	1998–2004	6	4	–	10
5 Bob Burnquist, Brazil	1998–2003	3	3	3	9
6 Rune Glifberg, Denmark	1995–2004	–	2	6	8
7 = Chris Senn, US	1997–2001	3	1	2	6
= Pierre-Luc Gagnon, Canada	2002–04	2	4	–	6
= Eric Koston, US	2000–03	3	1	2	6
10 = Neal Hendrix, US	1995–2003	–	2	2	4
= Mike Crum, US	1999–2003	–	2	2	4
= Kerry Getz, US	2000–01	1	2	1	4

* Medals won at the X Games 1–10 and 2003 Global X Games; includes Vert, Street, and Park, doubles and best trick

top 10 VERT SKATERS, 2004 (MALE)

SKATER / COUNTRY	WCS WORLD RANKING POINTS, 2004
1 Sandro Dias, Brazil	6,000
2 Neal Hendrix, US	4,375
3 Andy Macdonald, US	4,350
4 Lincoln Ueda, Brazil	4,275
5 Rune Glifberg, Denmark	4,150
6 Rodrigo Menezes, Brazil	4,025
7 Mike Crum, US	3,925
8 Bob Burnquist, Brazil	2,900
9 Jake Brown, Australia	2,875
10 Juergen Horrwarth, Germany	2,725

Source: World Cup Skateboarding (WCS)

top 10 VERT SKATERS, 2004 (FEMALE)

SKATER / COUNTRY	WCS WORLD RANKING POINTS, 2004*
1 Cara-Beth Burnside, US	2,900
2 Lyn-Z Adams Hawkins, US	2,700
3 Mimi Knoop, US	2,500
4 Holly Lyons, US	2,200
5 Tina Neff, Germany	1,450
6 Catherine Ashley, US	1,300
7 Ciara d'Agostino, US	1,200
8 Heidi Fitzgerald, US	700
9 Julia Bauer, US	650
10 Starr Quinn, US	600

* Total of points won in the Slam City Jam, Beach Games, and Vans Triple Crowns Finals

Source: World Cup Skateboarding (WCS)

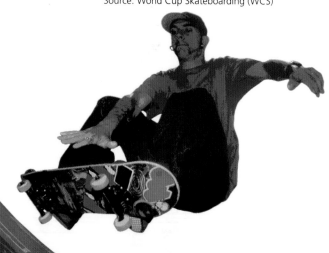

← Star turn
Through his innovative and often unique tricks and his appearance in bestselling video games, Tony Hawk (b. 1968) has clearly established himself as the world's best-known skateboarder.

top 10 STREET SKATERS, 2004 (MALE)

SKATER / COUNTRY	WCS WORLD RANKING POINTS, 2004
1 Rodil de Araujo Jr., Brazil	6,600
2 Ryan Sheckler, US	4,150
3 Greg Lutzka, US	3,770
4 Ronnie Creager, US	3,705
5 Austen Seaholm, US	3,540
6 Paul Machnau, Canada	3,475
7 Wagner Ramos, Brazil	3,375
8 Kyle Berard, US	3,230
9 Bastien Salabanzi, France	3,125
10 Dayne Brummet, US	3,110

Source: World Cup Skateboarding (WCS)

Ranking is arrived at by adding the points from a skater's four best results at North American WCS Points Events together with their best three results from WCS Points Events in Europe, Australia, Asia, and South America. Skaters have to take part in the World Championships in Dortmund, Germany, to win the No. 1 ranking.

top 10 STREET SKATERS, 2004 (FEMALE)

SKATER / COUNTRY	WCS WORLD RANKING POINTS, 2004*
1 Elissa Steamer, US	4,000
2 Vanessa Torres, US	3,800
3 Lyn-Z Adams Hawkins, US	3,100
4 Patiane Freitas, Brazil	2,850
5 Lauren Perkins, US	2,450
6 Alison Matasi, Canada	2,250
7 = Amy Caron, US	2,000
= Jessica Krause, US	2,000
9 Lauren Mollica, US	1,775
10 Elizabeth Nitu, US	1,700

* Total of points won in the Gallaz Skate Jam, Gravity Games, Vans Triple Crowns, and Canadian Open events

Source: World Cup Skateboarding (WCS)

Golf

top 10 LOWEST FOUR-ROUND WINNING TOTALS IN MAJOR CHAMPIONSHIPS

	PLAYER / COUNTRY	VENUE	YEAR	TOTAL*
1	**David Toms**, US	Atlanta, Georgia[#]	2001	265
2	**Phil Mickelson**, US	Atlanta, Georgia[#]	2001	266
3 =	**Greg Norman**, Australia	Royal St. George's, Sandwich[†]	1993	267
=	**Steve Elkington**, Australia	Riviera, California[#]	1995	267
=	**Colin Montgomerie**, UK	Riviera, California[#]	1995	267
6 =	**Tom Watson**, US	Turnberry[†]	1977	268
=	**Nick Price**, Zimbabwe	Turnberry[†]	1994	268
=	**Steve Lowery**, US	Atlanta, Georgia[#]	2001	268
9 =	**Jack Nicklaus**, US	Turnberry[†]	1977	269
=	**Nick Faldo**, UK	Royal St. George's, Sandwich[†]	1993	269
=	**Jesper Parnevik**, Sweden	Turnberry[†]	1994	269
=	**Nick Price**, Zimbabwe	Southern Hills, Tulsa[#]	1994	269
=	**Davis Love III**, US	Winged Foot, New York[#]	1997	269
=	**Tiger Woods**, US	St. Andrews[†]	2000	269

* As of Jan. 1, 2005

[#] US PGA Championship

[†] British Open Championship

The lowest four-round totals in the other two Majors are: US Masters: 270 by Tiger Woods, US, at Augusta, Georgia, 1997; US Open: 272 by Jack Nicklaus, US, at Baltusrol, 1980; 272 by Lee Janzen, US, at Baltusrol, 1993; and 272 by Tiger Woods, US, at Pebble Beach, 2000.

⊕ On the ball
Vijay Singh stands second to Tiger Woods for career winnings but in 2004 Singh knocked Woods from the top of the World Golf Rankings.

top 10 BIGGEST WINNING MARGINS IN THE MAJORS

	PLAYER / COUNTRY	YEAR	TOURNAMENT	VENUE	WINNING MARGIN
1	**Tiger Woods**, US	2000	US Open	Pebble Beach	15
2	**Tom Morris Sr.**, UK	1862	British Open	Prestwick	13
3 =	**Tom Morris Jr.**, UK	1870	British Open	Prestwick	12
=	**Tiger Woods**, US	1997	US Masters	Augusta	12
5	**Willie Smith**, US	1899	US Open	Baltimore	11
6 =	**Jim Barnes**, US	1921	US Open	Columbia	9
=	**Jack Nicklaus**, US	1965	US Masters	Augusta	9
8 =	**J.H. Taylor**, UK	1900	British Open	St. Andrews	8
=	**James Braid**, UK	1908	British Open	Prestwick	8
=	**J.H. Taylor**, UK	1913	British Open	Hoylake	8
=	**Ray Floyd**, US	1976	US Masters	Augusta	8
=	**Tiger Woods**, US	2000	British Open	St. Andrews	8

The biggest winning margin in the other Major—the US PGA Championship—was in 1980, when Jack Nicklaus won by seven strokes against Andy Bean at Oak Hill.

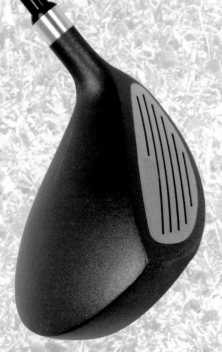

top 10 MONEY-WINNING GOLFERS

	PLAYER / COUNTRY	CAREER WINNINGS* ($)
1	Tiger Woods, US	45,142,737
2	Vijay Singh, Fiji	36,760,089
3	Phil Mickelson, US	29,557,928
4	Davis Love III, US	29,207,838
5	Ernie Els, South Africa	24,466,992
6	Jim Furyk, US	19,731,382
7	Nick Price, Zimbabwe	19,715,533
8	David Toms, US	18,942,915
9	Scott Hoch, US	18,455,984
10	Justin Leonard, US	17,639,781

* As of Jan. 1, 2005

Tiger Woods' winnings from his profession place him at the top of this list, while his total earnings from endorsements of everything from golfing equipment to motor vehicles have made him the world's richest sportsman.

top 10 PLAYERS TO WIN THE MOST MAJORS

	PLAYER / COUNTRY	BRITISH OPEN	US OPEN	US MASTERS	US PGA	TOTAL*
1	Jack Nicklaus, US	3	4	6	5	18
2	Walter Hagen, US	4	2	0	5	11
3	=Ben Hogan, US	1	4	2	2	9
	=Gary Player, South Africa	3	1	3	2	9
5	=Tom Watson, US	5	1	2	0	8
	=Tiger Woods, US	1	2	3	2	8
7	=Bobby Jones, US	3	4	0	0	7
	=Arnold Palmer, US	2	1	4	0	7
	=Gene Sarazen, US	1	2	1	3	7
	=Sam Snead, US	1	0	3	3	7
	=Harry Vardon, UK	6	1	0	0	7

* As of Jan. 1, 2005

top 10 GOLFERS WITH MOST WINS IN A US SEASON

	PLAYER*	YEAR	WINS#
1	Byron Nelson	1945	18
2	Ben Hogan	1946	13
3	Sam Snead	1950	11
4	Ben Hogan	1948	10
5	=Paul Runyan	1933	9
	=Tiger Woods	2000	9†
	=Vijay Singh	2004	9
8	=Horton Smith	1929	8
	=Gene Sarazen	1930	8
	=Harry Cooper	1937	8
	=Sam Snead	1938	8
	=Henry Picard	1939	8
	=Byron Nelson	1944	8
	=Arnold Palmer	1960	8
	=Johnny Miller	1974	8
	=Tiger Woods	1999	8

* All players from US except Singh, who is from Fiji

As of end 2004 season

† Includes Woods' British Open win which, since 1995, has been included as an official US PGA Tour event

Source: PGA

Having won eight Tour events in 1944, Byron Nelson went on to shatter the US record the following year with a stunning 18 wins. His remarkable year started on January 14, when he won the Phoenix Open, and by the time he won the Miami Four Ball at Palm Springs on March 11, he had achieved his fourth success of the season. This victory at Miami began a run of 11 consecutive tournament wins.

Horse Sports

top 10 **MONEY-WINNING** HORSES

	HORSE	WINS	WINNINGS ($)*		HORSE	WINS	WINNINGS ($)*
1	Cigar	19	9,999,815	6	Silver Charm	12	6,994,369
2	Skip Away	18	9,616,360	7	Captain Steve	9	6,828,356
3	Fantastic Light	12	8,486,957	8	Alysheba	11	6,679,242
4	Smarty Jones	8	7,613,155	9	John Henry	39	6,591,869
5	Pleasantly Perfect	8	7,349,880	10	Tiznow	8	6,427,830

* As of Jan.1, 2005

Source: National Thoroughbred Racing Association (NTRA)

List-leading horse *Cigar* achieved a total of 19 wins out of 33 starts—two in 1993 and 1994, 10 in 1995, and five in 1996—to gain his all-time North American record money total. Bred and owned by Allen Paulson, he retired as a six-year-old on October 31, 1996, at the end of a 16-race winning streak, tying a record set 46 years earlier by racing legend *Citation*. In 2002, he was elected to the Racing Hall of Fame.

top 10 **FASTEST TIMES** IN THE MELBOURNE CUP

	HORSE	YEAR	TIME (MIN:SEC)		HORSE	YEAR	TIME (MIN:SEC)
1	Kingston Rule	1990	3:16.30	7	Saintly	1996	3:18.80
2	Media Puzzle	2002	3:16.97	8 =	Kiwi	1983	3:18.90
3	Tawriffic	1989	3:17.10	=	Black Knight	1984	3:18.90
4	Might and Power	1997	3:18.30	=	Empire Rose	1988	3:18.90
5	Gold and Black	1977	3:18.40	=	Let's Elope	1991	3:18.90
6	Brew	2000	3:18.68				

Held at the Flemington Park racetrack in Victoria, the Melbourne Cup was inaugurated in 1861 and takes place on the first Tuesday in November, when most of Australia comes to a standstill at 3:20 pm to listen to the race. More than 200,000 spectators attend the meeting. Originally held over two miles, it went metric in 1972 and is now run over 3,200 meters—18.7 meters shorter than the original distance. The fastest time over two miles was 3 minutes 19.1 seconds by *Rain Lover* in 1968.

top 10 **TRAINERS** IN THE **TRIPLE CROWN** RACES

	TRAINER	KENTUCKY	PREAKNESS	BELMONT	WINS		TRAINER	KENTUCKY	PREAKNESS	BELMONT	WINS
1 =	Sunny Jim Fitzsimmons	3	4	6	13	7	Woody Stephens	2	1	5	8
=	D. Wayne Lukas	4	5	4	13	8 =	Sam Hildreth	0	0	7	7
3	Robert Walden	1	7	4	12	=	Jimmy Jones	2	4	1	7
4	James Rowe Sr.	2	1	8	11	10 =	Bob Baffert	2	3	1	6
5 =	Max Hirsch	3	2	4	9	=	Lucien Laurin	2	1	3	6
=	Ben Jones	6	2	1	9						

In 1995 D. Wayne Lukas, a former high school basketball coach, became the first to train the consecutive winners of all three Triple Crown races, with two different horses, *Thunder Gulch* and *Timber Country*. Sunny Jim Fitzsimmons is one of only two men (the other being Ben Jones) to train two different Triple Crown winners, *Whirlaway* (1941) and *Citation* (1948).

top 10 JOCKEYS WITH THE MOST BREEDERS' CUP WINS

	JOCKEY	YEARS	WINS		JOCKEY	YEARS	WINS
1	Jerry Bailey	1991–2003	14	=	Laffit Pincay Jr.	1985–93	7
2	Pat Day	1984–2001	12	=	Jose Santos	1986–2002	7
3	Mike Smith	1992–2002	10	=	Pat Valenzuela	1986–2003	7
4	Chris McCarron	1985–2001	9	10 =	Corey Nakatani	1996–2004	6
5	Gary Stevens	1990–2000	8	=	John Velazquez	1998–2004	6
6 =	Eddie Delahoussaye	1984–93	7				

Source: The Breeders' Cup

Held at a different venue each year, the Breeders' Cup is an end-of-season gathering with seven races run during the day, with the season's best thoroughbreds competing in each category. Staged in October or November, there is $13 million in prize money, with $4 million going to the winner of the day's senior race, the Classic. Churchill Downs is the most-used venue, with five Breeders' Cups since the first in 1984.

top 10 OLYMPIC EQUESTRIAN MEDAL-WINNING NATIONS*

	COUNTRY	GOLD	SILVER	BRONZE	TOTAL		COUNTRY	GOLD	SILVER	BRONZE	TOTAL
1	Germany/West Germany	35	19	21	75	6	Italy	7	9	7	23
2	United States	9	19	18	46	7	Switzerland	4	10	7	21
3	Sweden	17	8	14	39	8	Netherlands	9	9	2	20
4	France	12	12	11	35	9	USSR/UnifiedTeam/Russia	6	5	4	15
5	Great Britain	6	9	10	25	10	Belgium	4	2	5	11

* Combined total of medals won for Show Jumping, Three Day Eventing, and Dressage; including the discontinued events of high jump and long jump (1900), and the individual and team figures event (1920)

Hockey

top 10 GOAL-SCORERS IN AN NHL CAREER

	PLAYER	SEASONS	GOALS*
1	Wayne Gretzky	20	894
2	Gordie Howe	26	801
3	Brett Hull	18	741
4	Marcel Dionne	18	731
5	Phil Esposito	18	717
6	Mike Gartner	19	708
7	Mark Messier	25	694
8	Mario Lemieux	16	683
9	Steve Yzerman	21	678
10	Luc Robitaille	18	653

* Regular season only; as of end of 2003–04 season

Source: National Hockey League

top 10 GOAL-SCORERS IN AN NHL SEASON

	PLAYER / TEAM	SEASON	GAMES	GOALS*
1	Wayne Gretzy, Edmonton Oilers	1981–82	80	92
2	Wayne Gretzy, Edmonton Oilers	1983–84	74	87
3	Brett Hull, St. Louis Blues	1990–91	78	86
4	Mario Lemieux, Pittsburgh Penguins	1988–89	76	85
5	= Phil Esposito, Boston Bruins	1970–71	78	76
	= Alexander Mogilny, Buffalo Sabres	1992–93	77	76
	= Teemu Selanne, Winnipeg Jets	1992–93	84	76
8	Wayne Gretzky, Edmonton Oilers	1984–85	80	73
9	Brett Hull, St. Louis Blues	1989–90	80	72
10	= Wayne Gretzky, Edmonton Oilers	1982–83	80	71
	= Jari Kurri, Edmonton Oilers	1984–85	73	71

* As of end of 2003–04 season

In nine seasons with Edmonton Oilers, Wayne Gretzky only once scored fewer than 50 goals in a regular season (40 in 1987–88). Gretzky topped the points, goals, and assists lists in a season five times between 1982 and 1987.

top 10 PLAYERS WITH THE MOST NHL AWARDS*

	PLAYER	TOTAL
1	Wayne Gretzky	19
2	Bobby Orr	12
3	Dominik Hasek	10
4	Mario Lemieux	8
5	= Frank Boucher	7
	= Doug Harvey	7
	= Jacques Plante	7
8	= Ray Bourque	6
	= Ken Dryden	6
	= Bill Duman	6
	= Gordie Howe	6

* Based on total major awards won: Hart Memorial Trophy, Calder Memorial Trophy, Vezina Trophy, Lady Byng Memorial Trophy, James Norris Memorial Trophy, Frank Selke Trophy, and the Lester B. Pearson Award

The most prestigious annual award in the NHL is the Hart Memorial Trophy. It was presented to the NHL by Dr. David Hart, the father of Cecil Hart, the former coach of the Montreal Canadiens. The original trophy was retired to the NHL Hall of Fame in 1960 and replaced by the Hart Memorial Trophy. It is presented to the player judged by a panel of journalists to be the most valuable player of the year to his team.

top 10 GOALIES IN THE NHL

	GOALTENDER	SEASONS	GAMES WON*
1	Patrick Roy	20	551
2	Terry Sawchuk	21	447
3	Ed Belfour	16	435
4	Jacques Plante	18	434
5	Tony Esposito	16	423
6	Glenn Hall	18	407
7	= Martin Brodeur	12	403
	= Grant Fuhr	19	403
9	Curtis Joseph	15	396
10	Mike Vernon	19	385

* Regular season only; as of end of 2003–04 season

Source: National Hockey League

The first of Patrick Roy's career wins was in the 1984–85 season when he came on for one period for the Montreal Canadiens against Winnipeg Jets. He faced just two shots but received credit for the win. He was traded to the Colorado Avalanche, staying with them until his retirement in 2003. He won four Stanley Cups, two with each team, in 1986, 1993, 1996, and 2001 and was a three-time winner of the Conn Smythe Trophy. Coincidentally, Roy was born on the same day as one of the game's top goal-scorers, Mario Lemieux.

top 10 MOST SUCCESSFUL NHL COACHES*

	COACH	YEARS	WINS	LOSSES	TIES	PERCENTAGE WINS[#]
1	Scott Bowman	1967–2002	1,244	583	314	65.4
2	Toe Blake	1955–68	500	255	159	63.4
3	Ken Hitchcock	1995–2004	362	211	94	61.3
4	Fred Shero	1971–82	390	225	119	61.2
5	Glen Sather	1979–2004	497	319	125	60.0
6	Emile Francis	1965–83	388	273	117	57.4
7 =	Billy Reay	1957–77	542	385	175	57.1
=	Marc Crawford	1994-2004	369	264	108	57.1
9	Pat Burns	1988–2004	501	359	153	57.0
10	Al Arbour	1970–94	781	577	248	56.0

* Minimum qualification 600 regular season games

[#] Regular season only; based on percentage wins to end of 2003–04 season

Sather has the best record in Stanley Cup playoff games with an 89–37–0 / 70.6 percent record, while Bowman has won the most matches (353) in Stanley Cup playoffs.

the 10 LATEST STANLEY CUP WINNERS

YEAR	WINNER
2004	Tampa Bay Lightning
2003	New Jersey Devils
2002	Detroit Red Wings
2001	Colorado Avalanche
2000	New Jersey Devils
1999	Dallas Stars
1998	Detroit Red Wings
1997	Detroit Red Wings
1996	Colorado Avalanche
1995	New Jersey Devils

Source: National Hockey League

When Tampa Bay beat Calgary to win their first Cup in 2004, they were the first "first-time" winners since Dallas in 1999.

top 10 TEAMS WITH THE MOST STANLEY CUP TITLES

	TEAM	YEARS	WINS*
1	Montreal Canadiens	1916–93	24
2	Toronto Maple Leafs	1918–67	13
3	Detroit Red Wings	1936–2002	10
4 =	Boston Bruins	1929–72	5
=	Edmonton Oilers	1984–90	5
6 =	Ottawa Senators	1920–27	4
=	New York Rangers	1933–94	4
=	New York Islanders	1980–83	4
9 =	Chicago Black Hawks	1934–61	3
=	New Jersey Devils	1995–2003	3

* Since 1918 after the abolition of the challenge match format; up to and including 2004

The Stanley Cup was originally a challenge trophy in which any amateur team in Canada could challenge for the trophy over a single match. This was later changed to a best-of-three series. Following the formation of the professional National Hockey Association in 1910–11, the trophy was presented to their first champions, but challenges could still be made by any other team. Following the formation of a new league, the Pacific Coast Hockey Association (PCHA) in 1912–13, there began the first end-of-season series of games between the champions of the respective leagues. After the arrival of Portland, Oregon, in the PCHA in 1914, it was decided that the Stanley Cup was no longer restricted to Canadian teams, but was also open to teams from the United States who could challenge for the trophy, and in 1917 the Seattle Metropolitans became the first US team to win the Cup. The National Hockey league (NHL) succeeded the NHA in 1917–18, and that year saw the abolition of the challenge system. The NHL has had total control over the Stanley Cup since 1926.

top 10 GOAL-SCORERS IN THE STANLEY CUP

	PLAYER	GAMES	GOALS*
1	Wayne Gretzky	208	122
2	Mark Messier	236	109
3	Jari Kurri	200	106
4	Brett Hull	190	100
5	Glenn Anderson	225	93
6	Mike Bossy	129	85
7	Maurice Richard	133	82
8	Claude Lemieux	223	80
9	Jean Beliveau	162	79
10	Mario Lemieux	107	76

* Up to and including 2003–04 Stanley Cup

Despite playing with a shoulder injury, Mark Messier helped the Edmonton Oilers to their first Stanley Cup final in 1983; they lost to the New York Islanders. However, Messier played for the Oilers when they won a year later.

International Soccer

top 10 GOAL-SCORERS IN INTERNATIONAL SOCCER

	PLAYER	COUNTRY	YEARS	GOALS*
1	Ali Daei	Iran	1993–2004	103
2	Ferenc Puskás	Hungary/Spain	1945–56	84
3	Pelé	Brazil	1957–71	77
4	Sándor Kocsis	Hungary	1948–56	75
5	Gerd Müller	West Germany	1966–74	68
6	Majed Abdullah	Saudi Arabia	1978–94	67
7	=Hossam Hassan	Egypt	1985–2004	63
	=Jassem Al-Houwaidi	Kuwait	1992–2002	63
	=Kiatisuk Senamuang	Thailand	1993–2004	63
10	Imre Schlosser	Hungary	1906–27	59

* As of Jan. 29, 2005

Source: Roberto Mamrud, Karel Stokkermans, and RSSSF 1998/2005

If amateur appearances were included, Vivian Woodward (England) would figure on the list at No. 5 because he scored 73 goals for both the full and amateur England teams in 1903–14. The only two players on this list to win World Cup Winners' medals are Pelé and Gerd Müller. Between them, they scored 26 World Cup goals, with Müller's 14 making a record.

⬆ **ZZ at the top**

Despite securing the biggest transfer fee in soccer history, Zinedine Zidane has announced his retirement after the 2006–07 season.

top 10 TRANSFERS IN INTERNATIONAL SOCCER

PLAYER / COUNTRY	FROM	TO	YEAR	FEE ($)*
1 Zinedine Zidane, France	Juventus, Italy	Real Madrid, Spain	2001	64,200,000
2 Luis Figo, Portugal	Barcelona, Spain	Real Madrid, Spain	2000	56,200,000
3 Hernan Crespo, Argentina	Parma, Italy	Lazio, Italy	2000	51,300,000
4 Christian Vieri, Italy	Lazio, Italy	Inter Milan, Italy	1999	49,600,000
5 Gianluigi Buffon, Italy	Parma, Italy	Juventus, Italy	2001	46,200,000
6 Rio Ferdinand, UK	Leeds United, England	Manchester United, England	2002	45,200,000
7 Ronaldo, Brazil	Inter Milan, Italy	Real Madrid, Spain	2002	43,700,000
8 Gaizka Mendieta, Spain	Valencia, Spain	Lazio, Italy	2001	40,700,000
9 Juan Sebastian Veron, Argentina	Lazio, Italy	Manchester United, England	2001	39,600,000
10 Rui Costa, Portugal	Fiorentina, Italy	AC Milan, Italy	2001	39,400,000

* Figures vary slightly from source to source, depending on whether local taxes, agents' fees, and player's commission are included

Zinedine Zidane played a major part in putting France on the world soccer map at the end of the 20th century. He helped the French team to victory over Brazil in the 1998 FIFA World Cup Final with two first-half goals that set up a 3–0 victory. Two years later, he scored the extra-time winner against Portugal in the semifinal before going on to beat Italy in the final, also after extra time. His pivotal role in France's rise to world supremacy led Real Madrid to pay a world record sum for him in 2001.

top 10 PLAYERS WITH THE MOST INTERNATIONAL CAPS

	PLAYER	COUNTRY	YEARS	CAPS*
1	Claudio Suárez	Mexico	1992–2004	172
2	Mohamed Al-Deayea	Saudi Arabia	1990–2004	170
3 =	Adnan Kh. Al-Talyania	United Arab Republic	1984–97	164
=	Cobi Jones	US	1992–2004	164
5	Hossam Hassan	Egypt	1985–2004	163
6	Lothar Matthäus	West Germany/Germany	1980–2000	150
7	Sami Al-Jaber	Saudi Arabia	1992–2002	144
8 =	Mohammed Al-Khilaiwi	Saudi Arabia	1990–2001	143
=	Thomas Ravelli	Sweden	1981–97	143
10	Marko Kristal	Estonia	1992–2004	142

* As of Jan. 29, 2005

Source: Roberto Mamrud, Karel Stokkermans, and RSSSF 1998/2005

The first to amass 100 international caps was William Ambrose Wright, who played for England 104 times between 1947 and 1959. Mexican Claudio Suárez tops the table of male footballers, but US women's soccer player Kristine Marie Lilly has gained 294 caps.

top 10 COUNTRIES IN THE WORLD CUP

	COUNTRY	PLAYED	WON	TIED	LOST	FOR	AGAINST	POINTS*
1	Brazil	80	53	14	13	173	78	120
2	Germany/West Germany	78	45	17	16	162	103	107
3	Italy	66	38	16	12	105	62	92
4	Argentina	57	29	10	18	100	69	68
5	England	45	20	13	12	62	42	53
6	France	41	21	6	14	86	58	48
7	Spain	40	16	10	14	61	48	42
8	Yugoslavia	37	16	8	13	60	46	40
9	Uruguay	37	15	8	14	61	52	38
10 =	Netherlands	32	14	9	9	56	36	37
=	Sweden	38	14	9	15	66	60	37

* Based on two points for a win and one point for a tie; matches resolved on penalties are classed as a tie

Brazil has qualified for every World Cup since the first in 1930, coming third in 1938, second in 1950 at home (the only time Brazil has hosted the event), and winning the tournament on the first of five occasions in 1958, when they defeated host nation Sweden 5–2. Brazil's other wins were in 1962, 1970, 1994, and 2002.

top 10 US PLAYERS WITH THE MOST INTERNATIONAL CAPS

	PLAYER / YEARS	GOALS	CAPS*
1	Cobi Jones 1992–2004	15	164
2	Jeff Agoos 1988–2003	4	134
3	Marcelo Balboa 1988–2000	13	128
4	Paul Caligiuri 1984–98	5	110
5	Eric Wynalda 1990–2000	34	106
6	Claudio Reyna 1994–2004	8	105
7	Earnie Stewart 1990–2004	17	101
8	Joe-Max Moore 1992–2002	24	100
9	Tony Meola 1988–2002	0	99
10	Alexi Lalas 1990–1998	9	96

* As of Dec. 4, 2004

Source: Roberto Mamrud and RSSSF 2003/04

Caps are awarded when players appear in a senior international match against another country. Some countries award caps for every individual appearance, while others will issue only one cap per tournament, subject to a player's making an appearance in that tournament. Despite soccer's lower status compared with gridiron football, a number of US players have made their mark in the sport, with Los Angeles Galaxy player Cobi Jones (born 1970) the most prominent representation of the national team. He played in three World Cups (1994, 1998, and 2002), and has scored 15 goals for his country.

Motor Sports

top 10 DRIVERS WITH THE MOST FORMULA ONE WORLD TITLES

DRIVER / COUNTRY	WORLD TITLE YEARS	RACES WON	WORLD TITLES
1 Michael Schumacher, Germany	1994–2004	83	7
2 Juan Manuel Fangio, Argentina	1951–57	24	5
3 Alain Prost, France	1985–93	51	4
4 = Jack Brabbham, Australia	1959–60	14	3
= Jackie Stewart, UK	1969–71	27	3
= Niki Lauda, Austria	1975–84	25	3
= Nelson Piquet, Brazil	1981–87	23	3
= Ayrton Senna, Brazil	1988–91	41	3
9 = Alberto Ascari, Italy	1952–53	13	2
= Graham Hill, UK	1962–68	14	2
= Jim Clark, UK	1963–65	25	2
= Emerson Fittipaldi, Brazil	1972–74	14	2

top 10 FASTEST WINNING SPEEDS OF THE INDIANAPOLIS 500

DRIVER / COUNTRY	YEAR	SPEED (MPH)	SPEED (KM/H)
1 Arie Luyendyk, Netherlands	1990	185.981	299.307
2 Rick Mears, US	1991	176.457	283.980
3 Bobby Rahal, US	1986	170.722	274.750
4 Juan Pablo Montoya, Colombia	2000	167.607	269.730
5 Emerson Fittipaldi, Brazil	1989	167.581	269.695
6 Helio Castroneves, Brazil	2002	166.499	267.954
7 Rick Mears, US	1984	163.612	263.308
8 Mark Donohue, US	1972	162.962	262.619
9 Al Unser, US	1987	162.175	260.995
10 Tom Sneva, US	1983	162.117	260.902

Because American drivers start on the run and race around oval circuits, consistently higher average lap speeds are achieved than in Formula One. Car racing in the US on custom-built circuits dates back to 1909, when Indianapolis Speedway opened.

● **Ahead of the race**
Michael Schumacher has attained a level of statistical success in Formula One that is unlikely ever to be overtaken.

top 10 CART RACE WINNERS

	DRIVER / COUNTRY	CAREER	WINS*
1	Michael Andretti, US	1983–2002	42
2	Al Unser Jr., US	1982–99	31
7	Paul Tracy, Canada	1991–2004	28
3	Rick Mears, US	1979–92	26
4	Bobby Rahal, US	1982–98	24
5	Emerson Fittipaldi, Brazil	1984–96	22
6	Mario Andretti, US	1979–94	19
8	Danny Sullivan, US	1982–95	17
9	Alessandro Zanardi, Italy	1996–2001	15
10	Cristiano da Matta, Brazil	1999–2002	11

* From the establishment of Championship Auto Racing Teams (CART) in 1979 to end of 2004 season

top 10 DRIVERS WITH THE MOST NASCAR RACE WINS

	DRIVER*	YEARS	WINS#
1	Richard Petty	1958–92	200
2	David Pearson	1960–86	105
3 =	Bobby Allison	1975–88	84
=	Darrell Waltrip	1975–92	84
5	Cale Yarborough	1957–88	83
6	Dale Earnhardt	1979–2000	76
7	Jeff Gordon	1994–2004	69
8	Rusty Wallace	1986–2004	55
9	Lee Petty	1949–64	54
10 =	Ned Jarrett	1953–66	50
=	Junior Johnson	1953–66	50

* All US

As of end of 2004 season

top 10 FASTEST LE MANS 24-HOUR RACES

	DRIVERS / COUNTRIES	CAR	YEAR	WINNERS' AVERAGE SPEED (MPH)	(KM/H)
1	Helmut Marko (Austria), Gijs van Lennep (Holland)	Porsche 917K	1971	138.133	222.304
2	Jan Lammers (Holland), Johnny Dumfries, Andy Wallace (UK)	Jaguar XJR-9LM	1988	137.737	221.665
3	Jochen Mass, Manuel Reuter (West Germany), Stanley Dickens (Sweden)	Sauber Mercedes C9	1989	136.696	219.990
4	Dan Gurney, A. J. Foyt (US)	Ford GT Mk4	1967	135.483	218.038
5	Seiji Ara (Japan), Rinaldo Capello (Italy), Tom Kristensen (Denmark)	Audi R8	2004	133.885	215.418
6	Rinaldo Capello (Italy), Tom Kristensen (Denmark), Emanuele Pirro (Italy)	Bentley Speed 8	2003	133.233	214.418
7	Geoff Brabham (Australia), Christophe Bouchot, Eric Hélary (France)	Peugeot 905B	1993	132.574	213.358
8	Frank Biella (Germany), Tom Kristensen (Denmark), Emanuele Pirro (Italy)	Audi V8	2002	132.394	213.068
9	Klaus Ludwig, Louis Krages ("John Winter") (West Germany), Paulo Barilla (Italy)	Porsche 956B	1985	131.744	212.021
10	Chris Amon, Bruce McLaren (New Zealand)	Ford GT Mk2	1966	130.983	210.795

The *24 heures du Mans*, or Le Mans 24-hour Race, has been staged on the circuit at Le Mans, France, since 1923, when the average speed was 57.205 mph (92.065 km/h). Driven by a team of two or three drivers, the car that covers the greatest distance in 24 hours wins the race.

Motorcycling

top 10 RIDERS WITH THE MOST WORLD **500CC TITLES**

	RIDER / COUNTRY	CAREER	TITLES*
1	Giacomo Agostini, Italy	1964–77	8
2	Mick Doohan, Australia	1989–99	5#
3 =	John Surtees, UK	1952–60	4
=	Mike Hailwood, UK	1958–67	4
=	Geoff Duke, UK	1950–59	4
=	Eddie Lawson, US	1983–92	4#
=	Valentino Rossi, Italy	1996–2004	4
8 =	Kenny Roberts, US	1974–83	3#
=	Wayne Rainey, US	1984–93	3#
10 =	Umberto Masetti, Italy	1949–58	2#
=	Phil Read, UK	1961–76	2
=	Barry Sheene, UK	1970–84	2#
=	Freddie Spencer, US	1980–93	2

* As of end of 2004 season

The rider's only world titles

➔ High five
Despite a series of accidents, Mick Doohan won an unprecedented five consecutive world titles in 1994–98.

top 10 RIDERS IN THE 2004 **MOTOGP WORLD CHAMPIONSHIP**

	RIDER / COUNTRY	MOTOGP WORLD CHAMPIONSHIP POINTS
1	Valentino Rossi, Italy	304
2	Sete Gibernau, Spain	257
3	Max Biaggi, Italy	217
4	Alex Barros, Brazil	165
5	Colin Edwards, US	157
6	Makoto Tamada, Japan	150
7 =	Carlos Checa, Spain	117
=	Nicky Hayden, US	117
=	Loris Capirossi, Italy	117
10	Shinya Nakano, Japan	83

World Championship points are awarded to riders who finish in the top 15 positions. The winner receives the maximum 25 points, runner-up 20, third 16, fourth 13, fifth 11, and then one point less for each of the next finishers, down to a single point for the fifteenth rider.

top 10 RIDERS WITH THE **MOST GRAND PRIX** RACE WINS

	RIDER / COUNTRY	YEARS	WINS*
1	Giacomo Agostini, Italy	1965–76	122
2	Angel Nieto, Spain	1969–85	90
3	Mike Hailwood, Great Britain	1959–67	76
4	Valentino Rossi, Italy	1996–2004	68
5	Mick Doohan, Australia	1990–98	54
6	Phil Read, UK	1961–75	52
7	Jim Redman, Southern Rhodesia	1961–66	45
8 =	Anton Mang, West Germany	1976–88	42
=	Max Biaggi, Italy	1992–2004	42
10	Carlo Ubbiali, Italy	1949–60	39

* As of end of 2004 season

The UK's Barry Sheene won 23 races during his career and is the only man to win Grand Prix races at 50 and 500cc.

top 10 RIDERS WITH THE MOST RACE WINS IN A YEAR

	RIDER / COUNTRY	CLASS (CC)	YEAR	WINS*
1	**Mick Doohan**, Australia	500	1997	12
2 =	**Giacomo Agostini**, Italy	500	1972	11
=	**Valentino Rossi**, Italy	125	1997	11
=	**Daijiro Kato**, Japan	250	2001	11
=	**Valentino Rossi**	500	2001	11
=	**Valentino Rossi**	MotoGP	2002	11
7 =	**Mike Hailwood**, UK	250	1966	10
=	**Giacomo Agostini**	500	1968	10
=	**Giacomo Agostini**	500	1969	10
=	**Giacomo Agostini**	500	1970	10
=	**Anton Mang**, Germany	250	1987	10
=	**Fausto Gresini**, Italy	125	1987	10

* As of end of 2004 season

Sete of his pants
Newcomer Sete Giberneau took four first places in the 2004 season, but just missed out on his fifth first place to previous MotoGP champion Valentino Rossi.

top 10 FASTEST WINNING SPEEDS OF THE DAYTONA 200

	RIDER / COUNTRY / BIKE	YEAR	MPH	KM/H
1	**Mat Mladin**, Australia, Suzuki	2004	113.94	183.33
2	**Miguel Duhamel**, Canada, Honda	2003	113.83	183.20
3	**Mat Mladin**, Suzuki	2000	113.63	182.87
4	**Miguel Duhamel**, Honda	1999	113.47	182.61
5	**Kenny Roberts**, US, Yamaha	1984	113.14	182.08
6	**Scott Russell**, US, Yamaha	1998	111.78	179.89
7	**Kenny Roberts**, Yamaha	1983	110.93	178.52
8	**Scott Russell**, Kawasaki	1992	110.67	178.11
9	**Graeme Crosby**, New Zealand, Yamaha	1982	109.10	175.58
10	**Steve Baker**, US, Yamaha	1977	108.85	175.18

Source: American Motorcyclist Association

The Daytona 200, which was first held in 1937, forms a round in the AMA (American Motorcyclist Association) Grand National Dirt Track series. Until 2005 it was raced over 57 laps of the 3.56-mile (5.73-km) Daytona International Speedway. For the 64th event, held March 12, 2005, the race was extended to 67 laps and competed on Formula Xtreme-spec 600cc bikes.

Baseball Stars

top 10 PLAYERS WITH THE MOST RUNS

	PLAYER	YEARS	RUNS*
1	Rickey Henderson	1979–2003	2,295
2	Ty Cobb	1905–28	2,246
3 =Babe Ruth		1914–35	2,174
=Hank Aaron		1954–76	2,174
5	Pete Rose	1963–86	2,165
6	Barry Bonds	1986–2004	2,070
7	Willie Mays	1951–73	2,062
8	Cap Anson	1871–97	1,996
9	Stan Musial	1941–63	1,949
10	Lou Gehrig	1923–39	1,888

* Regular season only; as of end of 2004 season

The top run-scorer in baseball history, Chicago-born Rickey Henderson started his Major League career with the Oakland Athletics in 1979. Since then he has played with nine different teams in a 25-year career. He broke Ty Cobb's all-time run record in 2001 while playing with the Padres. Known as "The Man of Steal," Henderson was the 1990 American League MVP.

top 10 PLAYERS WITH THE HIGHEST CAREER BATTING AVERAGES

	PLAYER	AT BAT	HITS	AVERAGE*
1	Ty Cobb	11,434	4,189	.3664
2	Rogers Hornsby	8,173	2,930	.3585
3	Joe Jackson	4,981	1,772	.3558
4	Lefty O'Doul	3,264	1,140	.3493
5	Ed Delahanty	7,505	2,597	.3459
6	Tris Speaker	10,195	3,514	.3447
7	Ted Williams	7,706	2,654	.3444
8	Billy Hamilton	6,268	2,158	.3443
9 =Dan Brouthers		6,711	2,296	.3421
=Babe Ruth		8,399	2,873	.3421

* Calculated by dividing the number of hits by the number of times a batter was "at bat"; as of end of 2004 season

Second only to the legendary Ty Cobb, Rogers Hornsby also stands as the top-hitting second-baseman of all time, with an average of over .400 in a five-year period. Baseball's greatest right–handed hitter, slugging 20–plus homers on seven occasions, he achieved a career average of .358.

top 10 PITCHERS WITH THE MOST WINS

	PLAYER	YEARS	WINS*
1	Cy Young	1890–1911	511
2	Walter Johnson	1907–27	417
3 =Christy Mathewson		1911–30	373
=Grover Alexander		1900–16	373
5	Jim "Pud" Galvin	1875–92	364
6	Warren Spahn	1942–65	363
7	Kid Nichols	1890–1906	361
8	Tim Keefe	1880–93	342
9	Steve Carlton	1965–88	329
10	John Clarkson	1882–94	328

* Regular season only; as of end of 2004 season

Denton True "Cy" Young won almost 100 games more than the sport's next best pitcher. He topped 30 game wins five times and 20 game wins an amazing 15 times. He was a member of the Boston team that played in the first World Series in 1903, winning two games in a 5–3 series win.

top 10 PLAYERS WITH THE MOST HOME RUNS

	PLAYER	YEARS	HOME RUNS*
1	Hank Aaron	1954–76	755
2	Babe Ruth	1914–35	714
3	Barry Bonds	1986–2004	703
4	Willie Mays	1951–73	660
5	Frank Robinson	1956–76	586
6	Mark McGwire	1986–2001	583
7	Sammy Sosa	1989–2004	574
8	Harmon Killebrew	1954–75	573
9	Reggie Jackson	1967–87	563
10	Rafael Palmeiro	1986–2004	551

* Regular season only; as of end of 2004 season

George Herman "Babe" Ruth's career (1914–35) home run record was unbroken until Henry Louis "Hank" Aaron overtook him in 1974. His total of 714 came from 8,399 "at bats," which represents an average of 8.5 percent—considerably better than the next man in the averages, Harmon Killebrew, who averaged 7.0 percent.

top 10 PITCHERS WITH THE MOST STRIKEOUTS

	PLAYER	YEARS	STRIKEOUTS*
1	Nolan Ryan	1966–93	5,714
2	Roger Clemens	1983–2004	4,317
3	Randy Johnson	1985–2004	4,161
4	Steve Carlton	1965–88	4,136
5	Bert Blyleven	1970–92	3,701
6	Tom Seaver	1967–86	3,640
7	Don Sutton	1966–88	3,574
8	Gaylord Perry	1962–83	3,534
9	Walter Johnson	1907–27	3,509
10	Phil Niekro	1964–87	3,342

* Regular season only; as of end of 2004 season

Nolan Ryan was known as the "Babe Ruth of strikeout pitchers," pitching faster (a record 101 mph/162.5 km/h) and longer (27 seasons—1966 and 1968–93) than any previous player. As well as his 5,714 strikeouts, including 383 in one season, he walked 2,795 batters and allowed the fewest hits (6.55) per nine innings.

top 10 PLAYERS WITH MOST HOME RUNS IN THE WORLD SERIES

	PLAYER	HOME RUNS
1	Mickey Mantle	18
2	Babe Ruth	15
3	Yogi Berra	12
4	Duke Snider	11
5	= Lou Gehrig	10
	= Reggie Jackson	10
7	= Joe DiMaggio	8
	= Frank Robinson	8
	= Bill Skowron	8
10	= Hank Bauer	7
	= Leon "Goose" Goslin	7
	= Gil McDougald	7

Five of Reggie Jackson's total came in the 1977 Series against the Los Angeles Dodgers, a record for one World Series. Mickey Mantle's entire playing career (1951–68) was spent with the New York Yankees, during which he hit a career 536 homers.

top 10 HIGHEST-PAID BASEBALL PLAYERS, 2004

	PLAYER	TEAM	SALARY, 2004 ($)
1	Manny Ramirez	Boston Red Sox	22,500,000
2	Alex Rodriguez	New York Yankees	22,000,000
3	Carlos Delgado	Toronto Blue Jays	19,700,000
4	Derek Jeter	New York Yankees	18,600,000
5	Barry Bonds	San Francisco Giants	18,000,000
6	Pedro Martinez	Boston Red Sox	17,500,000
7	Mo Vaughn	New York Mets	17,166,667
8	Shawn Green	Los Angeles Dodgers	16,666,667
9	Mike Piazza	New York Mets	16,071,429
10	Jeff Bagwell	Houston Astros	16,000,000

Manuel Aristides Ramirez, born in the Dominican Republic in 1972, was baseball's top earner in 2004. He made his MLB debut for the Indians in September 1993 and in 2000 agreed to an eight-year deal worth $160 million to join the Red Sox. On his Red Sox debut at Fenway Park, he hit a three-run homer.

top 10 PLAYERS WHO HAVE TOPPED THE BATTING AVERAGES MOST OFTEN

	PLAYER / LEAGUE*	YEARS#	TIMES
1	Ty Cobb, AL	1907–19	12
2	= Honus Wagner, NL	1900–11	8
	= Tony Gwynn, NL	1984–87	8
4	= Rogers Hornsby, NL	1920–28	7
	= Stan Musial, NL	1943–57	7
	= Rod Carew, AL	1969–78	7
7	Wade Boggs, AL	1983–88	5
8	= Harry Heilmann, AL	1921–27	4
	= Roberto Clemente, NL	1961–67	4
	= Bill Madlock, NL	1975–83	4

* AL = topped the American League averages; NL = topped the National League averages

Since 1900

Ty Cobb topped the American League batting averages through a record nine consecutive years (1907–15).

Tennis

top 10 WINNERS OF WOMEN'S GRAND SLAM SINGLES TITLES

	PLAYER / COUNTRY	GRAND SLAM*				
		(A)	(F)	(W)	(US)	(TOTAL#)
1	**Margaret Court (née Smith)**, Australia	11	5	3	5	24
2	**Steffi Graf**, Germany	4	6	7	5	22
3	**Helen Wills-Moody**, US	0	4	8	7	19
4	=**Chris Evert**, US	2	7	3	6	18
	=**Martina Navratilova**, Czechoslovakia/US	3	2	9	4	18
6	**Billie Jean King (née Moffitt)**, US	1	1	6	4	12
7	=**Maureen Connolly**, US	1	2	3	3	9
	=**Monica Seles**, Yugoslavia/US	4	3	0	2	9
9	=**Suzanne Lenglen**, France	0	2	6	0	8
	=**Molla Mallory (née Bjurstedt)**, US	0	0	0	8	8

* A = Australian Open; F = French Open; W = Wimbledon; US = US Open

Up to and including the 2004 events

Margaret Court's first Grand Slam singles title was on home soil when she won the 1960 Australian Open. She became only the second woman after Maureen Connolly to win all four Grand Slam events in one year in 1970. The 1973 US Open was her final Grand Slam singles title.

top 10 MONEY-WINNING TENNIS PLAYERS (WOMEN)

	PLAYER / COUNTRY	WINNINGS ($)*
1	**Steffi Graf**, West Germany/Germany	21,895,277
2	**Martina Navratilova**, Czechoslovakia/US	21,194,804
3	**Lindsay Davenport**, US	18,694,975
4	**Martina Hingis**, Switzerland	18,344,660
5	**Arantxa Sanchez Vicario**, Spain	16,935,625
6	**Monica Seles**, Yugoslavia/US	14,891,762
7	**Serena Williams**, US	14,798,661
8	**Venus Williams**, US	14,503,591
9	**Jana Novotna**, Czechoslovakia	11,249,134
10	**Conchita Martinez**, Spain	11,009,539

* As of Jan. 1, 2005

◶ Court on court
Margaret Court (b. 1943) achieved her record total of 24 Grand Slam victories in the period 1960–73 and also won women's and mixed doubles at all four events.

top 10 WINNERS OF MEN'S GRAND SLAM SINGLES TITLES

PLAYER / COUNTRY		(A)	(F)	GRAND SLAM* (W)	(U)S	(TOTAL#)
1	**Pete Sampras**, US	2	0	7	5	14
2	**Roy Emerson**, Australia	6	2	2	2	12
3 =	**Björn Borg**, Sweden	0	6	5	0	11
=	**Rod Laver**, Australia	3	2	4	2	11
5	**Bill Tilden**, US	0	0	3	7	10
6 =	**Andre Agassi**, US	4	1	1	2	8
=	**Jimmy Connors**, US	1	0	2	5	8
=	**Ivan Lendl**, Czechoslovakia/US	2	3	0	3	8
=	**Fred Perry**, Great Britain	1	1	3	3	8
=	**Ken Rosewall**, Australia	4	2	0	2	8

* A = Australian Open; F = French Open; W = Wimbledon; US = US Open

\# Up to and including the 2004 events

Australia's Roy Emerson had held the record for the most Grand Slam singles titles since 1968, but Pete Sampras equaled his record of 12 wins when he won Wimbledon in 1999 and the following year; when he beat Pat Rafter to retain his title, it was his 13th and record-breaking title.

top 10 MONEY-WINNING TENNIS PLAYERS (MEN)

PLAYER / COUNTRY	WINNINGS ($)*
1 **Pete Sampras**, US	43,280,489
2 **Andre Agassi**, US	29,366,679
3 **Boris Becker**, West Germany/Germany	25,080,956
4 **Yevgeny Kafelnikov**, Russia	23,883,797
5 **Ivan Lendl**, Czechoslovakia/US	21,262,417
6 **Stefan Edberg**, Sweden	20,630,941
7 **Goran Ivanisevic**, Croatia	19,876,579
8 **Michael Chang**, US	19,145,632
9 **Gustavo Kuerten**, Brazil	14,609,954
10 **Lleyton Hewitt**, Australia	14,502,450

* As of Jan. 1, 2005

➔ Net profit
Andre Agassi has more than matched his tennis earnings with income from endorsements of sportswear, cell phones, and other products, establishing him as the world's wealthiest tennis star.

Water Sports

Golden boy
400-meter record-holder Ian Thorpe won three golds at the 2000 Olympics when he was just 17, and two at the 2004 Games—more gold wins than any other Australian.

top 10 OLYMPIC MEDAL-WINNING SWIMMERS (WOMEN)

SWIMMER / COUNTRY	MEDALS (GOLD)	(SILVER)	(BRONZE)	(TOTAL)
1 Jenny Thompson, US	8	3	1	12
2 Franziska van Almsick, Germany	0	4	6	10
3 = Shirley Babashoff, US	2	6	0	8
= Kornelia Ender, Germany	4	4	0	8
= Dawn Fraser, Australia	4	4	0	8
= Susie O'Neill, Australia	2	4	2	8
= Dara Torres, US	4	0	4	8
= Inge de Bruijn, Netherlands	4	2	2	8
9 = Dagmar Hase, Germany	1	5	1	7
= Krisztina Egerszegi, Hungary	5	1	1	7

List-leader Jenny Thompson (b. 1973) competed in individual and relay events in four consecutive Olympics (1994–2004) to amass her unrivaled collection of both golds and overall medals. Her closest rival, Franziska van Almsick, won her first Olympic medal in 1992 at the age of just 14.

top 10 OLYMPIC MEDAL-WINNING SWIMMERS (MEN)

SWIMMER / COUNTRY	MEDALS (GOLD)	(SILVER)	(BRONZE)	(TOTAL)
1 = Matt Biondi, US	8	2	1	11
= Mark Spitz, US	9	1	1	11
3 Gary Hall Jr., US	5	3	2	10
4 = Alexander Popov Unified Team/Russia	4	5	0	9
= Ian Thorpe, Australia	5	3	1	9
6 = Roland Matthes, Germany	4	2	2	8
= Michael Phelps, US	6	0	2	8
8 = Zoltán Halmay, Hungary	2	4	1	7
= Tom Jager, US	5	1	1	7
= Peter van den Hoogenband, Netherlands	3	2	2	7

* 1896–2004 excluding the 1906 Intercalated Games

Matt Biondi and Mark Spitz are tied for first place, but the latter's achievement (and greater tally of golds) is all the more remarkable because he won a record seven at the same games (Munich, 1972), setting a new world record in each event.

top 10 LONGEST-STANDING CURRENT OLYMPIC SWIMMING RECORDS

	SWIMMER / COUNTRY / EVENT	TIME (MIN:SEC)	DATE WHEN RECORD SET
1	**Heike Friedrich**, East Germany Women's 200-m freestyle	1:57.65	Sept. 21, 1988
2	**Janet Evans**, US Women's 400-m freestyle	4:03.85	Sept. 22, 1988
3	**Alexander Popov**, Unified Team Men's 50-m freestyle	0:21.91	July 30, 1992
4	**Krisztina Egerszegi**, Hungary Women's 200-m backstroke	2:07.06	July 31, 1992
5 =	**Yana Klochkova**, Ukraine Women's 400-m individual medley	4:33.59	Sept. 16, 2000
=	**Ian Thorpe**, Australia Men's 400-m freestyle	3:40.59	Sept. 16, 2000
7	**Inge de Bruijn**, Netherlands Women's 100-m butterfly	0:56.61	Sept. 17 2000
8 =	**Australia**, Australia Men's 4 x 200-m freestyle relay	7:07.05	Sept. 19, 2000
=	**Pieter van den Hoogenband**, Netherlands Men's 100-m freestyle	0:47.84	Sept. 19, 2000
=	**Yana Klochkova**, Ukraine Women's 200-m individual medley	2:10.68	Sept. 19, 2000

The 200-m freestyle event was first competed at the Mexico Olympics in 1968, when it was won by Debbie Meyer (US), establishing an Olympic record of 2 minutes 10.5 seconds. This was steadily trimmed to below 2 minutes, with Heike Friedrich's 1988 win at Seoul remaining unbeaten in all four subsequent Games.

top 10 OLYMPIC SAILING* COUNTRIES

	COUNTRY	MEDALS			
		(G)	(S)	(B)	(TOTAL)
1	**US**	18	22	18	58
2	**Great Britain**	23	14	10	47
3	**France**	16	11	14	41
4	**Sweden**	9	12	11	32
5	**Norway**	17	11	3	31
6 =	**Denmark**	11	8	6	25
=	**Netherlands**	7	9	9	25
8	**Germany / West Germany**	6	6	7	19
9	**Australia**	5	3	8	16
10 =	**New Zealand**	6	4	5	15
=	**Spain**	10	4	1	15
=	**USSR/Unified Team/Russia**	4	6	5	15

* Previously called Olympic yachting

As a result of poor weather conditions, the sailing events scheduled for the first modern Olympics (Athens, 1896) were canceled, but have been included since 1900. The US did not win its first gold medals until the Los Angeles Games of 1932, but has gone on to take the lead in the overall medal table.

the 10 LATEST WINNERS OF THE AMERICA'S CUP

YEAR	WINNING BOAT / SKIPPER / COUNTRY	CHALLENGER / COUNTRY	SCORE
2003	**Alinghi**, Russell Coutts, Switzerland	Team New Zealand, New Zealand	5–0
2000	**Black Magic**, Russell Coutts, New Zealand	Prada Luna Rossa, Italy	5–0
1995	**Black Magic**, Russell Coutts, New Zealand	Young America, US	5–0
1992	**America3**, Bill Koch, US	Il Moro di Venezia, Italy	4–1
1988	**Stars and Stripes**, Dennis Conner, US	New Zealand, New Zealand	2–0
1987	**Stars and Stripes**, Dennis Conner, US	Kookaburra III, Australia	4–0
1983	**Australia II**, John Bertrand, Australia	Liberty, US	4–3
1980	**Freedom**, Dennis Conner, US	Australia, Australia	4–1
1977	**Courageous**, Ted Turner, US	Australia, Australia	4–0
1974	**Courageous**, Ted Hood, US	Southern Cross, Australia	4–0

The 132-year US domination of the America's Cup came to an end at 5:21 am on September 26, 1983, when 37-year-old John Bertrand skippered *Australia II* to victory with a revolutionary boat designed by Ben Lexcen and owned by Alan Bond.

Winter Sports

top 10 SNOWBOARDERS WITH THE MOST FIS WORLD CHAMPIONSHIP MEDALS

	SNOWBOARDER / COUNTRY	YEARS	MEDALS (GOLD)	(SILVER)	(BRONZE)	(TOTAL)
1	**Nicolas Huet**, France	1999–2005	2	1	2	5
2	= **Mike Jacoby**, US	1996–97	1	2	–	3
	= **Helmut Pramstaller**, Austria	1996–97	1	–	2	3
	= **Jasey-Jay Anderson**, Canada	2001–05	3	–	–	3
	= **Antti Autti**, Finland	2003–05	2	–	1	3
6	= **Bernd Kroschewski**, Germany	1997	1	–	1	2
	= **Markus Hurme**, Finland	1997–2001	–	1	1	2
	= **Anton Pogue**, US	1997–2001	–	–	2	2
	= **Markus Ebner**, Germany	1999–2001	1	1	–	2
	= **Stefan Kaltschuetz**, Austria	1999–2001	–	1	1	2
	= **Mathieu Bozzetto**, France	1999–2003	–	2	–	2
	= **Dejan Kosir**, Slovenia	2001–03	1	1	–	2
	= **Kim Christiansen**, Norway	2001–05	1	–	1	2
	= **Simon Schoch**, Switzerland	2003	–	1	1	2
	= **Seth Wescott**, US	2003–05	1	1	–	2

Source: Fédération Internationale de Ski (FIS)

top 10 OLYMPIC FIGURE SKATING COUNTRIES

	COUNTRY	TOTAL MEDALS*
1	**USSR/Unified Team/Russia**	45
2	**US**	42
3	**Austria**	20
4	**Canada**	19
5	**Great Britain**	15
6	**France**	12
7	**Germany/West Germany**	11
8	= **East Germany**	10
	= **Sweden**	10
10	= **Norway**	6
	= **Hungary**	6

* Gold, silver, and bronze medals; up to and including 2002 Winter Olympic Games

Figure skating was part of the Summer Olympics in 1908 and 1920, becoming part of the Winter programme in 1924.

◀ **Snow business**
World champion snowboarder Jasey-Jay Anderson is Canada's best hope for gold at the 2006 Winter Olympics.

top 10 SKIERS WITH THE MOST ALPINE WORLD CUP TITLES

	SKIER / COUNTRY	YEARS	(OA)	(S)	(GS)	TITLES* (SG)	(DH)	(C)	(TOTAL)
1	Ingemar Stenmark, Sweden	1976–84	3	8	7	–	–	–	18
2	Annemarie Moser-Pröll, Austria	1971–79	6	–	3	–	7	1	17
3 =	Marc Girardelli, Luxembourg	1984–95	5	3	1	–	2	4	15
=	Pirmin Zurbriggen, Switzerland	1984–90	4	–	3	4	2	2	15
5 =	Vreni Schneider, Switzerland	1986–95	3	6	5	–	–	–	14
=	Hermann Maier, Austria	1998–2005	4	–	2	6	2	–	14
7	Katja Seizinger, Germany	1992–98	2	–	–	5	4	–	11
8 =	Gustavo Thoeni, Italy	1971–74	4	2	3	–	–	–	9
=	Phil Mahre, US	1981–83	3	1	2	–	–	3	9
=	Erika Hess, Switzerland	1981–84	2	5	1	–	–	1	9
=	Alberto Tomba, Italy	1988–95	1	4	4	–	–	–	9
=	Renate Goetschl, Germany	1997–2000	–	–	1	1	5	2	9

* OA = Overall; S = Slalom; GS = Giant slalom; SG = Super-giant slalom; DH = Downhill; C = Combined

The Alpine Skiing World Cup was launched as an annual event in 1967, with the addition of the super-giant slalom in 1986. Points are awarded for performances over a series of selected races during the winter months. As well as her 17 titles, Annemarie Moser-Pröll won a record 62 individual events in the period 1970–79, and went on to win gold for the Downhill event in the 1980 Olympic Games, when she achieved a record speed for women in the event of 61.887 mph (99.598 km/h).

top 10 SKIERS WITH THE MOST WORLD AND OLYMPIC NORDIC TITLES

	SKIER / COUNTRY	YEARS	TITLES* (ON)	(WC)	(TOTAL)
1	Bjørn Dæhlie, Norway	1991–98	8	5	13
2	Yelena Välbe, USSR/UT/Russia	1989–98	3	9	12
3	Larissa Lazutina, UT/Russia	1992–99	5	5	10
4	Gunde Svan, Sweden	1984–91	4	5	9
5 =	Galina Kulakova, USSR	1968–76	4	3	7
=	Lyubov Yegorova, UT/Russia	1992–94	6	1	7
7 =	Sixten Jernberg, Sweden	1956–64	4	2	6
=	Bente Skari (née Martinsen), Norway	1999–2003	1	5	6
9 =	Birger Ruud, Norway	1931–37	2	3	5
=	Veikko Hakulinen, Finland	1952–60	3	2	5
=	Eero Mäntyränta, Finland	1960–68	3	2	5
=	Raisa Smetanina, USSR	1976–88	4	1	5
=	Vladimir Smirnov, USSR/UT/ Kazakhstan	1988–98	1	4	5
=	Stefania Belmondo, Italy	1993–2002	1	4	5

* ON = Olympic Nordic gold medal; WC = World Championship gold medal

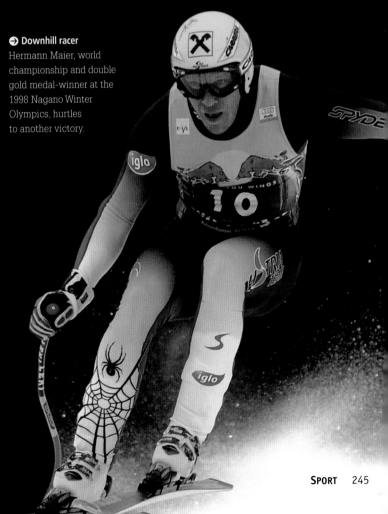

➔ **Downhill racer**
Hermann Maier, world championship and double gold medal-winner at the 1998 Nagano Winter Olympics, hurtles to another victory.

Further Information

THE UNIVERSE & THE EARTH

Asteroids
http://neo.jpl.nasa.gov/
NASA's Near Earth Object Program

Astronautics
http://www.astronautix.com/
Spaceflight news and reference

Comets
http://www.cometography.com/
Comet catalog and descriptions

Elements
http://www.webelements.com/
A guide to all the elements in the periodic table

Islands
http://islands.unep.ch/isldir.htm
Information on the world's islands

NASA
http://www.nasa.gov/home/index.html
The main website for the US space program

Oceans
http://www.oceansatlas.org/index.jsp
The UN's resource on oceanographic issues

Planets
http://www.nineplanets.org/
A multimedia tour of the solar system

Mountains
http://peaklist.org/
Lists of the world's tallest mountains

Space
http://www.space.com/
Reports on events in space exploration

LIFE ON EARTH

Animals
http://animaldiversity.ummz.umich.edu/site/index.html
Animal data from the University of Michigan

Birds
http://www.bsc-eoc.org/avibase/avibase.jsp
A database about the world's birds

Conservation
http://iucn.org/
The leading nature conservation site

Endangered
http://www.cites.org/
Lists endangered species of flora and fauna

Environment
http://www.unep.ch/
The UN's Earthwatch and other programs

Fish
http://www.fishbase.org/home.htm
Global information on fish

Food and Agriculture Organization
http://www.fao.org/
Statistics from the UN's FAO website

Forests
http://www.americanforests.org/
Information on the nation's trees and forests

Insects
http://ufbir.ifas.ufl.edu/
The University of Florida Book of Insect Records

Pets
http://petsforum.com/
Information about cats, dogs, and other pets

THE HUMAN WORLD

Death penalty
http://www.deathpenaltyinfo.org
US-specific data on the death penalty

Health
http://www.cdc.gov/nchs
Information and links on health for US citizens

Leaders
http://www.terra.es/personal2/monolith/home.htm
Facts about world leaders since 1945

Names
http://www.ssa.gov/OACT/babynames/index.html
Most common names from the Social Security Administration

Prisons
http://www.bop.gov
Public information on all aspects of the US prison system

Religions
http://www.worldchristiandatabase.org/wcd/
World religion data

Royalty, U.K.
http://www.royal.gov.uk/
The official site of the British monarchy, with histories

Rulers
http://rulers.org/
A database of the world's rulers and political leaders

US Presidents
http://www.whitehouse.gov/history/presidents/
The White House's biographies of every president

World Health Organization
http://www.who.int/en/
World health information and advice

TOWN & COUNTRY

Bridges
http://www.struct.kth.se/research/bridges/Bridges.htm
The longest bridges listed by type

Countries
http://www.theodora.com/wfb/
Country data, rankings, etc.

Country and city populations
http://www.citypopulation.de/cities.html
A searchable world guide to the world's countries and major cities

Country data
http://www.odci.gov/cia/publications/factbook/
The CIA World Factbook

Country population
http://www.un.org/esa/population/unpop.htm
The UN's worldwide data on population issues

Development
http://www.worldbank.org/
Development and other statistics from around the world

Population
http://www.census.gov/
US and international population statistics

Skyscrapers
http://www.emporis.com/en/bu/sk/
The Emporis database of high-rise buildings

Tunnels
http://home.no.net/lotsberg/
A database of the longest rail, road, and canal tunnels

US geography
http://www.usgs.gov/
US national and regional geographical information

CULTURE & LEARNING

Books
http://publishersweekly.reviewsnews.com
Publishers Weekly, the trade journal of American publishers

Education
http://nces.ed.gov
The home of federal education data

Languages of the world
http://www.ethnologue.com/
Online reference work on the world's 6,912 languages

Languages, online
http://global-reach.biz/globstats/index.php3
Facts and figures on online languages

Libraries
http://www.ala.org
US library information and book awards from the American Library Association

The Library of Congress
http://www.loc.gov
An online gateway to one of the world's greatest collections of words and pictures

The New York Public Library
http://www.nypl.org/
One of the country's foremost libraries, with an online catalog

Nobel Prizes
http://www.nobel.se/
A searchable database of all Nobel Prize winners

The Pulitzer Prizes
http://www.pulitzer.org
A searchable guide to the prestigious US literary prize

UNESCO
http://www.unesco.org/
Comparative international statistics on education and culture

MUSIC & MUSICIANS

All Music Guide
http://www.allmusic.com/
A comprehensive guide to all genres of music

American Society of Composers, Authors and Publishers
http://www.ascap.com
ASCAP songwriter and other awards

Billboard
http://www.billboard.com/
US music news and charts data

ClassicalUSA.com
http://classicalusa.com
An online guide to classical music in the US

Grammy Awards
http://www.naras.org/
The official site for the famous US music awards

Mobile Beat Magazine
http://www.mobilebeat.com
DJ song requests

MTV
http://www.mtv.com
The online site for the TV music channel

Recording Industry Association of America
http://www.riaa.org
Searchable data on gold and platinum disk award winners

Rock and Roll Hall of Fame
http://www.rockhall.com
The museum of the history of rock

Rolling Stone magazine
http://www.rollingstone.com
Features on popular music since 1967

STAGE & SCREEN

Academy Awards
http://www.oscars.org/academyawards/
The official "Oscars" website

Emmy Awards
http://www.emmyonline.org/
Emmy TV awards from the National Television Academy site

Golden Globe Awards
http://hfpa.org/html/
Hollywood Foreign Press Association's Golden Globes site

Hollywood.com
http://www.hollywood.com/
A US movie site with details on all the new releases

Internet Broadway Database
http://www.ibdb.com/default.asp
Broadway theater information

Internet Movie Database
http://www.imdb.com/
The best of the publicly accessible film websites; IMDbPro is available to subscribers

Internet Theatre Database
http://www.theatredb.com/
A Broadway-focused searchable stage site

Tony Awards
http://www.tonyawards.com/en_US/index.html
Official website of the American Theatre Wing's Tonys

Variety
http://www.variety.com/
Extensive entertainment information (extra features available to subscribers)

Yahoo! Movies
http://movies.yahoo.com/
Charts plus features and links to the latest film releases

COMMERCIAL WORLD

Development
http://www.undp.org/
Country GDPs and other development data from the United Nations Development Program

Energy
http://www.eia.doe.gov/
Official US energy statistics

Forbes magazine
http://www.forbes.com/
"Rich lists" and other rankings and business information

Fortune magazine
http://www.fortune.com/fortune
Information on US and global companies

International Currency Converter
http://www.oanda.com/convert/classic
Daily exchange rates for 164 currencies, from 1990 to the present

Labor, international
http://www.ilo.org/
The ILO's facts and figures on the world's workers

Labor, US
http://www.bls.gov
US Department of Labor statistics

OECD
http://www.oecd.org/
World economic and social statistics

Telecommunications
http://www.itu.int/
Worldwide telecommunications statistics

World Bank
http://www.worldbank.org/
World development, trade, and labor statistics

TRANSPORTATION & TOURISM

Air disasters
http://www.airdisaster.com/
Reports on aviation disasters

Aviation
http://www.aerofiles.com/
Information on a century of American aviation

Metros
http://www.lrta.org/world/worldind.html
A guide to the world's light rail and tram systems

National Parks
http://www.nps.gov
The official site of the US national park system

Railroads
http://www.railwaygazette.com/
The world's railroad business in depth

Road transportation
http://www.irfnet.org/
Facts and figures from the International Road Federation

Shipwrecks
http://users.accesscomm.ca/shipwreck/
A huge database of the world's wrecked and lost ships

Travel industry
http://www.tia.org
Stats on travel to and within the US

US and world tourism
http://www.towd.com/
Contact details for tourism offices for US states and countries around the world

World tourism
http://www.world-tourism.org/
The website of the World Tourism Organisation

SPORTS & LEISURE

Athletics
http://www.iaaf.org
The IAAF's statistics and rankings of the world's top athletes

Baseball
http://www.mlb.com
The official website of Major League Baseball

Basketball
http://www.nba.com
The official website of the NBA

Football
http://www.nhl.com
The official website of the NFL

Golf
http://www.pgatour.com
The Professional Golfers' Association (PGA) Tour

Hockey
http://www.nhl.com
The official website of the NHL

Olympics
http://www.olympic.org
The official website of the International Olympic Committee, with a searchable database

Sportscribe
http://www.sportscribe.com/cal.html
Details of forthcoming sporting events worldwide

Sports Illustrated
http://sportsillustrated.cnn.com/
Sports Illustrated's comprehensive coverage of all major sports

Yahoo Sport
http://dir.yahoo.com/Recreation/Sports/
The directory covering major and minor sports

Index

A

accidents
    accident-prone countries 65
    cause of death at work 65
    cause of injury at work 64
    injury, most common causes 64

advertising
    countries spending the most on 174

aid donors
    countries providing the most 168

air disasters
    caused by terrorism 196
    excluding terrorism 196

air speed records
    by jets 186

aircraft
    airlines with the most 194
    countries that suffered the greatest losses
      in World War II 74

airlines
    complaints against US airlines 195
    with most aircraft 194
    with most passenger traffic 195

airports
    busiest 194
    highest number, by country 194

albums
    albums of all time 114
    albums of all time in US 115
    at No 1. in US 115
    classical in US 122
    female solo singers, 2004 118
      most popular tracks, 2004 118
    Grammy awards
      "Album of the Year" 124
      "Best Classical Album" 122
    groups and duos, 2004 120
      most popular tracks 120
    longest in the US chart 114
    male solo singers, 2004 116
    soundtrack in US 129
    top US, 2004 115

America's Cup
    latest winners 243

amusement parks 199

animals see livestock, mammals, pets

animated films 156–7

armed forces
    countries suffering worst military losses in
      World War II 75

largest/smallest 76
ships 74

art see exhibitions, paintings

astronauts and cosmonauts
    countries with most spaceflight
      experience 18
    space shuttle flights, longest 18
    spacewalks, longest 19
    youngest in space 18

athletics (field)
    countries with most medals, 2004
      Olympics 215
    longest-standing current Olympic records 215
    outdoor records, longest-standing
      female/male 214
    world records, most recent 215

athletics (track)
    fastest men 213
    fastest milers 212
    fastest women 212
    most medals, by country, 2004 Olympics 212
    world records, latest 213

avalanches and landslides
    worst 30

awards see Grammy awards, MTV/VMA
    awards, Oscars

B

baseball
    American League titles, teams winning
      most 217
    batting averages, players who have topped
      most often 239
    College World Series titles, teams with most
      batting averages 217
    highest career batting averages, players
      with 238
    highest-paid players, 2004 239
    home runs, players with most 238, in the
      World Series 239
    National League titles, teams winning
      most 217
    pitchers with most wins 238
    runs, players with most 238
    strikeouts, pitchers with most 239
    teams with most major league wins 217
    World Series
      latest winners 216
      teams with most appearances 216
      teams with most wins 216

basketball
    NBA arenas, biggest 218, 219
    NBA players with highest points
      average 219
    NBA point scorers 219
    NBA titles, teams with most 218
    Olympic countries 218

beer-drinkers
    top-consuming countries 181

bestselling books
    hardback fiction/non-fiction in US,
      2004 100
    of all time 101

birds
    fastest 38
    heaviest flighted 38
    heaviest flightless 39
    longest migrations 39
    pet populations 44

births
    rate, countries with highest/lowest 56
    years with highest rate, in US 57

Blanchett, Cate
    top movies 151

boiling points
    highest/lowest 11

bones
    longest in body 52

books
    bestsellers, of all time 101
    hardback fiction/non-fiction in US,
      2004 100
    Pulitzer Prize for Fiction, latest winners 100

bottled water drinkers
    top-consuming countries 181

boxing
    latest boxers to win three or more world
      titles 220
    World Heavyweight Champions
      latest undisputed 221
      longest reigning 221
      oldest 221

brands
    Coca-Cola, countries where brand is top
      cola 175
    most valuable global brands 176

breakfast cereals
    top consuming countries 179

bridges
    longest 92

cosmetic surgery, procedures performed
    in the US 53
obese people, states in the US with most 53
organs, largest 53
see also diseases and illness
hurricanes
    costliest to strike the US 30
    worst 30

I

illness *see* diseases and illness
immigrants
    highest proportion countries 85
    to UK, countries of origin 85
Indianapolis 500
    fastest winning speeds 234
insects
    butterflies, smallest/largest 40
    fastest fliers 41
    spiders, deadliest 41
international soccer
    goal-scorers 232
    international caps, players with most
        in US 233
    transfers 232
    World Cup, countries in 233
islands
    largest 24
    largest lake islands 24
    most isolated 25
    smallest countries 24

J

Jews
    largest populations 78

K

Kidman, Nicole
    top movies 151

L

lakes
    deepest 23
    greatest volume of water 22
    largest 23
land speed record
    latest holders 187
landslides and avalanches
    worst 30

languages
    countries with most English speakers 96
    most spoken 97
    most spoken in the US 96
    online 97
    spoken by the youth of 2050 96
Le Mans 24-hour Races
    fastest 235
libraries
    largest 99
life expectancy
    countries where female exceeds male 59
    countries where male exceeds female 59
    highest/lowest countries 58
    smallest male/female disparity, countries 59
livestock
    types 46

M

magazines
    consumer, top in US 105
malaria
    countries with most cases 55
mammals
    fastest 37
    fastest-gestating 36
    heaviest marine 34
    heaviest terrestrial 42
    largest litters, wild 36
    lightest terrestrial 37
marine disasters 197
marriage
    highest rate, by countries 60
    lowest rate, by countries 61
    women/men marry at youngest age,
        by countries 60
meat
    countries with highest consumption
        of 178
melting points
    highest/lowest 11
meteorite craters
    largest 26
Metropolitan Opera House, New York,
    most frequently performed opera 123
mile
    fastest run 212
military losses
    countries suffering worst in World War II 75
    ships 74

Miramax movies 155
monarchs
    British throne, in line to 66
    longest reigning 68
MotoGP World Championship 236
motor sports 234–5
motor vehicles
    manufacturers 189
    producers 189
    see also cars
motorcycling
    Daytona 200, fastest winning speeds 237
    Grand Prix race wins, riders with most 236
    MotoGP World Championship, 2004,
        riders 236
    race wins, riders with most in a year 237
    World 500CC titles, riders with most 236
mountains
    Everest, first to climb 70
    highest 27
movie awards (Oscars)
    actors with most nominations 141
    animated films, latest winners 157
    "Best Actor" 140
    "Best Actress," latest 143
    "Best Actress," latest to win two 142
    "Best Picture," highest earning 144,
    "Best Picture," latest 144
    "Best Song" 129
    films to win/be nominated for most 145
    oldest winning actors 140
    oldest winning actresses 142
    youngest winning actors 141
movie directors 152–3
movie stars
    actors 148–9
    actresses 150–1
    see also movie awards
movie studios 154–5
movie-going
    countries 158
    most admissions 158
    most screens 158
movies
    all time 146
    animated 156–7
    biographical 138
    budgets 159
    documentary films 139
    genres 138–9

Acknowledgments

Special research: Ian Morrison (sport); Dafydd Rees (US); Louise Reip

Alexander Ash; Caroline Ash; Nicholas Ash; Emma Beatty; Roland Bert; Peter Bond; Nicolas Brasch; Thomas Brinkoff; Richard Chapman; Pete Compton; Luke Crampton; Philip Eden; Bonnie Fantasia; Christopher Forbes; Russell E. Gough; Robert Grant; Bob Gulden; Brad Hackley; Duncan Hislop; Andreas Hörstemeier; Richard Hurley; Todd M. Johnson; Larry Kilman; Jo LaVerde; Dr. Benjamin Lucas; Roberto Mamrud; Chris Mead; Roberto Ortiz de Zarate; Matthew Paton; Tony Pattison; Christiaan Rees; Linda Rees; Kathy Rooney; John Seech; Robert Senior; Karel Stockkermans; Mitchell Symons; Natacha Vassiltchikov; Lucy T. Verma

Academy of Motion Picture Arts and Sciences—
Oscar statuette is the registered trademark
and copyrighted property of the Academy
of Motion Picture Arts and Sciences
Ad Age Global
Advertising Age
Airports Council International
American Association of Port Authorities
American Forests
American Motorcyclist Association
American Pet Classics
American Society for Aesthetic Plastic Surgery
Amnesty International
Amusement Business
Arbitron
Art Loss Register
The Art Newspaper
Art Sales Index
Atlantic Oceanographic and Meteorological
Laboratory/National Oceanic and
Atmospheric Administration
Audit Bureau of Circulations
Automotive News Data Center
Billboard
BP Statistical Review of World Energy 2004
The Breeders' Cup
British Council
British Library
British Museum
Bureau of Labor Statistics
Business Week
Canada Geological Survey
Center for the Study of Global Christianity,
Gordon-Conwell Theological Seminary
Central Intelligence Agency
Christie's
Commission for Distilled Spirits
CRC Handbook of Chemistry and Physics
De Beers
Department of Agriculture

Department of Commerce
The Economist
*Encarta Webster's Dictionary of the
English Language*
Energy Information Administration
Euromonitor
FBI Uniform Crime Reports
Fédération Internationale de Football Association
Fédération International de Ski
Food and Agriculture Organization of the
United Nations
Forbes
Gemstone Publishing Inc.
Gold Fields Mineral Services Ltd.
Home Office (UK)
Initiative Global Adex 2004
Interbrand
International Agency for Research on Cancer
International Civil Aviation Organization
International Coffee Organisation
International Game Fish Association
The International Institute for Strategic Studies,
The Military Balance 2004–2005
International Labour Organization
International Olympic Committee
International Shark Attack File/American
Elasmobranch Society/Florida Museum
of Natural History
International Tea Committee Ltd.
International Telecommunication Union
Internet World Stats
Interpol
Joint United Nations Programme on HIV/AIDS
(UNAIDS)
League of American Theaters and Producers
Library of Congress
Lloyds Register-Fairplay Ltd.
Magazine Publishers of America
Major League Baseball
Metropolitan Opera
MRIB
MTV Video Music Awards (VMA)
Music Information Database
National Academy of Recording Arts and
Sciences (Grammy Awards)
National Aeronautics and Space Administration
(NASA)
National Basketball Association
National Center for Chronic Disease Prevention
and Health Promotion
National Center for Education Statistics
National Center for Health Statistics
National Center for Injury Prevention and Control
National Football League
National Hockey League
New South Wales Registry of Births, Deaths
and Marriages in Australia
New York Drama Critics Circle

Niagara Falls Museum
Nielsen Media Research
Nielsen/NetRatings
Nielsen Soundscan
The NPD Group
Office for National Statistics (UK)
Office of Aviation Enforcement and Proceedings
Office of Immigration Statistics
Office of Management and Budget
Organisation for Economic Co-operation
and Development
Organisation Internationale des Constructeurs
d'Automobiles
The Overstreet Comic Book Price Guide
Power & Motoryacht
Professional Golfers' Association
Publishers Weekly
Pulitzer Prize
Railway Gazette International
Recording Industry Association of America
Rentrak Home Video Essentials
River Systems of the World
Royal Astronomical Society (UK)
RSSSF
Screen Digest
Screen International
Social Security Administration
Sotheby's
Statistical Abstract of the United States
Stores
Times University Guides
Tony Awards
Tour de France
United Nations
United Nations Educational, Scientific
and Cultural Organization
United Nations Population Division
US Census Bureau
US Geological Survey
United World Chart, mediatraffic
Variety
Victorian Registry of Births, Deaths
and Marriages in Australia
Video Business
volcanolive.com
WebElements
World Association of Newspapers
World Atlas of Coral Reefs
World Bank
World Cup Skateboarding
World Economic Forum
World Gold Council
World Health Organization
World of Learning
World Tourism Organization

PUBLISHER'S ACKNOWLEDGMENTS

Dorling Kindersley would like to thank the following for their contributions: Design: Rebecca Painter, Mandy Earey

PACKAGER'S ACKNOWLEDGMENTS

The Bridgewater Book Company would like to thank Alison Bolus, Ursula Caffrey, Sarah Doughty, Nicky Gyopari, and Sara Harper for their editorial assistance, and Emily Wilkinson, Richard Peters, Lyndsey Godden and Chris Morris for their design work.

Picture Credits